35 in 10

Thirty-Five Ten-Minute Plays

Compiled and Edited

by

KENT R. BROWN

Dramatic Publishing

Woodstock, Illinois • England • Australia • New Zealand

35 in 10

TABLE OF CONTENTS

DOUBLE MANDIBLE

By
Julie Jensen

Double Mandible (originally entitled **Water Lilies**) was commissioned by Salt Lake Acting Company in 2001. It appeared on a bill with ten other short plays by Utah writers, produced January 24, 2002, as part of the Salt Lake City Winter Olympics. It also appeared in a volume of plays entitled *Cabbies, Cowboys and the Tree of the Weeping Virgin,* privately published, to commemorate Salt Lake Acting Company's contribution to the Olympic celebration.

CHARACTERS

BETTY: An enthusiastic, yet nervous water ballerina. Twin to Bella.

BELLA: A desultory, long-suffering water ballerina. Twin to Betty.

SETTING: The pool at the Olympics. The in-water segments should be performed behind a shoulder-high curtain. Mannequin legs can be used for some of the water ballet stunts.

COSTUMES: Both actors are dressed exactly alike: swimming suits, nose plugs, lots of makeup and lacquered hair. Each of them should also wear a large waterlily on top of her head.

DOUBLE MANDIBLE

AT THE CURTAIN: *It is a dark stage. SPOTLIGHT on BETTY. She is in front of a microphone.*

Part I: Before Competition

BETTY *(to AUDIENCE)*. Many people have asked me, "What is it with this water ballet?" And I am proud to answer. Water ballet has made America great. For example, water ballet incorporates all other sports—water sports and artistry sports. Go ahead, step right up, name any sport, any sport at all, and water ballet will incorporate some of its features.

BELLA *(off)*. Weightlifting.

BETTY *(to AUDIENCE, as if someone in the house answered)*. Weightlifting. Yes!

BELLA *(off)*. Marathon running.

BETTY *(again, as if another person in the house answered)*. Marathon running. Yes!

BELLA *(off)*. Greco Roman wrestling.

BETTY *(to AUDIENCE)*. Greco Roman wrestling. *Yes!* You see what I mean!

(BELLA enters. She is carrying some gear.)

BELLA *(to AUDIENCE)*. That is my sister. She has a reputation for intensity.

BETTY *(to AUDIENCE)*. ...What is more, ladies and gentlemen, water ballet is also the *first* art form. Before there was ground ballet, there was water ballet. But even before that. Before the human race walked on two legs, there was water ballet. Swimming around in the primordial ooze, there was water ballet. The little mermaids and the little mermen, no feet, just fins. They had water ballet.

BELLA *(to AUDIENCE)*. As you can tell, my sister is known for her passionate defense of her career. Our career.

BETTY *(to AUDIENCE)*. ...In conclusion, my fellow Americans, may I add the following: water ballet is not the thing that separates us from the animal kingdom, no, it is the thing that connects us to it. Thank you so very much. *(BETTY curtsies.)* Oh, and one more thing. I'm proud to be a waterlily. Proud, proud, proud.

(SPOTLIGHT out. BELLA claps. LIGHTS up.)

BETTY. Bella, for the love of Jesus, where have you been?

BELLA. I went to a movie.

BETTY. And left me to do the entire press corps by myself.

BELLA. I had to get my mind off things.

BETTY. You also missed our morning practice.

BELLA. No I didn't. I was at practice for the next part of my life.

BETTY. Bella! *This is the Olympics!*

BELLA. I had to get my mind off it.

BETTY. We are going to fail to medal because of you. Not because someone else beats us but because of your attitude.*(Practicing some water-ballet gesture.)* The judges will be scrupinizing us today.

BELLA. Scrutinizing.

BETTY. If there is a hidden hint of this attitude.

BELLA. A hidden hint of the truth?

BETTY. Yes. If there is a hint of it. They will see it. And they will kill us. *(BETTY twirls around and jumps in the pool.)*

BELLA *(to AUDIENCE)*. My entire life has been spent with my sister here, inside the womb and out. This kind of intensity, well, it can be wearing. *(BELLA jumps in the pool.)*

BETTY. I guess you know I threw up today.

BELLA. In the water?

BETTY. I threw up because you were not here. And I did not know if you would show up.

BELLA. You're just afraid of the Double Mandible.

BETTY. *Of course, I'm afraid of the Double Mandible! who would not be afraid of the Double Mandible?*

BELLA *(to AUDIENCE)*. Really, my sister is afraid to hang up her nose plugs. She has serious doubts about whether she exists. If she is not doing a torpedo twirl and a military salute in some container of water, she may not be alive. *(Some water-ballet gesture.)*

BETTY. Our entire life has been focused on this day. And where are you?

BELLA. I had some popcorn...

BETTY. Popcorn! Forty-four grams of fat.

BELLA. ...And tried not to think about it.

BETTY. Tried not to think about it!

BELLA. There is nothing to think about, Betty. Everything that could be thought has been thought. Years ago. *(Some water-ballet gesture. To the AUDIENCE.)* This is the thing about water ballet. You repeat the same two minutes of your life over and over again, tens of thousands, if not millions of times. And every time it is exactly the same, it sounds the same, it smells the same, it feels the same, it looks the same, it is, for all intents and purposes, exactly the same. Exactly. The. Same! And then, preposterous as it may sound, someone else sits out there and judges it. This part was more the same, this thing was less the same, and this is your grade for sameness. *(Some water-ballet stuff. To AUDI-ENCE.)* But even that is not the worst of it. The worst of it is the fact that this, this two minutes endlessly repeated, is the only thing that matters. The only thing about my life or my thoughts or my actions that matters. The only thing.

BETTY. Bella, couldn't you at least enjoy the show?

BELLA. Do you know what muscles in me are the most exhausted? Face. Face muscles. I have an exhausted face. From "enjoying" it too much. *(More water-ballet stuff.)*

BETTY. Promise me one thing, Bella. You will not throw the Double Mandible.

BELLA. I will not throw the Double Mandible.

BETTY. But we didn't practice the Double Mandible this morning.

BELLA. The first Double Mandible of the day is the best Double Mandible of the day. *(More water-ballet stuff. At AUDIENCE.)* What will become of my sister, I wonder, when repetition and grading are not a part of her day? Will she every morning make a thousand eggs and a thousand pieces of bacon? Trying to do each one just like the one before? Getting caught in an endless string of repetitions? *(Long pause. Some water-ballet stuff.)*

BETTY. Do not forget, Bella, if we do the Double Mandible, we'll be on the cover of *Sports Illustrated*. We'll have a whole segment of "60 Minutes" devoted exclusively to us. We'll be on the Wheaties box. We will be responsible for triggering a world-wide mania for water ballet. Young people all over the world will long to become waterlilies. They will look at us and…drool.

BELLA. Oh please, Betty.

BETTY. No one's expecting it. It's not even a rumor that we might try it.

BELLA. We'll try it, Betty. We'll do it.

BETTY. Oh, yes! Say that again, Bella.

BELLA. We'll try it, Betty. We'll do it.

BETTY. Oh, yes! I even love to practice, Bella, don't you?

(A military march comes on. The two of them are doing their routine. It goes on for several seconds. There are dives and feet in the air. Synchronized, energetic gestures. Finally they both go under the water, and then up pops BELLA alone. She has screwed it up. BETTY pops up next, livid. They finish the routine. LIGHTS out. End of Part I.)

Part II: After Competition

(LIGHTS up. BETTY is in a rage.)

BETTY. How can I forgive you? How can I ever forgive you?

BELLA. You don't have to, Betty.

BETTY. I might have to hate you forever.

BELLA. Blame me, go ahead. Blame me forever.

BETTY. No. I must not be drawn into negative thinking. *(Pause.)* But you threw it, didn't you, Bella?

BELLA. I blew it.

BETTY. You threw it.

BELLA. I didn't throw it.

BETTY. You threw it. You threw the Double Mandible. You wanted to rob me of the supremacy, the ultimateness. You ripped the waterlily crown from my heart.

BELLA *(to AUDIENCE)*. My sister is inconsolable. Like Niobe, all tears.

BETTY. How could you do it?

BELLA. Inevitability.

BETTY. But no, no. We must take control. We must not dwell on the failures of the past. We must put our minds on the future.

BELLA. Right, Betty, the future.

BETTY. The World Games are in June. I want to announce the Double Mandible ahead of time and do it there. We've got to start practicing. Now, Bella. Right now. *(Some water-ballet stuff.)* Oh, Bella, what do you say?

BELLA. I want to go to the Goose Necks of the San Juan.

BETTY. The what of the what? *(Some water-ballet stuff.)*

BELLA. Set up a little sunshade and live out my days as a desert animal with a view of the dry red earth.

BETTY. You can't quit.

BELLA. I will not swim again forever.

BETTY. We can't retire. We must continue this work. The Double Mandible. The World Games, after that the Goodwill Games.

BELLA. I'm gonna save the desert tortoise.

BETTY. You're not!

BELLA. I'm going to collect cicada songs.

BETTY. You are so full of...shit.

BELLA. I will be a person who never goes into the water again. I will never immerse myself in water, I will not even be near water deep enough to dive into. I will take showers, not baths. I will drink snow cones not water. I will live like a lizard on a red rock surrounded by juniper and sage. Me and all the dry creatures of the desert.

BETTY. You've lost your mind, haven't you?

BELLA. No. I'm going to find my mind. I've been doing this job since I was four. I am tired of it. I want to do something else with my life. Besides stick my head in the water and my foot in the air.

BETTY. You see no artistry in it. You never have. It is truly beautiful, and the entire world thinks so.

BELLA. The best thing about this job is that you retire early.

BETTY. If I could go out doing the Double Mandible on the day I die, I'd be a happy person.

BELLA. Are you ready?

BETTY. You're really leaving.

BELLA. I'm leaving this water. Yes. And forever.

BETTY. My whole life is about the Double Mandible that could have been.

BELLA. Not mine. Not ever mine. *(BELLA climbs from the water.)*

BETTY *(wailing)*. Bel-la!

(LIGHTS fade. SOUND of swimming and water lapping.)

END OF PLAY

CLASSYASS

By
Caleen Sinnette Jennings

Classyass premiered in 2002 in Actors Theatre of Louisville's 26th Annual Humana Festival of New American Plays. Timothy Douglas was dramaturg. The play was directed by Rajendra Ramoon Maharaj, and featured Jason Cornwell, Nikki E. Walker and Robert Beitzel.

CHARACTERS

AMA (or AMADEUS): Black college freshman.
BIG B (or BELINDA): Black woman, 20, dressed like a street person.
MILES: White college senior and radio-station manager.

SETTING: A small room that serves as a modest campus radio studio at Bellmore College.

TIME: The present. Early morning.

CLASSYASS

AT THE CURTAIN: *AMA speaks into the microphone with a suave broadcaster's voice.*

AMA. Okay Bellmore boneheads. That was Tchaichovsky's "1812 Overture." Bet those cannons busted a couple of you dozers. Perfect for 3:47 on a cold, rainy Thursday in finals week. It's the end of time at the end of the line. Study on, people. Bang out papers. Cram the facts. Justify that exorbitant tuition and make Bellmore College proud. *I'm feeling y'all!* Especially those of you studying for Calc 801 with Professor Cobb. Call me if you have a clue about question #3 on page 551. You're listening to Casual Classics, because you don't have to be uptight and white to love classical music! This is WBMR the radio station of Bellmore College. Miles Morgan is your station manager. I'm Ama, Amadeus Waddlington with you until six a.m. Guzzle that warm Red Bull and cold Maxwell House. Here's music to squeeze your brains by. It's Dvorjak's "New World Symphony" comin' atcha. *(He puts on the CD, grabs a beer and a huge textbook and sprawls out on the floor. A bold knock interrupts him. He shouts.)* Go to hell, Miles. I like "New World"! *(Another knock.)* Okay, okay. I'll play Beethoven's Symphony #1 next. Lots of strings, okay? *(Persistent knocking.)* Damn!

(AMA strides to the door and opens it. BIG B strides in, carrying shopping bags and waving several faxes.)

BIG B. You messed up, boy!

AMA. Excuse me?

BIG B. And your smart-assed faxes made it worse!

AMA. Do I know you?

BIG B *(examining the mike and CDs)*. I want a public apology.

AMA. Don't touch that. Listen, whoever you are...

BIG B. Whomever!

AMA. Whatever!

BIG B. You ain't got a clue who I am.

AMA. A fabulous person, no doubt, but you've got to go. This is a classical music show and I've got a killer calc final...

BIG B. Color me compassionate. You're shorter than I thought. But I figured right about you being a dumbass. I told you right here...

(BIG B shows AMA the faxes and he realizes who she is.)

AMA. Oh my God...you're...Big B! I thought you were...

BIG B. ...a brother. I know, 'cause I ain't hearing none of your bullshit. Well, I thought you was a white boy, and I was right.

AMA. Look, I don't know what you want...

BIG B. How long I been faxing you, moron? You said the "Gloria" was by Faure...

AMA. I told you one thousand faxes ago, "Gloria" is by Poulenc, and when I played it, I said Poulenc...

BIG B. ...Faure!

AMA. ...Poulenc!

BIG B. I know what I heard, you arrogant shithead.

AMA. Does that Big B stand for "bitch" or "borderline psychotic"?

BIG B. I ain't even 'pressed by you trottin' out them tired SAT joints. I'm down at the Palmer Street Shelter, which you knew by the headin' on the fax, and you just figured I didn't know shit about classical music.

AMA. Big B, I'm truly flattered that you even listen, but you don't...

BIG B. My Palmer Street crew wanted to come up here and kick your ass.

AMA. Whoa, whoa there. I'm sorry about our misunderstanding, okay?

BIG B. And that's s'posed to float my boat?

AMA. Let's be calm, okay B?

BIG B. Big B to you, and I know you ain't s'posed to be drinkin' beer up in here.

AMA. You never saw that.

BIG B. Now I got two things on ya. This gonna be what they call an interesting evening. *(She thumbs through his calculus book.)* This the shit probably got your brain too messed up to know your Poulenc from your Faure. *(She sips AMA's beer.)*

AMA. Don't do that. Suppose I have a social disease?

BIG B. Ha! Bet you still a cherry.

AMA. Suppose *you* have a social disease?

BIG B. I'll just call your dean and tell him I caught it sippin' outa your freshman-ass beer bottle.

AMA. What do you want from me?

BIG B. You made me look stupid in front of my crew.

AMA. Look, I'm just a nerd playing dead, white men's music. Why do you even listen to my show?

BIG B. So a sistah like me ain't s'posed to be a classical music affectionado.

AMA. It's "aficionado"…

BIG B. Boy, I'm feelin' better 'n better about bustin' yo ass.

AMA. This is like something out of Scorcese. If I apologize for the thing *I did not do*, will you go?

BIG B. Maybe. Or maybe I'll stay and watch you work awhile.

AMA. It's against the rules.

BIG B. Lots of things against the rules, freshman boy. Don't mean they ain't delicious to do.

AMA. If my station manager comes in…

BIG B. Tell him I'm studyin' witcha, that we putting the "us" in calculus.

AMA. Well, you don't exactly look like a student.

BIG B. Well, you don't exactly look like a asshole, but you the poster boy. Where you get "Ama" from anyway?

AMA. Wolfgang Amadeus Mozart. My dad's a classical musician.

BIG B. Oh yeah? Where he play at?

AMA. He sells insurance. No major symphony'll hire him.

BIG B. I know that's right. Oughta be called "sym-pho-ney" —like phoney baloney, right?

AMA *(patronizingly)*. That's very clever, but I've got a lot of work to do. How about I give you and your people at the shelter a, what do you call it, a "shout-out." Right in the middle of Dvorjak. How would you like that?

(AMA goes to the mike, but BIG B stops him.)

BIG B. How you gonna interrupt "New World Sym-
phony" and mess up everybody's flow? You crazy,
Amadeus Waddlington. You also a lucky bastard. Big
B like you. She gonna take it easy on you.

AMA. Why does your use of third person chill my blood?

BIG B. Take me to dinner and we cool.

AMA. What?

BIG B. Over there to the Purple Pheasant, where the president of Bellmore College eat at!

AMA. Are you crazy? I don't have that kind of...

BIG B. ...an' buy me a present...

AMA. ...a present? I'm broke!

BIG B. ...something, how they say it, "droll." Yeah,
"droll." Like a CD of "Dialogs of the Carmelites" by
Poulenc. I can see you 'n me sittin' up in the Purple
Pheasant, chucklin' over our little in-joke, sippin' a
half-ass California pinot grigio.

AMA. Who the hell writes your material?

BIG B. And pick me up in a shiny new car.

AMA. Hello? Freshmen aren't allowed to have cars.

BIG B. Beg, borrow or steal, my brother, but you better
have yo ass waitin' for me at the shelter tomorrow
night at 7:30. And don't shit in your khakis. My boys
will watch your back in the hood.

AMA. You're delusional.

BIG B. Oh, you just insultin' Big B now? You don't
wanna be seen with her?

AMA. I'd love to be seen with her...you! I'd give my
right arm to have the whole town and the president of
Bellmore see me escort you into the Purple Pheasant.
Hell, I'd even invite my parents. But I'm a scholarship
student with five bucks to my name.

BIG B *(sniffing him)*. Ya wearing cashmere and ya stank of Hugo Boss. Don't even try to play me, boy.

AMA. Maxed-out cards, Big B. I'm just a half-ass, wannabe freshman with a little gig, trying to make some headway with Mr. MasterCard. I'll apologize on air. I'll stamp your name on my forehead, I'll run naked down the quad and bark like a dog…

BIG B. …anything but take me out. You're a snob, Amadeus Waddlington. You a broke-ass, cashmere-wearin', shit-talkin' loser who don't know his Poulenc from his Faure… *(She finishes off AMA's beer.)* …and drinks lite beer! My crew was right. Ya need a beat-down.

AMA. Big B, please…

BIG B. See, I be down at the shelter, diggin' on ya voice early in the mornin'. People say you ain't shit. But you got a way a soundin' all mellow an' sexy. And when you spank that Rachmaninoff, oh yeah, baby! So when you screw up the Poulenc I send a friendly fax to point out yo error and help yo ass out…

AMA. And I appreciate…

BIG B. But you had to get up in my grill wit that, "what-do-you-know-about-classical-music-you-stu-pid-ass-homeless-crackhead" kind of attitude. *(She starts to leave.)* Well, Palmer Street crew will be very happy to whup yo behind.

AMA *(stopping BIG B from leaving)*. I didn't mean to give you attitude. I'm sorry. I'm broke, I swear! I'll show you my bills, I'll show you my bank statements. Isn't there anything else I can do, Big B? Please?

(Pause. BIG B looks AMA up and down, to his great discomfort.)

BIG B. Kiss me.

AMA. What did you say?

BIG B. I'm gettin' somethin' outa this deal. Kiss me.

AMA. But…

BIG B. Not one a them air flybys, neither. Gimme some tongue!

AMA. Oh God.

BIG B *(advances to him)*. Lay it on me, Amadeus Waddlington. Kiss me or kiss yo ass goodbye.

AMA *(backing away, near tears)*. This isn't Scorcese, it's John Woo.

BIG B. Come on, classyass, pucker up!

(BIG B tackles AMA and plants a long, deep kiss on him. When she lets him go, AMA steps back, looks at her, touches his lips, and faints. BIG B kneels calmly beside him. Her entire demeanor changes. Her voice is rich, cultured, her grammar impeccable. She sits him up and gives him a few light slaps.)

Hey! Hey! Ama? Damn it, Amadeus Waddlington, wake up!

(MILES MORGAN enters drinking a beer.)

MILES. Who are you, and what the hell did you do to Waddlington?

BIG B. He just fainted. Get something cold. *(MILES pours cold beer on AMA's face. AMA comes to.)* Have you sufficiently recuperated, Mr. Waddlington?

MILES *(to BIG B)*. Hey, you look familiar… Where do I know you from?… In the paper…from the shelter.

You're… Man you sure look…different! Oh my God… You're not going to tell your father about the beer, are you? I'm a fifth-year senior trying to graduate…

BIG B. Just make sure he's okay.

(MILES bends down to AMA who grabs him by the collar. They whisper urgently, while BIG B thumbs through the CDs and eavesdrops, greatly amused.)

AMA. Oh God. Oh God! I kissed her!

MILES. Way to go, man!

AMA. I'm gonna die.

MILES. She's that good, huh? Bet she's a knockout under all that stuff she's wearing. You all going to a costume party or something?

AMA. Don't you get it, Miles? I kissed her!

MILES. Lucky freshman bastard, kickin' it with Dean Stafford's daughter.

AMA *(after a beat)*. What did you say?

MILES. That's Belinda Stafford, Dean Stafford's youngest daughter! She dropped out of Bellmore to work at the shelter. It was all in the papers and everything.

BIG B *(hands AMA money)*. Thanks for the beer and the amusement, Mr. Waddlington.

AMA. Is it true? Are you really…?

BIG B *(removing her dirty garments and putting them in a bag)*. I work night shifts at the Palmer Street Shelter. You can imagine that some of the women find it hard to sleep. Your music and your incredibly boring commentary usually do the trick. Everything was fine until you responded so rudely to my fax. You assumed because it came from the shelter…

AMA. No…I just…I didn't…

BIG B. You're an arrogant, ill-informed elitist, Amadeus Waddlington. I've known guys like you all my life. It broke Daddy's heart when I dropped out of Bellmore, but your faxes reminded me exactly why I did it. So, I decided to teach you a lesson. You're not going to die from my kiss, but I hope you won't forget what it felt like to think that you were. *(She rips and scatters the faxes over his head and starts to exit.)*

MILES. Now, uh, Ms. Stafford, you wouldn't mention this to your father…

BIG B. I've got people without winter coats on my mind.

AMA *(rushes to her)*. Big B, I mean, Belinda, I mean Ms. Stafford, please wait. I get a lot of shit from people about this show and I thought you were just another brother hassling me. I don't have an attitude about the shelter because I've got too many poor folks in my own family. I'm sorry about the vibe. Can I make it up to you? Maybe put in some hours at the shelter.

BIG B. If you think you can handle it. I picked out some CDs for you to play. My people sleep well to Debussy. I'll be checkin' you! *(She puts on her headphones as she exits.)*

MILES. And you won't mention this to…

(MILES exits calling after BIG B. AMA suddenly re-members he's on air. He runs to the mike.)

AMA. Yo, my people, was that dope? Bet the "New World Symphony" woke yo asses up! Hey, I'm still waiting to speak to anybody with a clue to #3 on page 551 in Cobb's calculus class. Anybody? It's 3:59 on WBMR the voice of Bellmore College. I'm Amadeus Waddlington and this is Casual Classics, because you don't have to be uptight and white to love classical music. You don't have to be a snob either. I wanna give a shout out to my girl Big B. I think I'm in love, people. Yo, B, I apologize. "Gloria" was, is, and always will be Poulenc. I dig the lesson... *(He touches his lips.)* ...and I dig the way you taught it. I'll be down to lend a hand, you better believe that. And for the folks listening at the Palmer Street Shelter, here's a little Debussy to soothe you to sleep. Better times ahead, my people. Better times ahead.

(LIGHTS dim as sounds of Debussy come up.)

END OF PLAY

A MUSTACHE AND A MATTRESS

By
Nancy Gall-Clayton

A Mustache and a Mattress was first produced in 2001 by Love Creek Productions at the Creative Place Theatre in New York City.

CHARACTERS

ROSIE: A shopper, a woman with a mission.
BURT: A mustachioed man, also with a mission.

SETTING: A store. A mattress with a sign reading "Special" placed next to it.

TIME: The present.

A MUSTACHE AND A MATTRESS

AT THE CURTAIN: *ROSIE enters, sees the sign, and makes a delighted little gesture. She goes to the mattress, touches it, traces the pattern, looks around to make sure she's not being observed, and leans down to touch her face to the mattress. She looks at the tag, drops her pocketbook on the mattress, and quickly descends to check the "bounce factor." She is investigating this mattress every way but lying on it when BURT strolls in. ROSIE is so engaged she doesn't notice.*

BURT. Thinking of a new mattress?

ROSIE. Oh! Hello.

BURT. Thinking of a new mattress?

ROSIE. Thinking of a new person.

BURT. When it comes to mattresses—

ROSIE. It has come to mattresses.

BURT. And you've come to the best mattress store in town.

ROSIE. Your…uh…mustache.

BURT. You need a new mattress?

ROSIE. Yes, he's staying the weekend. What a beautiful mus—

BURT. For the new man.

ROSIE. No, no, not new.

BURT. Right, but he's staying the weekend. This weekend?

ROSIE. Yes, but—

BURT. Under your roof.

ROSIE. Under your nose is the most glorious mustache.

BURT. A new man is staying the weekend under your roof? You need a mattress, and we have an excellent one on special.

ROSIE. Not under my sheets, you understand. Well, they're my sheets, of course, but not *my* sheets. When did you start growing your—

BURT. A light sleeper? A man who tosses and turns? A man who stretches out? A tall man?

ROSIE. Yes, but not a new man.

BURT. An old man? Your grandfather perhaps?

ROSIE. Not exactly. How long have you had that mustache? If I may ask.

BURT. My whole life. This mattress has a lifetime warranty.

ROSIE. Absurd. The mustache, I mean. Not *the* mustache, the "mustache for life" comment.

BURT. Since puberty, I've had it since puberty. The mustache, I mean.

ROSIE. You've never cut it?

BURT. Trimmed, yes. Cut, no. A complimentary pad comes with this particular mattress. Quilted. Satin. Your choice of three colors.

ROSIE. Is it religious, Burt? I may call you "Burt," may I not? It's on your name tag in big navy blue curlicue letters like your you-know-what. It's not a secret or anything, is it?

BURT. I'm Burt.

ROSIE. I'm Rosie. Is it religious?

BURT. My mustache?

ROSIE. Certain religions don't believe in hair cutting.

BURT. I trim it.

ROSIE. Oh, yes, I forgot. Do you have other facial hair? Oh, sorry! That was personal.

BURT. We have three degrees of firmness.

ROSIE. In mattresses?

BURT. Firm, Very Firm, and Extraordinarily Firm.

ROSIE. May I touch it?

BURT. Be my guest.

ROSIE *(touching BURT's mustache)*. It's so…

BURT. The mattress!

ROSIE. I know what the mattress feels like. But I haven't sat on it. Will you join me? To test the firmness for two bodies, I mean.

BURT. If you insist.

ROSIE. What firmness is this one?

BURT. Extraordinarily Firm.

ROSIE. Please, let's sit. *(They sit.)* Aaahhhh. Let's lie back, shall we?

BURT. Well—

ROSIE. And face me, will you? I want to study that mustache.

BURT. Maybe I should get another sales representative for you.

ROSIE. But I want you! You're doing everything just right. *(ROSIE lies back and emphatically gestures for BURT to do the same.)* Please, Burt.

BURT. Frank usually has five-o'clock shadow. I could get Frank for you. His dinner break is almost up.

ROSIE. Don't trifle with me.

BURT. Don't trifle with me.

ROSIE. I'm not.

BURT. You're having a gentleman spend the weekend.

ROSIE. Yes—

BURT. I need to make my quota. It's the end of the month. Are you buying the mattress?

ROSIE. Dazzle me. Give me your sales pitch. Tell me everything. Talk!

BURT. May I sit up yet?

ROSIE. No.

BURT. I feel undignified making a sales presentation on my side.

ROSIE. All right. *(BURT sits up and ROSIE reluctantly follows suit.)* Do you use one of those little mustache brushes?

BURT. Yes.

ROSIE. A teeny comb?

BURT. Yes.

ROSIE. Ooooh.

BURT. This mattress has amazing inner springs, some of the best on the market.

ROSIE. May I jump on it?

BURT. No mattress should be jumped on.

ROSIE. To test the bounce factor.

BURT. This man you're buying mattress for... Is he stocky?

ROSIE. Have you heard of Clayton Bailey?

BURT. Is he stocky?

ROSIE. Clayton Bailey took the grand prize at the 1993 Bull Valley Mustache Festival in Hayward, California.

BURT. You're making this up!

ROSIE. Clayton's "stache"—as he calls it—measured—are you ready for this?

BURT. If you're ready to buy a mattress, I am.

ROSIE. Twenty-four inches.

BURT. No!

ROSIE. He's formulated a special organic protein formula for feeding mustaches.

BURT. My mustache doesn't eat.

ROSIE. But it has such potential!

BURT. Are you offering to be my Mustache Trainer?

ROSIE. May I?!?

BURT. I was kidding. Besides, you have that older man in your life.

ROSIE. *Other* man.

BURT. Same difference.

ROSIE. Wouldn't you love to go to a mustache festival?

BURT. Can you afford this mattress, or is all this some weird and perverted hair fantasy of yours?

ROSIE. Are you accusing me of being kinky?

BURT. Yes.

ROSIE. Thank you.

BURT. You're welcome.

ROSIE. Clayton Bailey's personal formula Mustache Grower—and I happen to have a jar in my pocketbook—lengthens and stiffens the hair and prevents it from getting snarled and tangled.

BURT. I do get the occasional mustache snarl.

ROSIE. Shall I get the jar out right now?

BURT. Please don't.

ROSIE. Even more important, the Mustache Grower works as a fire retardant.

BURT. This mattress is flame retardant.

ROSIE. So if you use the Mustache Grower and you sleep on this mattress, you'd—

BURT. Never catch on fire!

ROSIE. Right!

BURT. So you *are* buying the mattress for the mustache champion?

ROSIE. No, no! It's for my nephew. He's staying with me while his parents go to a wedding in Toronto. He's becoming a young man, and I don't want to stick him on the couch again. Does it come in king size?

BURT. King size won't fit just anywhere.

ROSIE. I want king size. It will be my mattress after the weekend.

BURT. The weekend with your nephew?

ROSIE. Exactly, and I was thinking that maybe he would be interested in a growing a mustache. Would you talk to him man to man about what's involved? How you decided, how you got started, what it's meant to you, that sort of thing.

BURT. Gosh, I don't know. I do think he'd like this mattress though. Any young man would.

ROSIE. Oh, yes, the mattress. Do you deliver?

BURT. Of course.

ROSIE. No, no. Do *you* deliver? You Burt with the curlicue stache.

BURT. Me personally? I never have.

ROSIE. What if I would only buy it if *you* personally deliver?

BURT. You'll buy this mattress in king size and extraordinarily firm and close the deal today?

ROSIE. Yes.

BURT. I could deliver it.

ROSIE. For my nephew.

BURT. I'd ride in the delivery truck. I couldn't lift it alone, of course—even though I am a weightlifter.

ROSIE. Oooooh! A weight-lifting mustachioed man. Do you have one of those undershirts with only one strap?

BURT. In flourescent blue.

ROSIE. Why don't you ride in the delivery truck with the mattress, stay to talk with my nephew, and then we'll all watch my video of the Mustache Festival. I'll make some lasagna. Have you ever had fresh Parmesan cheese, Burt? I grate my own. What do you say?

BURT. I love lasagna.

ROSIE. You're not married, are you?

BURT. No. Are you?

ROSIE. No.

BURT. Let me get my sales tickets.

ROSIE. In a minute. I want to feel it one more time.

(ROSIE pulls him onto the mattress and begins playing with his mustache.)

END OF PLAY

JUMPERS AND SPINNERS

By
Bruce Post

Jumpers and Spinners was first heard at the Westbeth Theatre in New York City in 1996.

CHARACTERS

JOE: A guy.
PETE: Another guy.

SETTING: A lunch break.

TIME: The present.

JOE. I still got to get the car home. I can't do anything about this spider with the car in a ditch on the side of the road. I look for the thing but I can't find it. I know it's in there but I can't find it. I wish I had long pants on and socks. I got nothing to cover my legs with so I build up my courage and I get in the car and I tear ass back home. I'm afraid to leave my feet and legs down on the pedals 'cause I'm sure the beast is hanging out up under the dash, that's where it came from the first time, and I thank my lucky stars I didn't kill myself driving home it's only a couple of miles but it was the longest trip I've ever taken I get back to the house I skid to a stop in the driveway and jump out of the car and even though I know the thing is probably just as terrified as I am, more, and it's wondering where the hell it went wrong by crawling through my window my heart is beating like a drum and my mind is racing. I got to have a car.

PETE. This guy I know thought he had a boil on his ankle. Went to the emergency room to get it lanced and when they opened it up all these baby spiders came out.

JOE. That's disgusting.

PETE. You should have captured it.

JOE. Capture it? The thing had me captured. I couldn't go anywhere. Still I had to go to the city that night and it was me or it. And of course I start with the nightmare fantasies and the paranoia and I think back to when we had all those pet spiders. Remember Bunky?

PETE. Bunky was a helluva spider.

JOE. Undefeated for two years.

PETE. It was a little one what got him. Bunky was too fast for the big ones. Remember that big wolf spider we threw at him? Thing was as big as a pancake but Bunky wore him down, waited him out then put the bite on him.

JOE. Bunky was 26 and 0.

PETE. 26 and 1. The last one got 'im.

JOE. True. I know about spiders. That only fuels my gruesome fantasies.

PETE. You can break all spiders down into two groups: jumpers and spinners. Bunky was a jumper. It was a spinner got him.

JOE. Bunky was a jumper. This beast in my car was a jumper.

PETE. Jumpers lay out web strands that are like trip lines, something hits the web, they know food is near. They wait completely still until the victim gets within range then they jump what would be for us the equivalent of forty feet from standing still and they put the bite on and back off and wait for the poison to paralyze then when the victim can't move anymore they slide over and sink the fangs into the gut and suck all the body fluids out 'til the victim is a dried-up husk and they do that while you're still alive.

JOE. What a way to go.

PETE. I always think that. Spiders don't feed on dead meat. Gotta be alive. Gotta be warm. I always have to go there, think about what it'd be like if I was small enough or the spider was big enough that I got caught in the web and the thing put the bite on me and then fed on me for a couple days, that's how long it would take, sucking all the fluid out of my body until I dry up and die.

JOE. The horror!

PETE. What's the matter? You're not eating.

JOE. I'm still eating.

PETE. It might be worse with a spinner. The spinners throw loops of web, like lassos, from far away, until they catch hold of a limb or some other protuberance and then it's like you got one hand tied to a tree and every couple a minutes they put a little bite on you until they bit you enough you start to paralyze then they lasso another limb and put the little bite on you until you're tied spread-eagle and they been puttin' the little bite on you all over then they feed on you for a week or so.

JOE. I should have gotten the chicken salad.

PETE. Are you kidding? That's terrific liverwurst.

JOE. You talked me into it.

PETE. That spinner fed on Bunky for a week and wasn't half done when you tossed it.

JOE. I couldn't bear to watch no more.

PETE. Spiders are always pregnant.

JOE. Shit, yeah, the male sticks it to the female then she puts the bite on him.

PETE. Kinda like your girlfriend. That one wolf spider dropped a brood in the cage, remember, and the eggs hatched and there musta been ten thousand baby spiders in there, and then the mother starts eating the babies. She hatched 'em for food. Brutal!

JOE. I got all these horrible things racing through my head, psyching me up for this job I got to do, so I get a can of bug spray, or maybe it was rodent spray, nasty poison, and I close the windows of the car and I empty the can into the car. I spray until I can spray no more. I close the doors and I go off to have more horrible fantasies...

PETE. Imagine the doctor slaps your butt, you take your first breath, he hands you to your mother... She sinks her fangs into your chest and sucks your vitals out.

JOE. I'm trying to eat here.

PETE. Sorry.

JOE. I have no choice but to get in the car and drive. I open the car door and it smells like a DuPont factory inside but I don't see no dead spider. I get a small broom and I whack away up under the dashboard, behind the seats, it's only a two-seater, there's not much room to hide, and I think I go over the interior pretty well. I'm feeling better about it. No bug, even one as big as my hand, could survive the chemical wash I put in there.

PETE. It's like nerve gas. It attacks their central nervous system. Everything breaks down and they shit themselves to death.

JOE. I go back inside to grab a bite and change my clothes. I'm still nervous about it but I'm feeling pretty sure I'll be alone in the car when I drive to the city. Wouldn't you know it, the sky starts to blacken and this big storm moves in. I grab my umbrella and my flashlight and I go out to the car. The sky opens up and it's raining cats and dogs and lightning is bursting bright white with thunder all around and I turn on the flashlight and I shine it down on the pedals in the car to see what I could see, and son of a bitch, I see one thick strand of silvery web reaching down from under the dashboard down right to the clutch and I know the beast is still alive. I curse a blue streak and I shake my fist at the gods and the storm and I'm getting soaked. It's got to be him or me, or her or me, whatever, I ain't driving that car with that thing waiting to jump on me. I got no more bug spray to speak of, but I'm gonna spray that thing with something, be it furniture polish, and I'm gonna spray direct 'cause I know she's at the top of that web strand, waiting for the doorbell to ring. I grab a can of something and the storm is right on top of me now, it's all dramatic and big flashes of lightning like some horror show which it is and I spray up that web strand and she drops to the floor, big as a trout, alive, and unhurt. *(He takes a breath.)* Annoyed, though. And I swear to God this thing jumps two feet in the air and across the console and on to the floor on the other side of the car. I nearly shit my pants. But I got to drive this car to the city and I tell myself I got to defeat this demon bitch and I go around to the other side of the car and open the door and I look down and I think I see little yellow eyes glaring up at me and I beat the thing with the flashlight except I only wing it and it jumps again! It jumps right out of the car, I told you it was a jumper, and on to the ground at my feet and lightning flashes and I can see the thing scurrying towards me and I jump this time and I land on it and I dance on it. The little fuck has had me chicken-shitted for half a day and I dance on its head. I Watusi on the thing and grind it into the gravel. And I beat my chest and roar. I shake my fist at the sky and shout my victory to the treetops. And I look down and the lightning flashes again and the thing is all crumpled and dead and it looks tiny. It's no bigger than a quarter. A nickel. And I'm standing there in the rain and I'm startin' to feel pretty small. But hey, fuck it, the thing is dead and my car is my own.

PETE. Good thing it wasn't a brown recluse.

JOE. What's that?

PETE. Deadly spider. Likes mammals. Big mammals. It has this amazing ability to grow as it feeds. I read in *Newsweek* they found this kid at some summer camp in Michigan, almost dead. He didn't show up for archery or something and they found him wrapped up in his bunk, nearly catatonic. He couldn't talk. They got a nurse and when they pulled the covers down they found this thing, this spider, sitting on his chest, sucking away. Big as a ripe plum. Pulsating. The fangs were so deep they were afraid to pull it off him. The nurse shot the thing with an epi pen and it jumped six feet in the air. The kid was spouting blood and they figure the thing was locked onto an artery. The thing jumped around for a few seconds until somebody stepped on it. They figure it had a pint of blood in it from the mess it made. The kid was the color of that moss over there.

JOE. You read that in *Newsweek*?

PETE. Yeah. Couple weeks ago.

JOE. We got spiders like that around here?

PETE. Not confirmed.

JOE. Yuck.

PETE. Anyway, you got rid of the spider.

JOE. Yeah. You want my sandwich?

PETE. No. You eat it. I'll shut up.

JOE. Here. You take it. Take the chips, too.

PETE. Didn't you buy a cookie?

JOE. It's in the bag. It's yours. I got to get back to work.

PETE. I ever tell you about the spiders in Missouri? The ones that hang forty-foot webs from telephone poles?

JOE. Enjoy my lunch.

END OF PLAY

FILM NOIR

By
Bathsheba Doran

Film Noir was produced in 2004 by Point B at the Blue Heron Arts Centre in New York City as part of "States of Undress: An Evening of Ten-Minute Bedroom Plays."

CHARACTERS

WOMAN: ⌐
⎬ The classic guy and girl from film noir—
⎬ *The Maltese Falcon* look.
MAN: ⌐

AUTHOR'S NOTES: This play was inspired by film noir of the 1940s. When writing it, I saw movement against those filmic locations—a rainy street under a lamppost, a private dick's office, a nightclub. The play is also about the limitations of roles, for actors and, relatedly, for men and women. In some ways, therefore, the play seems to take place on a film set and in a bedroom.

I do not specify any one of these locations, but encourage a non-realistic design that allows an audience to experience the piece on a number of levels, and affords the actors the possibility of moving through different spaces during the performance. At the very opening, however, the evocation of classic 1940s film noir should be absolutely clear, at least from the costuming.

Finally, above all, we are in a theater. While I specify no particular places in the text, the actors should play with addressing some lines to the audience, as well as to each other.

FILM NOIR

WOMAN. What'cha doin' under that lamppost?

GUY. Thinkin'.

WOMAN. About what?

GUY. 'Bout how sordid the underground is. Gambling, gangsters, women who'll destroy you to get at their husband's money.

WOMAN. You wanna light my cigarette? *(He does.)*

GUY. Nice stems.

WOMAN. I grew them myself.

GUY. I gave birth to the rain. I looked up at the weather and it didn't suit my mood, so I thought of rain.

WOMAN. I thought of stockings. I thought of what a man would want to see on my legs if he wanted to come between them. I thought of the hair I hadn't shaved off them. And then I thought of stockings. *(A beat.)*

GUY. You want to fight?

WOMAN. You want to fight and fuck?

GUY. You wanna solve a crime?

WOMAN. You want me guilty at the end or innocent? Or retrospectively understood?

GUY. How 'bout I'm jealous.

WOMAN. How 'bout it's my fault.

GUY. And mine.

WOMAN. Yeah, I play around 'cause you treat me like shit.

GUY. It beats pizza. *(A beat.)*

WOMAN. Sometimes I wake up, sit up, see me in front of the mirror, and a gun from nowhere blows my brains out.

GUY. I see me, walking down the street, collar up, cigarette between my lips like a necessary flaw.

WOMAN. I see parties. I see my dress. You jealous, him trying. *(Defiant.)* I'm sexy. I'm oblivious.

GUY. I'm pissed as hell getting loaded at the bar. Fellas all around me crackin' wise 'bout how they want a piece of you and I want to smash their jaws in. I look beautiful.

WOMAN. I'm dancing.

GUY. No one will ever know how big my penis is.

WOMAN. No one will ever know if I come or if I'm just faking.

GUY. They want a story though.

WOMAN. Love, loss…

GUY. Plot.

WOMAN. You want to try?

GUY. Well we've got the lamppost…

WOMAN *(sounding like a film noir voiceover)*. It was dark, and it was cold so…

GUY *(same)*. I showed up at Harry's bar.

WOMAN. Harry's. You never knew what you were going to find there. Diamonds or some lowlife scum.

GUY. That night I went looking for diamonds. And I found her.

WOMAN. She had tits you wouldn't believe and a voice that made you think home was a warm bed in the Pacific.

GUY. Oh I knew she was trouble. The minute she said—

WOMAN. Hi, Johnny.

GUY. But somehow I couldn't keep her off of my mind.

WOMAN. I told him I was in trouble.

GUY. And when a dame tells you that—

WOMAN. What's a guy to do when it's dark and it's cold on a Saturday night?

GUY. I knew I could take out her old man and make off with her in my arms—

WOMAN. And he wanted the diamonds. *(A beat.)*

GUY. Then that…

WOMAN. No good…

GUY. Double-crossing… *(A beat.)*

WOMAN. I loved 'er hair in the morning. Rumpled, confused.

GUY. She didn't know how sexy it was. They did. The lowlifes. The guys she called friends.

WOMAN. What could I do? All I had was my hair. And I needed—

GUY *(aggressive)*. Diamonds.

WOMAN. Arms to hold me when I die. *(A beat.)*

GUY. And me? You think I like walking from one scene to the next, feeling the cigarette burn my nostrils as I inhale without using my hands?

WOMAN. My lungs are dying and my children would hate me.

GUY. I think I might want to run a café.

WOMAN. Vegetarian.

GUY. I agree. Maybe a collective.

WOMAN. Political pamphlets.

GUY. Rice and beans.

WOMAN. We'd live above it.

GUY. Oh yeah?

WOMAN. I can't bake. I don't want to. Maybe I'd have a job. Singing.

GUY. Yeah, you sing, you bitch, and look who comes around.

WOMAN. The dogs.

GUY. I'm running the café, you got guys sniffing 'round you while I'm baking the bread.

WOMAN. I don't find a man who runs a café very attractive.

GUY. Oh no. You want Wall Street.

WOMAN. I want arms.

GUY. I got arms.

WOMAN. But how do you know which arms are the right arms? This is what we forget. All arms are strong. But there are pimples, and hairs...

GUY. And flab and stubble...

WOMAN. Does it matter if the stroking tickles?

GUY. Does it matter if the armpits smell? We go to a party...

WOMAN. No one knows...we're dancing.

GUY. The envy...

WOMAN. Pictures taken...

GUY. My smile just right.

WOMAN. My breasts must be fabulous if you were the one to loosen the strap, feel underneath, know what you were touching you can taste. My dress on your floor, my skin in your mouth, my hair on your face.

GUY. My cigarettes on your teeth.

WOMAN. Your tongue in my mouth.

GUY. My hands on your back.

WOMAN. And then the rest.

GUY. Small. Odd. Quaking. Glistening at the tip with humiliating eagerness.

WOMAN. Dark. Smelly. Horrendously embarrassing. Covered with hair.

GUY. We're covered in hair.

WOMAN. We're descended from apes. I mean think about it. We're descended from apes.

GUY. That's why the soles of our feet are so hard.

WOMAN. Sometimes I sneeze.

GUY. I wake up and I see my hat and I see my coat and I have rehearsal, see? And I walk along with my cigarette, and I'm like, what if I'm no good. I say my line and it doesn't sound like I can hear it. They say how's it going and I say fine.

WOMAN. I look in the mirror and I can see I'm sexy. I look in the mirror and I can see my face. And my skin is dying and my hair is thinning and I just say—it doesn't matter. I'm an actor and—

GUY. I'm an actor. I feel the camera. I can see how I laugh at jokes and it's sexy.

WOMAN. I'm an actor and I can feel vulnerable!

GUY. But only up to a certain point...

WOMAN. ...and then I'm a stone.

GUY. I am a stone. Something used to crack open a head.

WOMAN. Something that looks better if it's covered in water.

GUY. There's a million of them and they're all different and they're all the same. *(A beat.)*

WOMAN. How can I be? When I hold a pen and it falls from my hand because it's already written.

GUY. And I crave a bed. Not mine, not yours, just a bed that says home. Sleep. Let the arms around me be the arms I love.

WOMAN. Let the breath on my neck be the breath I know.

GUY. Let the morning be morning and the day be the day before bed, when we're whole, and the clothes on the floor be the clothes that we wear before we take them off again.

WOMAN. And let me cry without being a woman.

GUY. And let me shout without being a man.

WOMAN. Because if the days are so tiring

GUY. Then the nights must be sacred.

WOMAN. But it's dark and we're cold.

GUY. And my cigarette is killing me.

WOMAN. And if I put my arm around you—

GUY. Then will you think I want something?

WOMAN. And could you touch my back?

GUY. And could you taste my tongue?

WOMAN. Because…

GUY. Everybody's got an angle.

WOMAN. No good…

GUY. Double-crossing… *(Pause.)*

WOMAN. But there are diamonds out there.

GUY. And Paris and Rome.

WOMAN. And the underworld is sexy

GUY. And so's being alone.

(Pause. They're back where they started.)

GUY. Hey baby.

WOMAN. What'cha doin' under that lamppost?

END OF PLAY

CHIAROSCURO

By
Lisa Dillman

Chiaroscuro was commissioned and first produced in 1998 by Chicago's Rivendell Theatre Ensemble for its ten-minute play festival "Mommapalooza: Short Takes on Mom." It was a finalist for the 1999 Actors Theatre of Louisville National Ten-Minute Play Contest.

CHARACTERS

JEN: A daughter.
MOTHER: Jen's.

The characters can be played by a young woman and a middle-aged woman; a middle-aged woman and an older woman; or two middle-aged women.

SETTING: Ideally, the action should take place in empty space full of light and shadow, with specific lighting cues serving to enhance some of the transitions.

TIME: The present.

CHIAROSCURO

AT THE CURTAIN: *LIGHTS come up revealing JEN and MOTHER on opposite sides of the playing area.*

JEN. In the beginning. A woman with red, red lipstick and a voice full of jumps and trills and wonder tells me story after story night after night.

MOTHER. "...Soon the princess came to a clearing in the woods. And there, hunched upon a craggy stump, sat a gnome of questionable breeding. He had a wart the size of an egg on the tip of his nose and he was hairy from top to toe. Some might call him matted. He took one look at our princess and found her so enticing that for a moment he was tempted *not* to put a curse on her. But alas! Evil gnome tradition won the day. 'Oh, thou pretty aimless wench. Sit ye on my splintery bench. Bethink all words ye've spake before. From this day on ye'll speak no more.' "

JEN. Later... She and my stepfather yak away all through dinner—their conversations, their *banter* erupting out of them, surging, blasting, spluttering. They warble. They chortle. They tease. They research and excavate each other's day. Words are king and queen and the rest of the royal family too. Words are the real food; what's on their plates is just an excuse. During a pause that many wouldn't recognize as such, I break in. "Hey, what's that? What's *chiaroscuro*?" They look perplexed for a moment— Did you just hear something? What was that sound? —and, squinting, tell me I'd better just go look it up.

MOTHER. Keep up or give up.

JEN. I begin bringing the dictionary to the table with me. With the extra four inches, I am almost as tall as they are. It's a massive, a *weighty* tome—an abridged OED. Abridged, yes, but that's OK by me—it's the perfect height and I like the elevation. I hop on and off it at will, finding, then absorbing the words. The words. Torrents, deluges of them. Great avalanches and whirling siroccos of words. Words all day and late into the night. I believe God invented sleeping just to shut us up a while. Later... We play Poem-itation.

MOTHER. Whose socks these are I think I know... She's chucked them on the sofa though. *(Barest pause.)*

JEN. But Ma won't mind I leave them there... Since I'm a lazy so-and-so.

MOTHER. And yet she does not think it queer... To always lob her socks right here...

JEN. One: split infinitive. Two: Frost is too easy. And while we're at it, Gray's *Elegy* blows big juicy chunks.

MOTHER. There stands and sneers the tiny-minded queen... It's true she knows it all at age thirteen...

JEN. I'm only *twelve*.

MOTHER. Don't mess with meter. *(Regroups.)* Tom Gray is not a chucklefest, it's true... Still, he's a well-loved poet, unlike *you.*

JEN. Talk is incessant. Silence means you have nothing to say. Of course there are things we don't talk about. *(She sneaks a glance at MOTHER, who stands a little ways away rubbing her temples gently, in obvious pain.)* And times when all talk suddenly ceases for days on end. And question marks bank up in the corners of the rooms. When my mother wanders the house noise-lessly through the night. Then sleeps in patches through the following day in her shaded room, with the door closed and locked. And if I have to ask her some-thing…

(She taps the floor lightly with her foot—a knock.)

MOTHER. What?

JEN. Absolute specificity is vital. Or she will whimper and gnash at her pillow. *(Beat. Then with great deliber-ation.)* I was hoping I could borrow your car. For to-night. To leave approximately seven p.m. and return at midnight or before. With no driving over sixty-five miles per hour on the highways—certainly much less than that on the byways—and no alcohol or drug con-sumption taking place during the hours the car is en-trusted to my care. *(Beat.)*

MOTHER. Take it.

JEN. Later… My stepfather takes his leave. Conversa-tion-wise he'd already been gone a while. Dinners had become cacophonous with the sounds of mastica-tion—his and mine, usually, since my mother was so often among the disappeared. His voiceless but very present wish to be elsewhere sucked all words out of the dinner hour. I took the opportunity to catalog his faults. His baldness. His lack of energy. His haunted, hopeless eyes. His habit of sniffing the back of his hand. Obsessively. But most of all, his silence. There he sat—balding, sniffing inertia personified. A husk. Then one evening he didn't come to the table. And soon it was apparent he'd cleared out for good. Later…

My mother returns to the world. She drinks more wine than before. We play Limerick Impromptu.

MOTHER. There once was a man from Toledo... Who looked awfully good in his Speedo... He'd prance all around... Then pull the thing down... While the ladies all swooned, "Oh how neato!"

JEN. Aren't you bawdy.

MOTHER. Limericks are traditionally filthy. I cleaned it up because we're eating. Your turn. Go ahead.

JEN. I'd rather not.

MOTHER. Oh, come on!

JEN. There once was a mom from Seattle... About the male member she'd prattle... She'd slurp up her wine... Then sit there and pine... 'Cuz finding a man's such a battle.

MOTHER. There once was a mean, heartless daughter...

JEN. Yes?

MOTHER. That's enough for tonight. Consume your comestibles, you.

JEN. Meaning she's had enough to drink that the necessary end rhymes would be an impossible feat. Meaning I hurt her feelings. Meaning something else too. Something so integral to our relationship that I can't name it until years later: I *bore* her. The occasional limerick is a poor replacement for densely layered stories from the heady landscape of my school day. Since she can build an epic out of a fifteen-minute jaunt to the grocery store, she can't see why I don't do the same. She figures that I must be living the life of a veritable Candide out there in the world. And what a withholding little gob-shite I am for not laying out the rich tapestry of my misadventures. The truth is I'm *not* picaresque. And words don't thrill me anymore.

MOTHER. Oh, Jen! Tell Marcia about that *Dickensian* math teacher of yours! She does a *drop-dead* impression of this guy, Marcia. Go on, honey. Tell it.

JEN. *You* tell it. *(MOTHER turns away. With great animation she silently mimes the impression and tells the story.)* And then she *does*. And she tells it better than I could have. And she imitates the math teacher—she's only met him *once*—better than I can after having sat in his class a semester and a half.

MOTHER. I've just about decided you're *shy*.

JEN. Well, I'm not.

MOTHER. You won't let anyone know you.

JEN. *You* know me.

MOTHER. Is that true, sweetie? Do I know you? *(Beat.)*

JEN. Don't you? *(Beat.)* Later. *(Beat.)* Years later. I am home. Alone. It's been a long day. My feet hurt. I'm on my third glass of merlot. The phone.

MOTHER. It's me.

JEN. Hello, you.

MOTHER. Listen…do you…? What does *splungeree* mean?

JEN. Umm. Something to do with exploring caves?

MOTHER. I'm not sure.

JEN. Well, where did you hear it? Give me some context.

MOTHER. I went to the door to see the postman today, and when he forked over my mail I said to him, "Oh, nuts. Just a bunch of splungeree." *(JEN laughs.)* I couldn't think of the word for *catalogs*. I was standing there with a fistful of the things and I couldn't think of the word. *Splungeree*. I went inside and wrote it down.

I had to sit and meditate to get the word *catalog* to come back to me. It was floating out there in the mist for such a long time.

JEN. Later.

MOTHER. It happened again.

JEN. We begin to keep a list. We call it the List in the Mist. *Splungeree. Altocram. Zlit. Oppley.*

MOTHER. *Eggoline. Fedabush. Croomuttle.*

JEN. *Hohorgan. Denkaptu. Argenbach. Joroist.*

MOTHER. *Cabblefan. Chickley.* That thing you boil water in. The *trattalot.* I can't remember anything. I burned the bottom out of my *trattalot* this morning.

JEN. We play List/Mist/Gist. *(Reciting.)* In last week's o'erlooked *splungeree*…I found a *trattalot*…I knew it was the one for me… I'd wrecked my old teapot.

MOTHER. A teapot…the word comes to me…not always, but just now…

JEN. I long to make a spot of tea… But I've forgotten how. *(Beat.)* Later. A specialist informs her she's suffered a series of tiny strokes. Probably over a period of years. Painless. But finally measurable.

MOTHER. Don't let me get away with anything. *Correct me.* Tell me what it's supposed to be.

JEN. Yes. I will. Later… She gives up driving and spends most of her time in her garden. Her conversation for the most part makes sense. But she speaks in facts now.

MOTHER. It's your. Birthday. I sent you a card.

JEN. And then there are the holes. The ones less and less-often filled by even her transitory invented language.

MOTHER. Today I…sssssss…I…ohhh. Nothing.

JEN. I think of her often just before sleep. But she is young and her red, red mouth is a vivid patch in perpetual motion. I see her take a step away from me. Waving. And then another. Still waving.

MOTHER. The lilacs. Are early this year.

JEN. And the mist rolls up around her feet. She is blurred around the edges. But still she is waving.

(The LIGHTS slowly fade.)

END OF PLAY

A CHANGE OF PACE

By
Edward Pomerantz

A Change of Pace first appeared in *Ms* magazine in 1974 and had its first production at the Déjà vu Playhouse in Hollywood, Calif., in 1985. It was directed by Raymond Cole, and featured Shannon Sullivan and David Hunt Stafford. Subsequent readings of the play have been performed at Food for Thought, the dramatic reading series at the National Arts Club in New York City, featuring Daniel McDonald and four different actresses—Judith Light, Marlo Thomas, Barbara Feldon and Betty Buckley.

CHARACTERS

JERRY:

MARGO:
} An attractive couple in their 40s.

SETTING: A bedroom.

TIME: The present.

A CHANGE OF PACE

AT THE CURTAIN: *JERRY and MARGO are lying in bed in each other's arms. After a while:*

JERRY. Margo?

MARGO *(sleepily)*. Mmmmmm?

JERRY. You still up?

MARGO *(muttering)*. What is it?

JERRY. Nothing...I was just lying here thinking... *(Pause.)* Have you ever cheated on me? *(MARGO doesn't answer. We listen to her breathing.)* I mean... what right have I to assume you haven't? What right have I to be so sure of you? Especially now... Back to school after all these years...your whole life centered around the kids...around the house...around me. You must be coming into contact with all kinds of new people...all kinds of opportunities. *(Pause.)* ...Are you?

MARGO *(in her sleep)*. Am I what?

JERRY. Meeting new people... Having an affair.

MARGO *(turning over, making herself comfortable)*. I'll tell you in the morning.

(She goes to sleep. JERRY looks at her, then to himself:)

JERRY. Some English professor who's told you you have a talent for writing...a profound understanding of the human heart. Some kid...with a tattoo and an earring in his nipple—who punctuates your every word, your every breath with wow...and cool...and like that's really deep, man. *(A sigh.)* Well, it was inevitable, I guess.

(He leans over, kisses her ear.) Just try to keep things in perspective. Okay? I'd hate to see you get hurt.
(He turns over, goes to sleep. Long pause. Then lifting her head, MARGO turns and looks at him. She sits up.)

MARGO. You've got it all figured.

JERRY *(waking with a start)*. What?

MARGO. I said you've got it all figured.

JERRY. What are you talking about?

MARGO. My education. My extracurricular activities.

JERRY. I was only kidding.

MARGO. Kidding. First you tell me you have no right to make assumptions...no right to be so sure of me. Then you not only assume I'm having an affair but who I'm having it with.

JERRY. I was indulging myself—in fantasy.

MARGO. Some kid. Some English teacher. Some nice safe stereotype you can generalize, feel superior to.

JERRY. I wish I was dead. What do you want me to say?

MARGO *(stares at him)*. You don't think I have talent...a profound understanding of the human heart.

JERRY. I didn't say that. I was suggesting some English teacher might take advantage of that to get into bed with you.

MARGO. And that's all it would take.

JERRY. English teachers want to get laid like everybody else.

MARGO. That's your fantasy...your image of me. Instant pushover. For horny intellectuals. Tattooed boys with earrings.

JERRY. Oh for Christ's sake...

MARGO. What contempt you must have for me. What contempt you must have for yourself…being married to such a pushover.

JERRY. I'm sorry. Okay?… Let's go to sleep.

(He turns over. MARGO sits there for a moment. Then:)

MARGO. He's not an English professor.

JERRY. What?

MARGO. I said he's not an English professor. *(JERRY turns, looks at her.)* Or a kid.

JERRY. What does that mean?

MARGO. I'm answering your question. *(They stare at each other.)*

JERRY. Look. Forget I asked. Okay? If you're having an affair, terrific! We've been married forever. It's about time.

(He turns over and punches his pillow. MARGO waits for him to settle down.)

MARGO. Then you won't mind hearing the details.

JERRY. I don't want to hear the details.

MARGO. You just want me to hear your fantasies.

JERRY *(turning, angry)*. Look, what is this? Revenge?

MARGO. Revenge for what?

JERRY. You know. *(She looks at him bewildered.)* All the times you think I've screwed around. *(She stares at him dumbfounded for a moment, then she laughs.)* What's so funny? *(She laughs again.)* What's so funny?!

MARGO. Think you've screwed around. Oh, Jerry…

JERRY. What does that mean?

MARGO. Every time you've been with a woman I know it. That night…when you come home…all that week… you're a better lover. We fuck more often. Why do you think I've never said anything to you? If it didn't pay off for me I'd have left you long ago. *(He looks at her stunned.)* What a fool you take me for… I've lived with your infidelities for years. If it hasn't been other women, it's been your fantasies…your projects…your constant preoccupation and love affair with yourself. Most of the time I'm not here at all for you. Even when you're with me you're not with me. I just exist—as your mirror, your tape recorder.

JERRY. I don't believe this. I don't believe this is happening.

MARGO. His name is David.

JERRY. Who?

MARGO. My new person. The one you inquired about.

JERRY. Oh my God. I think I'm going to be sick.

MARGO. He's an ex-Marine. In my philosophy class. Works nights as a bartender while he gets his PhD. He's killed people. Enemy soldiers his own age. He's thirty-two.

JERRY. You're just dying to tell me all this, aren't you? You've been lying there…waiting.

MARGO. If you weren't prepared for the answer you shouldn't have asked the question. *(They stare at each other.)* For years I thought going to bed with another man would mean the end of us…that it would have to be him or you. I know otherwise now… For years I thought all men brought your appetite…your violence to bed with them… I'm not complaining. It's always excited me… *(She shrugs.)* Now I know there's something else… Something different.

JERRY. And something tells me I'm going to hear all about it.

MARGO. Your fantasies underestimate me. I want you to know who I am…what my capacities are.

JERRY. If there's one thing I'll never do again it's under-estimate you.

(They stare at each other.)

MARGO *(slowly, quietly)*. I've learned things. I've learned that you can make a man happy and not feel like a slave…a nymphomaniac. I've learned to locate and honor my appetite…my violence. *(JERRY stares at her.)* I've learned to do things…sexy things…things only whores and Orientals are supposed to know how to do.

JERRY. What kind of things?

MARGO *(a shrug)*. Things. With thumbs. And knotted silk handkerchiefs. *(He stares at her dumbstruck. She smiles.)* If you like I'll teach them to you. *(He turns away. She laughs.)* I've learned to be generous…with all of my body. With you I've always held back, re-sented giving until I got, only gave when I got first. I'm sorry about that. Until I met him, I had no idea there was another way. Until I met him, I had no idea you could make love to someone and still belong to yourself… That's why I agreed to try the others.

JERRY *(looks at her)*. Others?

MARGO. His brother. And his friends. *(JERRY stares at her.)* When he first suggested it, I was insulted. I felt like a prostitute…an object. But then I saw it his way. How could he be so selfish…so possessive…to keep me all to himself… *(She laughs.)* As it turned out, his brother and his friends are as sexy as he is… Sensi-tive…intelligent… I'm sure you'd like them.

JERRY *(quietly)*. How many of them are there—all to-gether?

MARGO. Just four.

JERRY. I don't believe you.

MARGO. My only regret is there isn't more of me to go around.

(She smiles. A long pause as they stare at each other, then:)

JERRY. Oh no...Oh no... You had me going there for a minute...but that did it... That last one about the brother and the friends... You blew it, baby.

MARGO. Would you like to meet them?

JERRY. I'm warning you, Margo. A joke is a joke.

MARGO. You overestimate my sense of humor.

JERRY *(visibly shaken, trying to control himself)*. Okay... *(Holding his hand up in truce.)* Okay. One fantasy deserves another. We're even now. Let's go to sleep. *(He turns over and lies there taut. MARGO sits there. A long moment, then JERRY continues, laughing:)* Thumbs... Knotted silk handkerchiefs... *(Turning to her.)* Where did you get that shit?

(A long moment before she answers.)

MARGO. I read a book.

(She turns over and goes to sleep. JERRY remains still, looking at her, as the LIGHTS dim and the curtain falls.)

END OF PLAY

MA IN HER KERCHIEF

By
Janet Kenney

Ma in Her Kerchief was originally produced at The 6th Annual Boston Theatre Marathon, Boston Playwrights' Theatre, Boston, Mass., in 2004. It was directed by Susan Kosoff, and featured Kippy Goldfarb and Helen Mc-Elwain.

CHARACTERS

ANDREA: A newly married woman in her 20s.
RUTH: Andrea's mother-in-law, late 50s or so.

SETTING: The living room of Andrea and her husband, Jack. A small suburban home. The place is ready to go for Christmas. There is a picture window behind the tree. A mantel, bare. Boxes of ornaments.

TIME: Christmas morning, two a.m. The present.

MA IN HER KERCHIEF

AT THE CURTAIN: *The tree lights are all off. RUTH is standing at the window beside the tree. She is in her bathrobe. A silky scarf covers her head. What bit of hair shows is wispy and nearly gone. After a moment, RUTH starts to sift through the ornament box. Pause, then ANDREA, in bathrobe and slippers, enters. She startles RUTH.*

RUTH. Oh! Andrea. I thought—Jack's asleep?

ANDREA. You can't hear the snoring?

RUTH. You'll get used to that.

ANDREA. I doubt it.

RUTH. I never did. To Dave's, I mean.

ANDREA. Any sign of Santa?

RUTH. Not yet. But it's only two. He's probably in Spain, or Iceland.

ANDREA. Probably.

RUTH. Can we turn on the tree lights?

ANDREA. Of course— *(She does so.)*

RUTH. I didn't want to, well, I'm not paying the bill—

ANDREA. Don't be silly. Did you have a nice nap?

RUTH. My last Christmas, and I'm sleeping through it.

ANDREA. Well, we'll have a busy day tomorrow. It was smart to take a nap.

RUTH. When the children were young, Dave used to keep a little jingle bell in his pocket and ring it once in a while. The kids would scream and dash up the stairs.

ANDREA. Dave's funny.

RUTH. He's easy with people, not like me.

ANDREA. Oh, now don't say that—

RUTH. I can't live here if you're going to be using that tone with me.

ANDREA. Sorry.

(RUTH pulls a string of white lights out of the box, starts to work on the mantel.)

RUTH. Do you think I should have divorced Dave?

ANDREA. I couldn't know a thing like—

RUTH. Was I too hard on him? He looked so handsome at the wedding. How do they put that in the paper? "Survived by ex-husband"?

ANDREA. I really don't know. What would you like it to say?

RUTH. I'll get back to you on that one. Open your present, will you?

ANDREA. But it's not—all right, if you want. *(She opens a large package. It's a sweater; one of those embroidered/appliquéd Christmas jobs. It's ghastly.)* Oh, I love it!

RUTH. Take it back—

ANDREA. No, no, I love it—I'll wear it tomorrow—

RUTH. Andrea: every little thought shows on your face.

ANDREA.	RUTH.
Oh! I hate that! I've always been like that—I'm—	It's fine, don't worry about it—
sorry, it's a very sweet gift, it's just a little loud for me, and I'm always hot, especially tomorrow when I'll be cooking the turkey, and that takes all day— Right. Sorry.	It's fine, return it, I don't mind. Please, please return it.

ANDREA *(re: the decorating)*. Maybe we should do this in the morning. *(But RUTH persists.)* Well, here, let me help you with that.

(The two of them work at the mantel.)

RUTH. Thank you for not doing it without me.

ANDREA. Jack said it was your favorite thing to do. He said you said, "the mantel draws the eye in the room, past the tree, past the gifts, because it's a permanent part of the house. It's the part that stays after the holidays, therefore it's the most important part of the decorating, and should have some dignity and solidity to it."

RUTH. God, I'm long-winded.

ANDREA. Oh, no, I—

RUTH. I'm teasing. Have I never teased you before?

ANDREA. I don't think so.

RUTH. I'll have to tease you again sometime.

ANDREA. All right.

RUTH. It'll give us something to look forward to. *(Re: a box of ornaments.)* Oh, these. Dave came home with these one night.

ANDREA. They're nice.

RUTH. They are. He'd been out celebrating; the "silly season," you know, and usually he'd come with these God-awful pieces of tacky junk. They went into the trash before morning. And he'd come home with an entire box of candy canes, dozens of canes, and he'd just hand them to the kids, before dinner, and if I tried to take them away, he'd say, "Oh, Ruth, relax, it's Christmas," as if a person should be ill or drunk because— "Oh, Ruth, it's Christmas." What do you call me?

ANDREA. What?

RUTH. You never call me anything. You—I just realized that.

ANDREA. Oh, well. "Mrs. Driscoll."

RUTH. No!

ANDREA. I do, yeah.

RUTH. Of course, that's *your* name, now.

ANDREA. Yes, yes it is.

RUTH. That's funny. I just don't think I ever—

ANDREA. When I first met you, I said, "It's lovely to meet you, Mrs. Driscoll," and you didn't correct me, didn't say, "Oh, call me 'Ruth,'" or call me, whatever, "Mother," or something—

RUTH. Well, I'm not your mother—

ANDREA. Some of my friends call their mothers-in-laws "mother," but—

RUTH. That's just silly. It's a gratuitous and obvious attempt at unearned intimacy, don't you think so?

ANDREA. Yeah. Yes, sure.

RUTH. What would you like to call me?

ANDREA. Oh, whatever you want me to call you.

RUTH. We left it at "Mrs. Driscoll"?

ANDREA. After that, I just said "Hi, _____." "How are you, _____?" "How are you feeling, _____?" Like that.

RUTH. Did you? Just that big pause like that?

ANDREA. Not a pause, no, more like a blank.

RUTH. Ruth. My name is Ruth. Let's just go with that. Please. Call me "Ruth."

ANDREA. Fine. Ruth.

RUTH. No, that won't do. Then Jack will call me "Ruth." Then Stephanie will call me "Ruth." No, I don't want my own children to call me "Ruth."

ANDREA. I'm sure they won't—

RUTH. One of the women in my chemo group—

ANDREA. The Tuesday night—

RUTH. No, the Wednesday—that's the "Death and Dying" group on Tuesday.

ANDREA. Oh, right—

RUTH. There's a woman in that group, and her name is Janine. A nice name, but somehow or other along the way, her daughter has come to call her "Janine." How do you suppose that happened?

ANDREA. Maybe she asked her to—

RUTH. What would prompt a parent to have her children call her by her—you live your whole adult life being this person's parent—rearrange everything, spend all your time, give up anything, anyone, do any—all because of that, what is that, a title? "Mother"? A job? A life. It's a life. You don't give that up lightly. Your mother wouldn't like it if you called me "Mother"—

ANDREA. She's not that fussy. I think as long as I continued to address her as "Mom," she wouldn't—

RUTH. Is "Mother" formal? Is it too formal that Jack and Stephanie call me "Mother"?

ANDREA. No. Yes. It seems a bit, yeah, Victorian, I guess.

RUTH. What should they call me?

ANDREA. I think it's a little late to get them to change, now.

RUTH. I guess I'm running out of time—

ANDREA. That's not what I—

RUTH. Well, I am.

ANDREA. How about some warm milk? My mom used to put vanillin and sugar and—

RUTH. I'd just throw it up.

ANDREA. If you don't go to bed, Santa won't come.

RUTH. My God, you're a pretty girl. You and Jack will make such pretty babies. And I'll never—I'm so sorry for that. I don't believe in angels; don't know if there's any—I'm not sure...but, if there is such a thing, if there's a lingering, a hovering...I'll be one, and I'll watch over them all the days of their lives.

ANDREA. I'll let them know that.

RUTH. Good. I'm going to give you a proper Christmas present.

ANDREA. No, that's—

RUTH *(takes off her diamond ring)*. I want you to have this.

ANDREA. No, no, I can't—

RUTH. It's going to fall off anyway.

ANDREA. Stephie should have this.

RUTH. Oh, please. Have you seen the size of that rock she's got? I only kept wearing it to annoy Dave. You and Jack will always struggle for money. Some people just do, I'm sorry to tell you. The good news is, you don't care.

ANDREA. We don't.

RUTH. But turquoise is not a proper engagement ring.

ANDREA. We can't see spending a year's salary on a—

RUTH. Keep it.

ANDREA. I really don't think it's right for me. Really, and Stephie would—she'd—and Jack—

RUTH *(overlapping on "she'd")*. Will you take this ring—with this ring—take this, and keep it and cherish it and cherish—and cherish...

ANDREA. I will. Certainly, I will. I won't take it off 'til I give it to my daughter.

RUTH. Ah, what's wrong with me? I'm all sappy tonight.

ANDREA. It's a sad night. It's all about waiting, you know? Nights are long sometimes, that's all.

RUTH. They're gonna get longer, missy. They're going to get very long. You two children are wonderful to—

ANDREA. Please, please, we want you here. It's our wedding present, your staying.

RUTH. That's a lousy present. Will you take back that sweater?

ANDREA. I will.

RUTH. Fine. Good. Thank you.

ANDREA. Thank you.

RUTH. Thank you, what? We should finish that sentence.

ANDREA. I don't know—

RUTH. Call me something.

ANDREA. Thank you, Mrs. Driscoll.

(RUTH hands over the gathered mantel decorations and ANDREA takes over. RUTH, tired, sets herself in a comfy chair and watches...and supervises.)

END OF PLAY

18 HOLES

By
David MacGregor

18 Holes premiered in 2003 as part of Hearlande Theatre Company's "Play-By-Play" at the Studio Theatre at Oakland University in Rochester, Mich. It was directed by Mary Locker, and featured Neil Necastro and David Haig. That same year, it was voted "Audience Favorite" at the Barebones Theatre Group's 3rd Annual 15-Minute Play Festival in Charlotte, N.C.

CHARACTERS

STEVE: 20s to 40s.
JOHN: 20s to 40s.

SETTING: A golf course.

TIME: The present.

18 HOLES

AT THE CURTAIN: *STEVE and JOHN approach each other from opposite sides of the stage, each wearing golf attire and pulling their clubs on pull carts. They will play a faux round of golf, perhaps actually hitting some kind of balls, but perhaps not. The end of each hole can be indicated in any number of ways: movement by the actors, a shift in lighting, or a sound effect of a ball hitting the bottom of the cup.*

STEVE. Hey, how you doing?

JOHN. Just happy to be here. You good to go?

STEVE. Are you kidding me? I've been looking forward to this all week.

JOHN. Then let's do it.

STEVE. All right. Show me how it's done, big man.

FIRST HOLE

JOHN. ...so I'm out walking with Alex the other day and he finds this stick and he's just having a ball with it, right? And then pretty soon he's done playing with the stick, so he kisses it, sets it gently on the grass, and says, "Bye stick!" And I'm standing there watching all this and I'm thinking, "Either he's missing something, or I am."

STEVE. It's probably you.

JOHN. Yeah. That's what I'm afraid of. I used to know what he knows, but somewhere along the line, I must have forgot it.

SECOND HOLE

STEVE. ...so you remember that whole thing when Princess Diana died?

JOHN. Sure.

STEVE. Well, I remember watching all that on TV and people are just going nuts, you know, weeping and crying and leaving flowers everywhere, and as I'm watching it I realized that I didn't feel a damned thing. You might as well have told me that Yosemite Sam or Daffy Duck died. On the other hand, the whole World Trade Center thing, I'm watching that on TV and I'm just crying like a baby. Explain that to me.

JOHN. Well, the World Trade Center, those were real people. Princess Diana, you're right, she was kind of like a cartoon character. She got packaged and marketed just like any other product...just like any other celebrity.

STEVE. Yeah. Maybe that's it. Because I remember thinking, I probably won't die when my chauffeur-driven Mercedes slams into a concrete abutment while I'm being chased by paparazzi.

JOHN. Probably not.

STEVE. Hey, is that wind coming more towards us or more from the side?

THIRD HOLE

STEVE. ...yeah, Taylor's all worried about me getting old and dying, so I told him I'd have myself cloned.

JOHN. That's not going to do him any good. He's what, eight years old? And if they clone you, you'd be a baby.

STEVE. Well, that's part of this deal we worked out. See, right now, I'm the dad. But I'll get myself cloned in twenty years or so, then he can be my dad. And then we'll just keep going like that. I'll be the dad, then he'll be the dad, and so on. I think it would be a pretty good deal, actually. If you knew that somewhere down the road, your child would become your parent, hey, you're gonna make sure you're a pretty good parent.

FOURTH HOLE

STEVE. ...it's Ding Dongs.

JOHN. No, it's King Dons.

STEVE. King Dons? What are you talking about?

JOHN. They're called King Dons. I swear to God. In fact, originally, they were called King Dongs, then they changed it.

STEVE. You're making that up.

JOHN. I'm not. I'm telling you, I wish I'd saved a box of King Dongs. You tell people about them today and they look at you like you're nuts.

FIFTH HOLE

JOHN. ...if you want to find an attractive woman, or man for that matter, it's really just a question of how much money they come from. Richer people are better looking than poor people because wealthy men marry attractive women and breed with them. It's that simple.

STEVE. Well, I agree with you to a certain extent. You go to the low end kind of shopping malls and you're going to see some pretty scary specimens of humanity. The better class the mall is, the better looking the people get.

JOHN. Right.

STEVE. But only up to a point. When you get to the really high-end malls, that's when it starts getting scary again.

JOHN. You know, you're right. What do you think's going on there?

STEVE. Inbreeding. The very very wealthy are kind of required to only marry the very very wealthy. And if you confine yourself to that small a genetic pool you're just asking for trouble.

JOHN. Yeah, it's tricky. Hey, there's the cart girl. You want a candy bar or something?

STEVE. Yeah, that sounds good.

(JOHN waves his hand in the air.)

SIXTH HOLE

(STEVE and JOHN munch on candy bars.)

STEVE. …so what I usually do is I wait until Karen goes to bed and then slip one in the VCR.

JOHN. You're kidding.

STEVE. No.

JOHN. Does she know you're doing this?

STEVE. Well, I think it's one of those deals where she doesn't really want to know.

JOHN. You have to wait until your wife goes to bed before you can watch Akira Kurosawa films?

STEVE. She doesn't like Orientals. It's like this phobia.
She knows it's wrong, she knows it's silly, but she just
can't help herself. So I sit in the dark with the sound
turned down low and watch *Yojimbo* by myself.

SEVENTH HOLE

STEVE. ...it won't matter anyway, because in a hundred
years or so, women will be ruling the world.

JOHN. Oh yeah? Why's that?

STEVE. Virtual reality. Once they perfect those virtual reality machines, it's all over for men running the show.
They'll just stay at home, day and night, plugged into
their machines, blowing things up and having sex with
Marilyn Monroe.

JOHN. You don't think the women will be plugged in too,
eating virtual fudge and finding the perfect pair of virtual shoes?

STEVE. Nah, women aren't as fetishistic as men. I think
it'll be all for the best, really. I just hope I live long
enough to get one of those machines.

EIGHTH HOLE

JOHN. ...you know what kind of women I find really attractive? New moms.

STEVE. How new exactly?

JOHN. Well, with a six-month-old, say. I see them walk-
ing around the neighborhood with their strollers and
I'm telling you, they are just radiant. They're glowing.
The way they walk, they've got their chins up, they're

strutting along, and they just seem so damned happy. I find that really attractive.

STEVE. I've always been attracted to pigeon-toed women, myself.

JOHN. Pigeon-toed? Really?

STEVE. Yeah. I'm not sure why. Probably because with their toes pointed in a little, it kind of accentuates their buttocks.

JOHN. Like when women Rollerblade.

STEVE. Yeah! I love seeing women on Rollerblades, wobbling down the sidewalk.

JOHN. Well, maybe it's that wobbly thing that attracts you. They look like they'd be pretty easy to run down and ravish. It's your primordial instincts kicking in.

STEVE. Could be. You gotta love those primordial instincts.

JOHN. Hey, they're the only reason we're here in the first place.

NINTH HOLE

STEVE. ...so for your money, who do you think is the single-most imitated or mimicked person in the entire history of humanity?

JOHN. Boy...um...Yoda?

STEVE. I don't think he qualifies as a person.

JOHN. Oh. Who would you say?

STEVE. I'd go with Curly from the Three Stooges...you know, the whole, "Ooh, a wise guy" thing. When you think about it, it's a helluva legacy.

JOHN. Moe, Larry, the cheese!

STEVE. Exactly!

TENTH HOLE

JOHN. ...anyway, I finally decided to look it up and it turns out the whole story about Catherine the Great and the horse is just a myth.

STEVE. That's too bad. It really gave her life a punchy ending.

JOHN. Well, I suppose it was a little unbelievable... I guess it's just the kind of thing you want to believe is true.

ELEVENTH HOLE

STEVE. ...the best job I ever had was when I was a teenager, picking up trash at the carnival.

JOHN. Come on. Picking up trash was the best job you ever had?

STEVE. I'm dead serious. I'd get there early in the morning and get my sawed-off hockey stick with a nail stuck in the end of it and just go through the whole carnival. After a couple of days, I was so good with that stick that I could nail cigarette butts with just one stab. And the thing is, what's so great about it, is you start picking up the trash and the place looks like a cyclone hit it. But a couple of hours later, you look behind you and there isn't a speck of paper anywhere. You can see what a difference you made because it's right in front of your eyes. It was just real satisfying. I haven't had a job since that made me feel that way.

TWELFTH HOLE

JOHN. ...anyway, she's looking at the lasagna and saying I burned it and I'm saying it's not burned, it's caramelized. And you know what? She bought it.

STEVE. That Food Network is a godsend.

THIRTEENTH HOLE

JOHN. ...well, from an historical perspective, the guys you really need to watch out for are the ones with facial hair.

STEVE. Oh yeah?

JOHN. Sure. Prussian generals, Islamic fundamentalists, suburban cops, guys like Hitler and Charles Manson and Geraldo. They've got some issues going on.

STEVE. You think it's a masculinity thing? They need to prove they're men by growing beards and mustaches and making everyone else's lives miserable?

JOHN. Could be. My question is, does being a prick make you want to grow facial hair, or does growing facial hair turn you into a prick?

FOURTEENTH HOLE

(JOHN and STEVE look upward.)

STEVE. What is that?

JOHN. Looks like a turkey vulture.

STEVE. You think?

JOHN. I'm pretty sure.

STEVE. Where was it we saw that treefrog climbing out of the irrigation pipe?

JOHN. Crooked Creek?

STEVE. Yeah. Man, what the hell was he thinking about?

FIFTEENTH HOLE

JOHN. ...all I'm saying is that from an experience stand-point, I'd be kind of interested to know what it feels like to perform fellatio.

STEVE. Huh. I don't think I'll be able to help you out there.

JOHN. Well, it's not like I'm going to do it. I'm just talking about the sensation. It would be interesting to see what it's like, that's all.

SIXTEENTH HOLE

STEVE. ...you can take it from me, if humanity survives another ten thousand years, you're not going to see any road kill at all.

JOHN. What are you saying, cars will be programmed to avoid animals?

STEVE. No, I'm saying road kill will be naturally selected against. Those animals that stay away from roads or bright lights are the ones that will breed. Cars and trucks have only been around for a hundred years or so, so the animal population hasn't had time to adjust.

JOHN. So really, this is the Golden Age of road kill.

STEVE. You're damned right it is!

SEVENTEENTH HOLE

JOHN. ...the thing is, you're not supposed to say it, but slavery actually helped civilization along.

STEVE. In what way?

JOHN. Every way. Before there was slavery, what did you do to people you defeated in battle? You killed them and ate them. But once they made them slaves, and it didn't matter who it was, blacks, whites, Orientals, Egyptians, whoever, once they had slaves doing the grunt work, it left other people more spare time to think about stuff and invent things like zippers and microwave ovens. That's why guys like Aristotle and Saint Paul were all for slavery. They could see it really moved things along.

STEVE. You know, you really should hit the talk-show circuit. You'd be the breath of fresh air they need.

EIGHTEENTH HOLE

JOHN. ...well, let me think...I'd have to say a novocaine shot up into the roof of my mouth when I was about ten years old. I remember the dentist saying, "This might sting a little." How about you?

STEVE. It was in our basement. I'm maybe twelve or thirteen, the lights are out, and my brother winds up for a slap shot using a glow-in-the dark Superball. Caught me right in the left testicle.

JOHN. Jesus. *(JOHN putts a long one, and his body English helps guide the ball into the hole.)* Yes! I knew I'd make one today. It just took me eighteen holes to do it.

STEVE. So what did you shoot?

JOHN. Oh, I don't know. Ninety-something, probably.

STEVE. Are we on for next week?

JOHN. Sure. I'll give you a call.

STEVE. All right. *(STEVE embraces JOHN in a hug.)* I love you, buddy. I don't know what I'd do without you.

JOHN. Yeah, I know.

STEVE. See you next week.

(JOHN and STEVE head off in different directions. STEVE exits as JOHN's cell phone rings. He reaches into his pocket and pulls it out.)

JOHN. Hello?… Oh, hi hon…no, we just finished. I'm walking to the parking lot right now…what did we talk about? Oh…nothing. See you in a few.

(JOHN puts his phone back in his pocket and exits.)

END OF PLAY

COFFEE BREAK

By
Jerry Thompson

Coffee Break premiered in 2003 with the Provincetown Theatre Company under the direction of Robert Seaver, and featured Peter Scarbo Frawley and Deborah Peabody. It was also produced at the Academy of Performing Arts in Orleans, Mass., and was chosen for the 2003 Last Frontier Theatre Conference in Valdez, Alaska.

CHARACTERS

AL: Early 70s.
ANNA: Early 30s.

SETTING: The back of a modest home in a small New England town.

TIME: The present, late June. About nine a.m.

COFFEE BREAK

AT THE CURTAIN: *AL is painting a door. Downstage of him are two sawhorses standing side by side. A plank is laid across them. ANNA approaches carrying two cups of take-out coffee.*

AL. Took ya long enough! Whaddya do, stop at the beauty parlor fer a manicure? *(ANNA, used to this sort of abuse, does not respond. She places coffee cups on the plank and sits down beside them. AL goes over to a window on the back of the house. Examines the window. Turns to ANNA. Angry. Shouting:)* How many times have I told ya that ya gotta prime the window muntins* before ya putty 'em?

ANNA. Probably a hundred times.

AL. Then why the hell didn't ya prime 'em yesterday, after ya took out the broken glass? Ya can't glaze a window if it ain't primed! I tole ya—the putty won't stick! Jesus! *(Pulls off his hat and hurls it on the ground, moves to the plank. Sits down. Removes the top from the coffee cup. Sips coffee.)* Sometimes you make me so goddamn mad! Now we're goin' ta be here an extra day waitin' fer the damn primer ta dry!

ANNA *(calm, even tone)*. I did prime the muntins. You better take a closer look.

AL. Whaddya talkin' about? *(Gets off the plank. Goes to the window and examines it.)* Look here, there ain't a

---

* Strips of wood separating panes of glass in a window sash.

drop a paint on these muntins? Now we got ta paint 'em and wait all day fer it ta dry before we can putty 'em. These people want us outa here. They're goin' ta be pissed!

ANNA. I used linseed oil. You said it worked better. You better put on your glasses, Al.

AL *(examines the window more closely. Touches the muntin)*. Oh, yah. Yah. I guess ya did. *(Returns to the plank and sits down, picks up the coffee cup and sips.)*

ANNA *(trying to maintain control after AL's tirade)*. Al, if you keep flying off the handle like that, you're going to have a heart attack. You don't have to yell all the time to get the job done right.

AL. I'm the boss. I have to yell. People always try ta take advantage of their boss. It's jus' human nature. Like you! Moseyin' in ta work every mornin' like ya ain't got a care in the world. I got responsibility. I got ta make sure the job keeps movin' along.

ANNA *(angry)*. Responsibility? Responsibility? I've got a three-year old daughter. Wouldn't you call that responsibility?

AL. Yeah. *(Pause.)* Yeah a 'course I would but ya got ta...

ANNA. You know full well that the reason I come moseying in here late is because I've got to drop Tina off at daycare. And you manage to make up for the lost time by keeping me here every day 'til five-thirty cleaning brushes.

AL. You ain't on vacation ya know! This ain't Disney World! This is the real world. *(Pause.)* When I was your age I could go out drinkin' whiskey and go carousin' all night long—sleep maybe two hours and still be ta work on time.

ANNA. Yeah you've mentioned that a few times.

AL. Workin' with a jackhammer—breakin' up pavement ta lay sewage pipe...

ANNA. Shook the guts right outa ya.

AL. Yeah, an' lunchtime...

ANNA. You'd eat and then puke.

AL. That's right. How'd you know?

ANNA. I'm psychic.

AL. You and your fancy words.

ANNA. Did you ever stop to think that it might have been the whiskey and lack of sleep that...

AL. It was the goddamn jackhammer—shook the guts right outa me!

ANNA. Forget about that damn jackhammer. That was a hundred years ago. Let's get back to the matter of you yellin' at me all the time.

AL. I yell at ya because things ain't goin' right fer me, and it's 'cause a you.

ANNA *(imitating his masculine voice)*. Things ain't goin' right fer me, and it's 'cause a you! *(Normal tone.)* What's that supposed to mean?

AL. It's 'cause you're a girl.

ANNA. At least you got the gender right. But what does my being a woman have to do with things not going right for you?

AL. I'm not getting as many jobs as I used to. There's a lotta competition out there now. Young bucks comin' along, takin' work away from me—guys that don't know a paintbrush from a toothbrush, but they're gettin' mosta the work. I got a grand total a two jobs lined up. Two jobs! Don't ya see? It's June and I got a grand total a two jobs lined up. Used ta be—this time a year—the phone'ed be ringin' off the hook. I'd have—maybe ten jobs lined up fer the summer. I figure it's 'cause a you bein' a girl that I ain't gettin' jobs. *(Pause.)* Ya see people don't want a girl paintin' their house. It don't make a good impression.

ANNA. Oh, I see, it's my fault that you're not getting work. Well you don't have to worry about that any-more.

AL. Whaddya mean?

ANNA. I'm leaving.

AL. Where ya goin'?

ANNA. I'm quitting. Two weeks and I'm out of here.

AL. Outa here? Jesus, Anna! Things ain't that bad! Maybe I was exaggeratin' a little. I'll get more work.

ANNA. It's got nothin' to do with how much work you've got. It's got to do with you being a bastard.

AL. Bastard? This ain't like you. You never used that kinda language around me before. And ya wanna leave me? Are you all right? Is it your daughter? Jeez, if ya need some time off...

ANNA. I said I'm leaving because your temper—because I don't want to take any more of your crap.

AL. Come on, Anna, don't talk like that.

ANNA. You're going to have to get used to it if you want me to stay around for the next two weeks. For two years I've been listening to your bullshit. Two weeks and I'm outa here. In fact, I'll leave now if you want me to.

AL. What'id I do? Did I say somethin' ta make ya want ta swear at me—ta make ya want ta quit? No! I don't want you to leave now! A'course I don't. You're the best worker I ever had. I seen ya raise a thirty-two foot ladder by yerself!— By yerself! I haven't been able to do that fer ten years. You're strong. You're a good worker and you learn fast. *(Pause.)* I don't understand. I taught you everything I know, and now yer jus' goin' off an leavin' me?

ANNA. It's a little late for the praise, Al. You've never given me credit for doing anything right. *(Mimicking his masculine voice.)* "Use the tip of the brush when you're cuttin' in! Paint the butts a the shingles first! Jus' slop it on! This ain't the Taj Mahal!" *(Normal voice.)* Al, everybody says you're a good guy. But they've only got it partly right. You are a good guy, but the fact is, you're a bastard to work for.

AL. Will ya stop talkin' like that. It ain't natural—a girl talkin' to her boss—usin' that kinda language? You been drinkin' 'er smokin' that funny weed? *(Pause.)* You don't understand what it's like bein' a boss. I hired a guy once. The first mornin' I gave 'im five bucks ta go get us coffee—and he never came back with the coffee. Never saw 'im again! Took off with the five bucks! How ya s'posed ta treat that kinda guy?

ANNA. More than likely you chewed him out the first five minutes he was on the job. He probably knew— right from the start—that it wasn't going to work out. I don't blame him. If I didn't have a daughter to raise, I'd have quit working for you the first day.

AL *(pauses trying to gain composure)*. Leavin' me! Jesus! I'm sufferin' with sickness and you want ta walk out and leave me. They say that I got…

ANNA. I know you're sick!— You're a damn despot. All despots are sick.

AL. This ain't like you. Come on. I ain't kiddin'. I ain't well. I probably ain't gonna be around fer long.

ANNA. What are you talking about?

AL. I prob'ly got cancer.

ANNA. Probably got cancer? What does that mean?

AL. Yeah, it's very serious. It's— Let's see—it's what they call cancer a the es-coficus 'er somethin' like that.

ANNA. Jeez, Al, Why didn't you say something? If I'd known, I wouldn't have called you—you know. I wouldn't have given you a hard time. The doctor told you that you've got cancer of the esophagus? Why didn't you say something?

AL. People got their own problems. They don't wanna hear somebody talk about dyin'.

ANNA. Dying? Come on, Al, What's going on? *(Pause.)* Are you trying to lay a guilt trip on me because I said I'm leaving? Are you telling the truth?

AL. A'course I am.

ANNA. Aw, Jeez, Al. But what's your treatment plan? There's got to be a treatment plan.

AL. I ain't got a treatment plan. I'm jus' goin' ta keep on workin'.

ANNA. Why? That's ridiculous. You don't have a death sentence. These days, there's all kinds of cure for cancer. What did the doctor tell you?

AL. Nothin'.

ANNA. Nothing? Who told you you've got cancer? Have you been to a doctor, Al?

AL. No. But I told Louis at the paint store that I been havin' trouble swollowin' and—you know—that I had a sore throat and he said his uncle had the same problem. Turned out, it was cancer a the es-coficus. It was only a matter a months before he...

ANNA. Oh, for God sake, Al! I'm sure Louis at the paint store is a very good diagnostician but you just might want to get a second opinion. Like, maybe, see a doctor!

AL. You could at least show a little sympathy fer your old boss, who is maybe dyin' a cancer.

ANNA. Okay, you've got my sympathy. So now go see a doctor. In the meantime, I'm leaving you in two weeks.

AL. I'll go see a doctor, but can't we talk about you leavin'? I got two jobs ta finish up. I need ya fer at least three—four more weeks. I can't do that high work anymore. Don't ya see? I need ya.

ANNA. Here I come to work pissed off at you—can't stand the thought of listening to you shoot your mouth off—and now you've got me feeling sorry for you— Suppose I do stick around for another month. Then what are your plans? Are you going to retire?

AL. No. I wouldn't know what ta do with myself. I liked havin' ya work for me, right from the first day. You learn't fast and ya got a lot a spunk. Yer strong too. I can't climb like I used ta. The first time I saw ya go up a ladder I said to myself, "Jesus, Lord, look at her go! Jus' like a trapeze artist." You were havin' the time a yer life—thirty feet in the air. I jus' loved watchin' ya—longin' ta be up there with ya—but I knew I couldn't do it anymore. I can't climb like I used ta. I guess it's age—you start ta get afraid a things. Now I like havin' my two feet on the ground or maybe paintin' off a stepladder. *(Pause.)* I guess ya just don't like this kinda work. Ya acted like ya loved it.

ANNA. Are you kidding? I worked in an office for three years, answering the phone, sorting, filing, billing. But at the end of the week! Hell—at the end of the year—I felt like I hadn't accomplished a thing. But this kind of work is different. When we arrive at an old house like this, it looks like a sad, worn-out old woman in ragged clothes. She's in need of a bath and a haircut and maybe a touch of blush to her cheeks from a steady hand to restore some cheer to her sagging face. Don't you see, Al? What we do is magic! She's young again. She's beautiful! *(Pause.)* Aw, forget it! You don't know what I'm talking about.

AL. I never thought about it like that. I sorta know what yer sayin'. But I don't see why ya have ta quit.

ANNA. I told you, Al, you're a rage-aholic, and I can't take it anymore. My daughter means everything to me and your temper tantrums put me in a sour mood and it's got so that I go home and take it out on her. So that's it! I'm done.

AL. Come on, Anna, I can change. *(Pause.)* What are ya goin' ta do fer work? You goin' ta work fer one a them young hotshots?

ANNA. I'm going into business for myself. I've got four jobs lined up.

AL. Jeez. I guess the whole world's changin'. Girls goin' inta the paintin' business while I'm bein' forced outa the paintin' business.

ANNA. Yes, the world's changing, Al, and you'd better get used to it.

AL. How 'bout you stick' around fer a month so I can paint them two houses. I'll try ta cut out yellin' at ya.

ANNA *(pauses, looking at AL, deliberating)*. Well, maybe, I could stay on for a couple of extra weeks—that is—if you cut out the yelling.

AL. That's good, Anna. That's good. I could really use the help. *(Sips his coffee, gathering his thoughts.)* I was wonderin' if maybe you could use some help—you know—with them jobs ya got. I can't climb so good anymore, but I'm still good at cuttin' in windows and paintin' trim.

ANNA *(looks at AL. There is compassion in her voice)*. Sure, Al, I could use a good painter—as long as he was even-tempered—had the right disposition and got to work on time.

AL. That wouldn't be a problem.

ANNA *(stands up)*. Now let's get back to work. Oh yeah —pick up those coffee cups. Leaving a mess makes a bad impression. *(Stands up and moves to the window. Picks up the paintbrush, dips it in the paint, taps the brush and begins painting the window.)* And remember! *(Mimicking his masculine voice.)* Use the tip of the brush when you're cuttin' in. And paint the butts a the shingles first! Jus' slop it on! This ain't the Taj Mahal!

AL *(stands up. Picks up the coffee cups and drops them in the trash bucket)*. Yeah. Yeah. Yeah.

(Moves to his paint pail. Picks up the brush and begins to wipe the bristles on the inside rim of the pail. Picks up the paint pail. He moves to the door and resumes painting.)

END OF PLAY

THE SASMANN AESTHETIC

By
Jules Tasca

The Sasmann Aesthetic was first produced in 2000 by American Playwrights Theater, Inc., at the John Houseman Theatre in New York City.

CHARACTERS

DR. GRACE BULLOCK: A woman in her early 40s.
HOWARD SASMANN: A man in his 30s.

SETTING: The office of Dr. Grace Bullock at the Morrisville State Psychiatric Hospital. A desk and chairs suggest the office.

TIME: The present.

THE SASMANN AESTHETIC

AT THE CURTAIN: *DR. BULLOCK sits at the desk and peruses a folder. She pushes the button on the intercom.*

DOCTOR. Would you please tell Mr. Sasmann to come in.

(After a beat, HOWARD SASMANN enters. He is a well-built man who wears a pullover shirt and a pair of form-fitting white pants. The DOCTOR rises and greets him.)

DOCTOR. Howard Sasmann, I'm Dr. Bullock.

HOWARD. Good morning, Dr. Bullock.

DOCTOR. Good morning.

HOWARD. I was supposed to see a Dr. Eric Gutig, I believe.

DOCTOR. I'm his associate. Dr. Gutig's caught up in an emergency right now.

HOWARD. You mean the guy in the restraints who's yelling he's Jesus?

DOCTOR. We don't discuss other patients, Mr. Sasmann.

HOWARD. I understand a professional ethic, Doctor. But your Jesus is obviously mentally ill. I'm not. Let me clear that up right now. I don't really belong in a crazy house.

DOCTOR. *Mr.* Sasmann, this is a hospital, sir.

HOWARD. I stand corrected, Doctor. It is a hospital. All I'm trying to say is that there's nothing wrong with me.

DOCTOR. All right. But can we just talk for a while?

HOWARD. I'll talk all you like, but there's nothing the matter with me.

DOCTOR. Married?

HOWARD. *No,* I'm not.

DOCTOR. Girlfriend?

HOWARD. I date a couple of girls, yes. And they're both upset over this, too. It got into the papers.

DOCTOR. So I read.

HOWARD. I need to explain to them that there's nothing the matter with me. The papers made me into an evil person.

DOCTOR *(sitting).* All right. Then let me hear it from you. What're you doing here at Morrisville State Hospital?

HOWARD. You know what I'm doing here. You have my file.

DOCTOR. You tell me in your own words. Sit.

HOWARD *(sitting).* It was a deal. It was a deal my lawyer made with the judge. Coming here kept me out of jail. I agreed to come here as an outpatient to keep from going to prison. And I have to continue coming here until I'm deemed cured, Dr. Bullock. Does that correlate with what you have in that folder?

DOCTOR. It does.

HOWARD. And there's nothing wrong with me. Prison. That judge threatened me with prison. Oh, I don't say I don't possess the same quirks as every man, but psychologically, there's nothing wrong with me.

DOCTOR. Often... Often we perceive that nothing's wrong, Mr. Sasmann, because a person falls into a pattern of behavior that brings pleasure or security. But, in many cases, certain behaviors are...are destructive to a person's life and he or she doesn't see that if he...

HOWARD. It's not destructive. It's harmless. Harmless. And I lost my job over this harmless.

DOCTOR. You taught English at Community College.

HOWARD. Until I was arrested. And now I'm unemployed.

DOCTOR. Why do you think it's okay for you to go to the beach and...

HOWARD. It's harmless, I tell you. I've done it for years.

DOCTOR. And almost always have gotten away with it.

HOWARD. Away with what? Most of the girls smiled.

DOCTOR. But not all. And the judge called it assault, Mr. Sasmann.

HOWARD *(rising)*. It is not—*not*—assault, Doctor, to kiss someone. Assault. Jesus. There's nothing—absolutely nothing—violent about Howard Sasmann. I wouldn't know how to be violent. *(He turns away from the DOCTOR, pause.)*

DOCTOR. Look, Mr.... May I call you Howard?

HOWARD *(turning back to her)*. Please...

DOCTOR. Howard, I don't know if most people would agree that what you're doing is acceptable.

HOWARD. Most people live in a narrow band of the spectrum of life, Doctor. I don't.

DOCTOR. *Uh*-huh.

HOWARD. Is that uh-huh agreement or disapproval? Most people...

DOCTOR. Howard, let's look at this realistically. You go to the beach and…and you…kiss women's buttocks…

HOWARD. Yes.

DOCTOR. Then you run off.

HOWARD. Run off. The way you say it. I just go on my way. Run off. You make it sound pathological.

DOCTOR. Then you say it. You tell me in your own words what this is all about. *(Pause.)* Howard…

HOWARD. I…I…I like women's buttocks, Doctor. In my sexual map, a woman's buttocks are the main roads, thoroughfares and railroad lines. Do you understand?

DOCTOR. You're saying you have a fixation on a woman's…

HOWARD. Why do you make everything sound so clinical? Fixation. Come on, Doctor. In Africa, men are attracted to elongated lips. So much so that women insert pieces of wood under the skin to stretch them even longer. In Japan, men prize a woman's neck and so dresses are designed to flatter and display a woman's neck. Here in the U.S., dresses are cut low and bras amply push up the mammary flesh for those men with a propensity for breasts. And on the beach, women wear thongs and bikinis, so that men who admire that anatomical splendor, a woman's rear, might partake of its beauty. Beauty, Doctor. Oh, God, when did beauty become pathology?

DOCTOR. Howard, you're correct. There's nothing wrong with a person, male or female, having a certain fetish, but in the case of…

HOWARD. There, you did it again.

DOCTOR. Did what again?

HOWARD. You're making it all sound like something from a medical case history. Fetish...fetish...

DOCTOR. A fetish is simply a...

HOWARD. I know what a fetish is, Doctor.

DOCTOR. Then go on. Tell me what it is. Why you feel this compulsion...

HOWARD. I suppose you can't think any other way. Compulsion. Now it's a compulsion. Your job is to make a malady out of every human whimsy that this repressed society looks askance at. Why is it a compulsion? Beauty attracts human beings. And, I might add, the most sophisticated of human beings. It's supposed to. You call that profound attraction a compulsion?

DOCTOR. You said you've been doing it for years and years...

HOWARD. Dr. Bullock, I've been shaving my face for years, too. And I've been eating corned beef on rye for years. I don't consider those actions to be compulsions. I like a clean shave, and I love the taste of corned beef, and when I go to the beach and I see—excuse me, Doctor, the perfect ass...I enjoy going up and kissing it. It brings me pleasure. It makes me excited for my girlfriends. It's not a matter of compulsion, though it's compelling. It's not a fetish, but a defining female attraction. Dr. Bullock, try to understand, that to me the admiration of a tanned, oiled, shimmering derriere is a matter of...of...

DOCTOR. Of what?

HOWARD. Of aesthetics.

DOCTOR. Aesthetics?

HOWARD. Aesthetics. Yes. You know how a beautiful sunset captures the human eye simply because it's beautiful. You stop. You watch as the mighty wings of fire spread and float beneath the ocean's blue. It brings peace and tranquility. A woman's buttocks well formed is just another object of beauty on this earth: the firm rounded flesh where almost touching halves create the curved path of the split; the straight lines of the legs veering up to meet the delicate arcs; the tantalizing cross where the buttocks sensually crease atop the line of the thigh. Good God. It's the perfect human confluence of geometric forms in the body, Doctor. And when I kiss that anatomical precision, my kiss is a salute to the wonderment of nature's sculptural handiwork. *(Pause. DR. BULLOCK stares at him a long beat.)* Doctor? Dr. Bullock? Is something wrong?

DOCTOR. No. No. I...I understand what you're saying.

HOWARD. I'm sorry for getting myself all worked up.

DOCTOR. That's perfectly all right, Howard. You're giving me your perspective. I understand. You have this spontaneous desire to...

HOWARD. Desire...desire's okay. Yes, desire. I have a simple desire...

DOCTOR. Regardless of the terminology we use, Howard, you can't go to the public beaches and just... just salute women's buttocks as if they were the stars and stripes.

HOWARD. But you agree there's nothing wrong with me?

DOCTOR. People can't just go off and act out all the desires they have.

HOWARD. You didn't answer my question.

DOCTOR. I'm not a judge and jury. I'm a doctor. Just because you're more articulate than the average nuisance at the beach...

HOWARD. Nuisance?

DOCTOR. ...doesn't change the fact that you're going to have to exhibit self-control.

HOWARD. I told you most of those girls smiled afterward, I swear to you, Doctor. It was just misfortune that this last time, the woman happened to be a lieutenant in the police department. Just my luck; a cop with a hall-of-fame rear end. Doctor, listen to me. For one question, can we be Howard and Grace?

DOCTOR. Go ahead.

HOWARD. Thank you...Grace...Grace, have you...have you ever looked at a man's body and seen some part of that body that attracts you? *(Pause.)* Doc...I mean, Grace?

DOCTOR. How's this going to address your dilemma? Of course, women look at men's bodies and find them the object of...well...in fact, when I go to the tennis club, I see one fellow who must work out. He has an outstanding physique and I always look and...and...and admire.

HOWARD. You see. You see.

DOCTOR. But I have the self-control not to go up to him in the middle of a forehand and kiss him.

HOWARD. Which part of this fellow's body attracts you the most?

DOCTOR *(rising)*. I'm Dr. Bullock now.

HOWARD. Okay. Okay. I'm sorry. I just wondered.

DOCTOR. So what else would you like to say? I have to write up a summary of this visit.

HOWARD. How many visits must I make before you consider informing the courts that my lips are no longer a threat to society?

DOCTOR. I can't say right now. But I do want to prescribe a tranquilizer.

HOWARD *(slowly rising)*. A tranquilizer?

DOCTOR. It'll help calm the compulsion—sorry, but that's the nomenclature.

HOWARD. Doctor, come on. Tranquilizers?

DOCTOR. Just during the beach season, Howard, show the judge you're doing something. What am I going to report that we discussed—aesthetics? *(She writes the prescription.)*

HOWARD. You're right. A prescription. The judge'll like that. This is a good idea. A prescription. I'll fill it and I don't even have to take it, right? I'll show the courts my pills. Yes. It's a good idea. *(She hands him the prescription.)* Thank you.

DOCTOR. You're welcome, Howard.

HOWARD. Two weeks...all right...two weeks...all the killers running loose and she handcuffs me on the beach and reads me Miranda. What a mess, Doctor.

DOCTOR. Now...now...don't worry. I think we can work this all out. *(She pats his behind gently as she says this. He turns and looks at her.)* I'm sorry. I'm sorry. I didn't mean to be familiar.

HOWARD. That's...that's all right. I understand. *(He smiles.)*

DOCTOR. I don't know what came over me.

HOWARD. I'm not embarrassed.

DOCTOR. I apologize.

HOWARD. I said I understand. So this guy at the tennis court then, you...

DOCTOR *(cutting him off)*. Two weeks, Mr. Sasmann... please...please...I have other patients... *(HOWARD raises his hand as if to apologize for lingering and to say goodbye. Then he exits. She crosses downstage as the lights fade.)* Jesus Christ, what in hell came over me? What?

END OF PLAY

BUYING A BRASSIERE

By
Rebecca Ritchie

Buying a Brassiere premiered at The Alleyway Theatre, Buffalo, N.Y., in 2000. It was part of Pandora's Box Theatre Company's "Escaping the Box" festival of one acts and monologues by women. In 2001, it was a finalist in the Actors Theatre of Louisville National Ten-Minute Play Contest.

CHARACTERS

DIANE: A woman with breast cancer who is shopping for underwear.
MARIE: A French Canadian underwear fitter.

SETTING: The lingerie department and a dressing room in a department store.

TIME: The present.

AUTHOR'S NOTE: Diane must deliver her lines with *joie de vivre* and a sense of self-kery. If this play isn't funny, don't even try it.

BUYING A BRASSIERE

AT THE CURTAIN: *Blackout. In the blackout, Spotlight up on DIANE, who stands on a soapbox-sized riser, DL, facing slightly left. In blackout, MARIE stands on a similar riser DR, facing slightly right.*

DIANE *(to AUDIENCE)*. I'm considering buying a brassiere. —The decision unsettles me. It reminds me of visiting Student Health thirty years ago: Then, if you didn't use birth control, you weren't having sex. Now, if I don't buy this brassiere, I must not have cancer. *(Pause.)* I find myself on the lingerie floor of a large department store. There is a bower of bras the size of a football field: purple bras, cheetah-print bras, push-up bras, strapless bras. And lace, lace everywhere. —But I don't see what I'm looking for. —So I go up to the counter and wait for a clerk, and when she stops chewing gum long enough, I say, "Do you have a fitter?" And she says, "A fitter?" And I say, "For a bra." When she still looks clueless, I point to an advertisement in a Plexiglas stand. "Ohhh…" she says, "that kind of bra. —You'll have to wait for Marie." And she points to a chair against the wall. —I'm not in a hurry. In fact, I'm not completely committed to buying this brassiere. I'm keeping a low profile, so I don't arouse the interest of the Red Beast. It's crouching out there, waiting for the slightest opening: arrogance, or complacency, or a thoughtless moment of joy. —You'd be surprised how even the most benign activity, like shopping for this brassiere, could cause the Beast to lunge for the jugular. —So my mind is definitely not made up. Not by a long shot.

MARIE. You are the customer that desires the fitting?

DIANE. Marie is French Canadian and about two hundred years old. She wears a tailor's measure around her neck and has the demeanor of a drill sergeant.

MARIE. Wait here. I'll get the key.

DIANE. This surprises me, since dressing rooms in this store generally aren't locked. But I've decided to devote the whole afternoon to deciding whether to buy this bra. So I wait in my chair, watching the other women zigzagging along the aisles, doing that little click-clack thing with the hangers. Finally, Marie comes back with a bunch of keys on a chain.

MARIE. This way.

DIANE. I follow her to the far end of the lingerie department where she unlocks a narrow door edged in gilt.

MARIE *(pulls a foot of chain link from her pocket and turns the key)*. *Voici.*

DIANE. You keep it locked?

MARIE. For privacy. In here, you are *complètement comfortable*.

DIANE. Inside, it's a pink and satin boudoir. Pink curtains draped around the mirror. A pink vanity table with a little chair. And everything that isn't pink is gold. It's like something out of a French courtesan's nightmare. And all for me. Perfectly private. —Well, except for Marie.

MARIE. Here is the jacket.

DIANE. And she hands me a pink, satin bed jacket from the 1940s and waits for me to put it on. *(To MARIE.)* With you here?

MARIE. I see this all the time.

DIANE. Well, I don't get naked with *anybody*. Not anymore.

MARIE. I will check the storeroom.

DIANE. And she goes through an archway into a walk-in closet the size of Cleveland. There are shelves and shelves of bras.

MARIE. Right or left?

DIANE. Right or left what?

MARIE. Right or left side?

DIANE. Oh, I say, finally catching on. *(To MARIE.)* Both.

MARIE. Both! *Alors*, you can't mean both!

DIANE. Why not? I ask, because if there is one thing certain in this life, it is both.

MARIE. Both!

DIANE. She looks so distraught that I find myself apologizing. *(To MARIE.)* Sorry.

MARIE. Can't be helped.

DIANE. Marie disappears in the storeroom, and I take off my blouse, and when she comes back, I'm wearing a slipper-satin bed jacket with faded jeans in a room reeking of sexual fantasy, feeling like an ass. —Marie has an armload of green boxes.

MARIE. Just let me measure you.

DIANE. While she wraps the tape measure around my midriff, she steals a little glance under the bed jacket.

MARIE. *Mon Dieu!* How did that happen?

DIANE. Haven't the foggiest. *(To AUDIENCE.)* She rummages among the bras and comes up with a big white bra. No lace. And whatever the word "cleavage" means to you, this is not it. *(To MARIE.)* No thanks.

MARIE. Just try it on.

DIANE *(to MARIE).* No. *(To AUDIENCE.)* I'm beginning to feel claustrophobic in that room, the way I feel in an MRI machine searching for stray cells devouring my liver. *(To MARIE.)* I'm thinking black. Or red, even. With lace. The kind of stuff you've got out there. *(To AUDIENCE.)* And I indicate the outside world where women are breathing fresh air and searching for sales.

MARIE. That is different merchandise.

DIANE. I'm aware of that. But that's what I'm looking for. Color. Décolletage. Sex appeal.

MARIE. Our buyer does not believe in sex appeal for our special clientele.

DIANE. If all you've got is big white bras, I'm not interested.

MARIE. Off-white?

DIANE. No.

MARIE. Beige? Crème? Ocher?

DIANE. I'll look elsewhere, thanks.

MARIE. Wait! Wait! There may be an exchange from another branch! Another buyer!

DIANE. I hear her ripping open boxes and rattling plastic bins. Finally, she reappears with a bra in her hand. It is black. Lace appliquéd with birds and flowers. And through the scalloped edge runs a satin ribbon tied in a perfectly frivolous bow. —I feel the moist breath of the Red Beast on my neck, and I hesitate.

MARIE. It may not be your size.

DIANE. What do you mean, size? I haven't got a size. This is all smoke and mirrors.

MARIE. It must be proportional. —What kind of form do you wish?

DIANE. "Form" in the business is a euphemism for prosthesis. *(To MARIE.)* What kind of forms do you have?

MARIE. We have silicone, foam, sports, latex teardrop leisure, birdseed—

DIANE. Birdseed? *(To AUDIENCE.)* I have visions of avian diners feasting on my breasts. *(To MARIE.)* Silicone. Top of the line. *(To AUDIENCE.)* I try on the bra with the silicone breast forms, which feel uncannily like human flesh. —The bra fits! I am Cinderella, not some ugly stepsister, and I don't have to cut off any more body parts for this beautiful bra to go home with me. I glance in the mirror. Suddenly, I have curves where one short year ago, there were curves. In the interim, there were six surgeries, a long-line surgical bra, four drains, two failed reconstructions, socks stuffed into a brassiere, and raw, healing scars—two of them, running from my armpits to my breastbone. —But now, once again, there are curves. Luscious, lifelike, silicone lace-covered curves.

MARIE. Wear it. You'll feel like a million dollars.

DIANE. And I do. I feel like the seventeenth-century trollop this pink room was made for. —I haven't looked this good since I was sixteen. —I dress quickly, the better to admire my image in the gold-framed mirror, and sure enough, the lace peeks through the silk of my blouse, demure yet sensual. —I would buy it all instantly, but I hear a warning snarl from the Red Beast as it bares its teeth. *(To MARIE.)* How much does all of this cost?

MARIE. Let's see.

DIANE. Preserving my privacy to the last, Marie glances out the door of the dressing room to check that the coast is clear, then locks the pink room behind us. I follow her to the counter. Two lines of women wait impatiently, satin lingerie dripping from their fingers. Marie takes me to the head of the line—her private client—and rings up my purchases: One bra, $48; two breast forms, $740. —She hesitates, one manicured finger hovering over the cash register—

MARIE. Acch! This new register! —Where is the key for mastectomy product?

DIANE. All eyes turn to me. One woman clutches the cross around her neck. A young mother glances at my chest and away again, holding her baby so tightly the infant screams. If my grandmother had been alive and shopping for underwear, she would have spat on the ground three times to keep away the Evil Eye. —I suddenly understand why Marie put me in that little pink room and locked the door. *(Pause.)* I glance at the other women. I am the only adult in a playground full of children, and I pity their innocence. They don't understand that I just won the Triple Crown of survival: Life. Hope. Vanity. *(Pause.)* Screw the Beast. I'm buying this brassiere. —I pay for my purchases and head for Couture Fashions. What I really need now is a sequin jacket and some dancing shoes.

END OF PLAY

STAIRWAY TO HEAVEN

By
Gregory Fletcher

Stairway to Heaven premiered at Manhattan Theatre Source in 2004. It was produced by Gary Garrison and Brian Otano, directed by Janice Goldberg, and featured Ari Butler and Allison Goldberg. Previously, the play was workshopped with director Kathy Plourde and actors Ryan Bethke and Julie Miller. At the 2004 national Kennedy Center/American College Theater Festival, it was directed by Jon Royal, featured Kaitlin Yikel and Brian Watkins, and was chosen the winner of the 2004 National Ten-Minute Play Award.

CHARACTERS

ELISA: 17 years old.
GIL: 16 years old, Elisa's brother.

SETTING: The carpeted stairway of a family home.

TIME: The new century, 2000.

STAIRWAY TO HEAVEN

AT THE CURTAIN: *GIL, wearing a dark suit, is lying down on his back. His sister, ELISA, also dressed in dark colors and wearing a skirt, starts down the stairs. Her hair is pinned up in the messed-up look.*

ELISA. Get up. *(No response.)* I said, get up. Now!

GIL. So go.

ELISA. Like—I'm in a skirt.

GIL. Like—I'm gonna look? Gross.

ELISA. You're sixteen, of course you'll look.

GIL. In your dreams.

ELISA. Shut up. Why don't you go up to Mom so she can see how wrinkled your suit's getting. You should iron it.

GIL. And you should brush your hair.

ELISA. It's supposed to look like this, you jerk. Move!

GIL. Just go if you're going.

ELISA. If you look, that's sexual harassment, and sexual harassment leads to sexual abuse, and statistics show that one out of five women are sexually abused by a family member—

GIL. I can't believe you're quoting your term paper to me. That is so lame.

ELISA. I got an A+ on that paper. Gil, enough! If you don't move, you are so dead meat!

GIL. Two deaths in one week? Doubt it.

ELISA. Please. Go see Mom.

GIL. I'll see her when she comes down.

ELISA. I don't want her to be alone.

GIL. She's probably dressing, let her be.

ELISA. She's dressed, you're dressed, we're all dressed! Dressed and waiting. *(Sighs.)* And waiting. Go on, at least while I'm making Mom and me a cup of tea.

GIL. Oh, la-de-da, so adult. When did you grow up all of a sudden?

ELISA. When do you think?! *(GIL looks away.)* She needs you.

GIL. No, his…when I had to go up for his dress shoes, for the funeral home…his closet…I could…you can still…

ELISA. Smell him?

GIL. Yeah.

ELISA. Okay, so come down with me, I'll make you your first cup of la-de-da tea. You'll like it.

GIL. No.

ELISA. What?

GIL. Too many…the photo magnets on the refrigerator.

ELISA. Oh. Well, you can wait at the dining-room table.

GIL. His chair. Waiting to be pulled out.

ELISA. The living room?

GIL. The recliner. His impression…

ELISA. Still on the cushion, yeah. The back yard? Never mind. The hammock. Even in the garage. His car.

GIL. I could feel him on the steering wheel.

ELISA. Then go in your room, at least you're safe there. I'll call you when it's ready. *(GIL doesn't move.)* In your own room?

GIL. Every trophy. Every ribbon. He's there, cheering me on.

ELISA. For someone who's dead, he sure is all around. *(She finally gets it.)* Except here.

GIL. So go. Scram. *(ELISA doesn't move.)* Elisa, I don't need your permission to be here.

ELISA. Look, Gil, I know you're upset—we're all upset—but no need to... I'm just saying, when things start changing around here—

GIL. Yeah, duh, they already have.

ELISA. I mean it, lose the attitude.

GIL. Stop talking down to me.

ELISA. F you.

GIL. You're using the f word?

ELISA. It was a letter.

GIL. Used in a complete sentence with a subject and verb.

ELISA. I didn't use the word.

GIL. And of all days, I can't believe you.

ELISA. It was a fucking letter.

GIL. Oh my God!

ELISA. I didn't...stop, you made me.

GIL. I should fucking wash your mouth out. *(Gasps in shock.)* Oh my God!

ELISA. You watch it!

GIL. I didn't mean it!

GIL & ELISA. I don't want Mom to hear that kind of language!

GIL. Jinx, you owe me a Coke!

ELISA. Gil, you're gonna have to grow up. And fast.

GIL. Oh, like you're my authority figure now? My role model?

ELISA. Well, I am the eldest, and it only makes sense now that—

GIL. By a year, big deal. I'm the only man of the house now.

ELISA. Don't think so. It's Mom, dope.

GIL. Wrong equipment. Do I have to explain it to you?

ELISA. You can't even say the word.

GIL. Mom is not the man of the house and neither are you.

ELISA. Yeah, well—

GIL. Yeah, well, what?!

(They take a breath and calm down.)

ELISA. If you really want to be the man of the house, then go see Mom. Being the man means putting others first.

GIL. I just want to get this over with. When Howie Levy's dad died, they didn't drag it out with viewings and services, he was in the ground the next day.

ELISA. They don't believe in embalming.

GIL. You don't even know the Levys.

ELISA. They're Jewish. It's a Jewish thing.

GIL. Oh. Well, makes more sense. I think when you die, you should get to be dead.

ELISA *(carefully)*. Billy should've been invited.

GIL. Billy—what…why…I mean, he—he's not that close to Dad.

ELISA. To you. Special friends and loved ones…to comfort us in time of…oh, relax, no reason to clam up.

GIL. I just don't know why you think…I mean, it's…if—

ELISA. You're very close, you gonna deny it? Come on, Gil, when Mom and Dad went away with the church group, I know you guys—

GIL. It was a bath; we were in and out!

ELISA. Morning, noon and night? Please, if you weren't my brother, I'd think it was pretty hot.

GIL. Why do you bring this up like you got some power hold over me? You don't.

ELISA. Because you're gonna...you're gonna need someone special, you jerk! To confide in, to cry with, to get
through this. And since you don't let me in...I can't
even think of the last time we shared something important...really talked together.

GIL *(finally admitting)*. Did Dad know? Me and Billy?

ELISA. Why not? He's totally up on things.

GIL. *Those* things? No way, he's a Republican.

ELISA. Maybe, but only financially. I mean, down deep,
he's practically a hippie. He plays Led Zeppelin.
Played, whatever. I'm sure he was bound to talk to you
about it.

GIL. What he was bound to talk about was how Eddie's
too hands-on with you.

ELISA. At least we're out in the open.

GIL. Yeah, too open. Like we haven't all seen?

ELISA. As in Mom and Dad?

GIL. No, as in the entire neighborhood.

ELISA. Liar!

GIL. And he doesn't respect women.

ELISA. What do you know about it?

GIL. I know it's not right. You should respect yourself
more.

ELISA. You too! I hear you'll experience a huge relief
when you come out of the closet. Like a heavy burden
lifts from your shoulders.

GIL. Write a term paper on it, why don't you. You're just
too scared not to have a date for the prom.

ELISA. Like *you're* gonna ask Billy to your prom?

GIL. Like you need a boyfriend in order to feel whole?

ELISA. Be proud of who you are.

GIL. Practice what you preach.

ELISA. Preach what you practice!

GIL. Elisa, enough—

ELISA. Homosexual shame is so twentieth century, get with it!

GIL. Hold your voice down.

ELISA. All right. I'll talk to Eddie about it. When you talk.

GIL. That's the last thing Mom needs right now.

ELISA. She can handle it. We can all handle it. As long as you're—you're, you know, playing it safe. Are you? Playing it safe?

GIL. Are you and Eddie...playing it safe?

ELISA. Yes, Dad, we are. Are you and Billy? *(No response.)* Well?

GIL. Yes, Dad, we are. We're not stupid, you know.

ELISA. Okay...I'm relieved. Good.

GIL. Yeah. Me, too.

ELISA. Cool.

GIL. So.

ELISA. Dad for each other then? On an as-needed basis?

GIL. People would shit if I brought Billy to the prom.

ELISA. That's what people do—they shit. *(GIL takes ELISA's hand.)* You've got Dad's hands, you know. Throw your hand open, palm up.

GIL *(opening his hand)*. Weird, huh?

ELISA. Do it again? *(GIL opens his hand again.)* Identical.

(ELISA takes his hand, and they sit holding hands for a good long moment.)

GIL. Good. Okay.

ELISA. Okay what?

GIL *(standing and buttoning his jacket)*. I'll be up with Mom. How do I look?

ELISA. Like the man of the house.

GIL. Yeah, you too.

(GIL smiles and exits up the stairs. ELISA exits down the stairs.)

END OF PLAY

PLAYTIME

By
Kent R. Brown

Playtime premiered at the Boston Marathon in 2004. It was sponsored by SpeakEasy Stage Company, directed by Elaine Theodore, and featured Roxy Wongus and Cheryl Singleton. It was also a winner of the 2004 "Short & NEAT Play Festival," sponsored by the New England Academy of Theatre.

CHARACTERS

MAUREEN: Late 30s. Has lead a hard life. Compassionate. Bitter. Needy. Dressed in clothes purchased at
   Goodwill and church thrift shops.
NICOLE: Early teens. Maureen's daughter. A runaway. A
   survivor. Also dressed by Goodwill and hand-me-
   downs. Carries a knapsack.

SETTING: Playground park: Teeter-totter, swings,
   benches, merry-go-round, trash can...whatever can be
   comfortably provided.

TIME: The present, summer. Midnight. Bright moonlight.
   Warm breeze.

PLAYTIME

AT THE CURTAIN: *MAUREEN is seated on a bench, a picnic basket by her side. On the ground is a large garbage bag stuffed with assorted items and pieces of clothing for NICOLE. For several moments, MAUREEN sits patiently on the bench. Then...*

MAUREEN. Nicole, I'm not gonna sit here all night. Midnight is late in the day for me. I'm gonna pick my butt up off this bench, take this lovely picnic lunch I made you...and go. *(Beat.)* I've got good things in the bag, honey. *(Beat.)* Nicole...you there? Don't make me feel stupid.

(After another moment, MAUREEN gathers up the garbage bag and the picnic basket. As she begins to leave, NICOLE enters. She is as far from MAUREEN as she can be.)

NICOLE. What did you make? Did you bring me any books?
MAUREEN. You do this every time. You make me beg. You shouldn't do that, Nicole. I'm your mother. I don't have to be out here. I don't have to come.
NICOLE. Yes, you do.
MAUREEN. No, I don't!
NICOLE. Yes, you do!

(Beat. MAUREEN returns to the bench, puts down the garbage bag and picnic lunch basket and sits. NICOLE doesn't move.)

NICOLE *(cont'd)*. Where'd you get the picnic basket? It's cool.

MAUREEN. First Baptist.

NICOLE. They're nice at First Baptist.

MAUREEN. The folks at First Baptist, they don't ask a lot of questions. They just give you stuff. You say a coupla prayers, makes 'em feel good. The ones at the Congregational Church, they talk to you so they can get to know you better. Hell, I don't want nobody to know me any better.

NICOLE. How are you feeling, Mama? You getting your beauty sleep?

MAUREEN. Do you want me to give all this stuff back? I could maybe sell it myself maybe and—

NICOLE. I cut my arm. Yesterday. I fell down some stairs, the ones up behind Pitkin Drugs? Out back? I fell down. See?

(NICOLE extends her arm to MAUREEN, who glances over.)

MAUREEN. What were you doing on those stairs? Are you staying in those apartments there, Nicole? Those are terrible places, you know that?

NICOLE. I might not live, I might get blood poisoning. Randy Black did.

MAUREEN. I know Randy Black. He's a viper. A despicable human being. Nothing can kill him. And his mother's no better.

NICOLE. She's a real good cook. Randy got a chocolate pie from her three days ago. I had a piece for breakfast. Uuummm good!

(The tension between mother and daughter is palpable. This is a ritual they play out. To see who is the weakest, who wants the other the most. MAUREEN indicates the basket and the garbage bag.)

MAUREEN. What do you want me to do with all this?

NICOLE. Just leave it on the bench. Step back. Over there.

(NICOLE points to a spot some distance from the bench. MAUREEN complies. NOTE: if the setting and props permit, the continuing action/blocking should integrate the playground equipment, positioning NICOLE on the bars, perhaps; or both could be seated on either end of a teeter-totter. It is important that NICOLE puts an obstacle between herself and MAUREEN. This is done out of habit. She behaves this way with anyone. She lives defensively.)

NICOLE *(cont'd)*. Don't move now. You move and I'm gone! I'm fast. I've got everything I need. Don't need you! You don't move! You don't touch me!

MAUREEN. I know the rules. I'm not movin'. 'Sides, you're too fast for me.

(NICOLE crosses to the bench and begins to look through the items: sweaters, sweatshirts featuring a major university such as Michigan or Alabama, a few pair of sweat pants, two pair of sandals. The clothes are old, well used.)

MAUREEN *(cont'd)*. I thought you could cut the sweats if you wanted. For shorts. For the rest of the summer... maybe keep one for the fall? The sweatshirts should fit. Got those for seventy-five cents each.

NICOLE. That's a good price. *(Holding up one of the sweatshirts.)* Hey, look at me! I'm going to Michigan (appropriate school). Gonna get me some learnin', right, Mama?

MAUREEN. Got to finish high school first.

NICOLE. Nope. Don't have to. I'm already too smart for my own good, that's what you said.

MAUREEN. You have everything you need? Where are you stayin' now? In case I have to contact you.

(MAUREEN takes one step toward NICOLE. NICOLE moves quickly. She is highly accomplished in the art of disengagement.)

NICOLE. You do this every time! Every time! You get me lookin' one way and come at me from the other! I can't trust you.

MAUREEN. I just want to… Come here. Just let me hold your hand.

NICOLE. No.

MAUREEN. Please?

NICOLE. Don't beg! Begging is weak. Begging is dirty. Begging means you don't have enough. We don't beg in this household, Nicole! That's what you always told me. Did you bring any pop?

MAUREEN. It's in the basket.

NICOLE. All right.

(MAUREEN moves slowly to the picnic basket and removes the contents.)

MAUREEN. I made you some chicken salad. No onions. And two peanut butter and jelly sandwiches.

NICOLE. I don't like grape. I hate grape. I'll scrape the grape off, you know that.

MAUREEN *(laughing)*. Don't get your panties in an up-roar. I didn't do you any grape.

NICOLE. What kind?

MAUREEN. Guess.

NICOLE. I'm not a little girl anymore, Mama. I wash my face every day. I even know how to get a ride on the road. I know how to keep drivers happy.

MAUREEN. Don't tell me such stuff. You lie! I don't wanna know. *(Stepping back from the bench so NICOLE can approach safely.)* Eat this nice picnic lunch I fixed you.

(NICOLE moves to the picnic basket and begins to eat. She is ravenous.)

NICOLE. You want to know, Mama. Every mama wants to know. "Don't let 'em touch you, sweetie. Look both ways before you cross the street. Don't get in an eleva-tor alone with a man. Don't look a man in the eyes, he'll think you're interested in him." Well, I do look 'em in the eyes, Mama. My hormones are raging! They're smelly and stinky, Mama, and they burp a lot. But they feel good. Real good. *(Sees a can of pop.)* Strawberry, thanks.

MAUREEN. You finished shockin' me now? Ready for some apples? Granny Smiths, and three hard-boiled eggs, a jar of olives and two bananas.

NICOLE. Got 'em. Right here.

(NICOLE "fires" the bananas at MAUREEN as if they were pistols.)

MAUREEN. And some Twinkies. *(Beat.)* Happy birthday, sweetie.

NICOLE. It's not my birthday, Mama. You know that. You gettin' old in the head?

MAUREEN *(beat)*. You ever going to come back home?

NICOLE *(talking with her mouth full while keeping one eye on MAUREEN)*. Did you bring me any books? And magazines? Who's hot 'n who's not? Got to keep up. Gonna be an American Idol some day. Famous. Real famous. Famous for something…just don't know what it is yet. But I'm not gonna sit around here talkin' to you all night, that's for sure. I got things to do, people to see.

MAUREEN. I forgot the books.

NICOLE. You can bring 'em next time, books on the Romans and the Vikings! None of that Young Miss stuff. Give me war, death, sex and destruction! I wanna be just like a big person.

MAUREEN *(beat)*. I like your hair. You look good.

NICOLE. Amber cut it for me. She cuts mine, I cut hers. She's nice. She's my new best friend. I've got a lot of friends, Mama. Can't keep 'em all straight. You want a banana? Here.
(NICOLE places a banana on the ground half way between herself and MAUREEN, then steps back.)

MAUREEN. Where are you sleeping, Nicole? I won't tell the police. *(Beat.)* I won't tell Marty.

NICOLE. Don't you mention his name! *(NICOLE viciously stomps on the banana.)* Farty Marty! Farty Marty! Does he know you're out here? Did you take two buses like I told you? Is he out there in the dark *(Calling.)* You out there, Farty Marty? *(NICOLE pulls a knife from her pocket.)* I got me a knife. Wanna see it, wanna see it? You come at me and I'll slice you in half!

MAUREEN *(beat)*. Do I know Amber? *(Beat.)* Do you always have a knife, sweetie? That's dangerous.

NICOLE. I suspect you don't know my friends, Mama. And of course I have a knife, you think I'm stupid? On the streets and no knife? It's dangerous out here, Mama. Don't you watch television?

MAUREEN. Where did you meet Amber?

(NICOLE continues looking through the garbage bag, pulling out numerous items and flinging them over the bench, on the grass, anywhere. She also remains alert to her mother and to her surroundings.)

NICOLE. At the tennis club, where I meet all my friends. Out and around, Mama. Shawna, and Dougie, and Raphael. I like Raphael a lot. He's my new best boyfriend. Bobby could be—I love Bobby's hair, Mama—but I don't like his laugh. Laughs real high up, like a girl. *(NICOLE takes out a bunny doll that has seen its day.)* Hey, Roscoe, what's happenin', bunny boy? Let's see what Mama put in my goody bag, OK? Hey, you got me some pajamas, Mama! Thanks. *(NICOLE steps into her pajama bottoms.)* I can trade these with Amber. She's got two belts I want. And some suspenders. Suspenders are cool. *(NICOLE reaches into the bag and pulls out a package wrapped in birthday paper appropriate for a young child. A gaudy outsized bow flops over the edges.)* It's not my birthday, Mama. I told you that. *(NICOLE puts the package on the bench.)*

MAUREEN. You still leavin' next month?

NICOLE. Frank and Billy and Sarah Lynne and little Roscoe here and me and Jeffrey are thinkin' maybe we'll go to Los Angeles. Walk along the Avenue of the Stars. Go to Universal Studios. Get discovered. Get me a great tan. On the beach. Naked! Fall in love with a movie star. Just your everyday run-of-the-mill American dream. What's in this package, Mama?

MAUREEN. I don't want you leavin'. It's not good to be out and around at your age.

NICOLE. Of course it's not good, Mama. I'm still a punk kid. But it's all a part of life, right? That's how we learn what you can take and what you can't. Like you and Farty Marty. You keep takin' what Farty Marty keeps throwing your way and you keep coming back for more. Why do you do that, Mama?

MAUREEN. You lost a little weight, maybe, since last month? You look good.

NICOLE. You been to the dentist like I told you to? I bet Dr. Johnson said, "Looks like a broken jaw to me, Maureen. That sure must hurt."

MAUREEN. There are things you don't understand!

NICOLE. And I bet you said, "No, Dr. Johnson, I just ran into a tree playin' hide 'n seek with my baby girl." *(With passion.)* You're too old to be playin' hide 'n seek, Mama. I'm not your baby girl anymore! You see me standin' here? Do I look like a baby girl to you?

MAUREEN. He doesn't mean it, Nicole.

NICOLE. How can he not mean it, Mama? He walks over to you and smashes his fist right into your face! Did you think he was just shadowboxing on his way out to the kitchen to take out the trash, and you just happened to be standing in front of him with a big smile on your face?

MAUREEN. I hit back.

(NICOLE is suddenly very tired. And frightened. And very much the little girl. She begins to put items back into the garbage bag.)

NICOLE. I know, Mama. You hit him good. Both of you are real good hitters. I've been watchin' for a long time. Both of you gonna get in the hall of fame. I'm proud of you. You can take a hit and keep on tickin'. That's an old commercial, Mama. About a watch. They were doin' golden-oldie commercials on television this week.

MAUREEN. Where do you watch television?

NICOLE. In the woods, Mama. In the trees with the other monkeys!

MAUREEN. Where are you living, Nicole?

NICOLE. No one else reads but me, Mama. They just sit around watchin' TV and snortin' crap and—

MAUREEN *(overlapping)*. Nicole, you answer me this instant!

NICOLE. —sayin' how they're so smart and everyone else is so dumb and how they should be makin' a lot of money but the system wants to keep 'em down! I gotta get me away from here!

(MAUREEN sits on the edge of the bench.)

MAUREEN. Oh, baby, don't—

NICOLE. All I do is the cooking, Mama. Anybody mess with me and I'll put doo-doo in their hamburgers. *(Beat.)* I gotta go. You follow me...I'll never come here again. You got Farty Marty in a car out there somewhere? He follows me, I'll kill him. You know I will. *(NICOLE continues to put everything back into the garbage bag)*

MAUREEN. You don't do things with men, do you, sweetie?

NICOLE. Blah, blah, blah.

MAUREEN. You can't make it easy for men.

NICOLE. Time to go, Mama. I heard this song before. Thanks for all this stuff.

MAUREEN. Most men are nice enough. Your daddy was. He was nice. But some men are mean, not right in their hearts.

NICOLE. Amber says you're scared you won't know who you are if you don't have a man in your life. She watches Oprah. Why don't you leave? Just leave. When he's out drunk, you get his keys and you start driving. Drive until the road stops, Mama. Then get out of the car and start walkin' 'til you drop. Then start crawlin' 'til you can't crawl anymore. *(NICOLE is exhausted. She sits on the other end of the bench, an apple in her lap.)* You ready to do that and I'll go with you any-where. Just like Thelma and Louise, only we'd be Maureen and Nicole! But we'd make it, right, Mama?

MAUREEN. I think I'm going to kill him, Nicole.

NICOLE. Hey, there's an idea.

MAUREEN. I've thought about it.

NICOLE. You'll need some energy.

MAUREEN. I've done it in my head.

NICOLE. Want a bite of my apple?

MAUREEN. If I don't...stop him for good...he'll come after me.

NICOLE. Walk out. Slam the door! That's all you need to do.

MAUREEN. You walk away, he wins! I won't let him win! He just sits and laughs at me. "You leavin' me again, Maureen?" He knows I'll come back. 'Cause that's what we do. We fight. We yell. We scream. That's what keeps me going! I'm gonna get him, Nicole, for all the things he's done to me. *(Beat.)* And to you.

NICOLE. You know he's never touched me, Mama. You know that. This is just about you and Marty. And you must like it, Mama. And that's…not good, I don't think.

MAUREEN. I'll fix my famous potato salad…the one you really like with the little green olives all cut up…and we'll sit down and have a talk. Just like families do. All three of us. Turn off the television, pull up our chairs. And be civilized. And if it starts up again—and he hasn't been drinking, Nicole, not for a week now…almost a week, I think…coupla days now—but if it starts up again then you and me will take his keys and open the door and we'll…we'll just…leave. Marty'll understand. Will you?

(NICOLE refers to the package.)

NICOLE. What's in this thing, Mama?

MAUREEN. When he's sleeping…

NICOLE. Where'd you get the ribbon?

MAUREEN. I'll just get the frying pan from the kitchen…

NICOLE. My birthday isn't until next month, Mama.

MAUREEN. Then he won't come after us. 'Cause he'll be dead. *(Beat.)* I'm so tired, sweetie.

(NICOLE steps behind MAUREEN and fixes her hair. She touches her mother lovingly.)

NICOLE.You talk that every time I come out here! You've killed Farty Marty a thousand times. I've got to fix dinner, clean out the trailer and do everyone's laundry and then I have to read my books and learn new vocabulary words because I don't want to sound like trash anymore and then I've got to pillage—that's one of my new words—pillage a few tasty morsels—that's another one— from the grocery stores to hold up my end of the trailer commune thing. And all you got to do is kill little old Farty Marty. Does that seem fair to you?

MAUREEN. I won't be here for your birthday next month, baby.

NICOLE. 'Course you will. 'Cause it's my birthday. Mama? *(Beat.)* Has anything happened? Mama?

MAUREEN. Just blowing off a little steam, sweetheart. Just talking to Doctor Nicole. You're a good listener. *(MAUREEN reaches her hand up and touches NICOLE's hand. Then she brings NICOLE's hand to her lips, then to her cheek.)*

NICOLE *(beat)*. You need a haircut, Mama. Bad. Maybe I'll get you a coupon for your birthday. Would you like that? Mama, let go. Next month you can do my hair, OK? *(Beat.)* Let go of my hand, Mama. *(NICOLE tries to pull her hand away. MAUREEN holds on tight.)* Let go, Mama! Let go! *(MAUREEN releases NICOLE's hand. NICOLE stands back.)* Don't you touch me! You know the rules! I make all the rules! *(Beat.)* You gonna be here next month?

(MAUREEN rises from the bench.)

MAUREEN. Take the basket with you, OK? Happy birthday.

NICOLE. I'll leave a note.

MAUREEN. I got to go now, baby.

NICOLE. Tell you where to meet me, OK? OK?

MAUREEN. You be good.

(MAUREEN exits. For a moment, NICOLE is motionless. Then she calls off.)

NICOLE. Mama? Come back here! Where you goin'? Mama? You comin' back? *(LIGHTS begin to fade. The birthday package is left unopened on the bench.)* Mama? I don't want you to leave. Come back here right now...or I'll leave you, Mama. I swear I will. You know I will. Mama?

END OF PLAY

PARTIAL POST

By
Mark Guarino

Partial Post was first produced in 1997 at the Curious Theatre Branch in Chicago. It was directed by Julieanne Ehre, and featured Ed Dzialo and Melissa Culverwell.

CHARACTERS

A: A woman.
B: A man.

Both are in their forties and should not be conventionally attractive. They should look weary, as if they've been shut inside this house for years. They should be simply dressed.

SETTING: A bare stage with only a round, wooden table and two chairs. A window behind it suggests a dark, dreary, snowy day outside. There is a door leading outside. No colors at all should be visible. Everything— the clothing of the characters, the walls, the props— should blend together in a mix of blacks, grays and whites.

TIME: The present.

PARTIAL POST

AT THE CURTAIN: *LIGHTS up. B is at the table, trying to write with a pen. A is standing.*

A So you're writing a letter!
(Beat. B looks up at A. His pen has run out.)

B. Got a pen?
(A walks to him and pulls a pen from behind B's ear and hands it to him.)

A. You're writing a letter. How...1940s of you. A letter. What precious muse must spur you to action! You think? Yes... A Big Man With a Letter. A Big Man With a *Heart*. Postman must make that route bound and gagged by now. All led with the smell of the stamp that he knows to be yours. *(A pause.)* Whatta sap.

B. Who?

A. Oh, who knows. Me, especially. But I'd probably point to that postman. You think? He hates you, surely. Through pain, stains, heat and snow, he's got to trudge your little *affections* every week, every hour to that same address. He's not your slave.

B. No?

A. I am. You think? *(A pause.)* Me.

B. You're not. Especially.

A. Oh. Well...I thank that. I guess I'm a little special like my mama always said I am. I had six toes on each foot when I was born and they made me a queen, she said. We celebrated imperfections back then. We advertised misnomers. We relished in idiosyncratic methods of living that were contrary to the general populi. *(A pause.)* Barf. That was the first six months. Problem was, baby hadda walk. Now two toes in a pill bottle in a crazy lady's house. But hey. The feeling's still there—to be special? I am *that,* you know.

B. I know.

A. Oh, sorry. You're penning again. *(A pause.)* What does it ever say?

B. "Dear."

A. Oh baby, I know that. "Dear Her. Boo Hoo." A sad tale of lament, I'm sure. A tug. A soppy string of eloquent mash.

B. You don't know what it is.

A. Tell me. Baby, for once, isn't it time? You think? *I* do.

B. I know.

A. *I* do. Isn't it a sign of respect, do you think, that maybe I should know what's inside'a your heart?
(B puts his pen down.)

B. I-can't-think.

A. Maybe I'm just a Mason jar you screw shut every night to keep the air out. Fresh air.

B. I'm almost done.

A. I know. *(A checks her watch.)* About that time. For X's and O's. For Met-a-phors, don't you know. Yes. To sign off again is the most creative time, to shine, to *shine,* don't you think? Let's see you do it.

B. No. Make coffee.

A. Oh, the grounds are all caked. It's not to be drunk. Now you...

B. It's personal. Sweet. It's mine.
(A tries to look at his letter.)

A. No, no...

B. Sweet, please.

A. No, can't...

(B folds the letter.)

B. It's done.

A. No. It won't be done. It gets mailed and all those workers touch it, holiday help maybe, college kids. Then it all goes along in a sack across town, in a plane to a plant where it's manhandled again. Your letter. Second your hands shut the chute, it's buried alive in a stack for all to start touching— Nothing's yours anymore. Not her.

B. I know that.

A. Her fingers touch it last. Or do they? I doubt everything. You should too.

B. I don't have to. She reads. She opens them, I know, like a reminder as a clock might be, a chime in time, always mine, always mine...

A. Rung dead. Her brittle hands. By now, not moist or like spoons. Weighty fingers. Hard. *(A beat. Re: the letter.)* Where does that go to?

B. Fort Wayne.

A. Ha! You ever think she'd do that? End up in a town with a fort? Beauty can be sad. She lives it. You should see.

B. You don't know her.

A. I can hear the paint peeling on all four walls of her house. And boots dropping off a husband who wants dinner now. And a bathtub faucet thundering to keep out the sounds of everything else. Is that your beauty— Fort Wayne? Am I? *(A pause.)*

B. You're a beautiful comedienne.

A. Ingrate. Jokes are for the weak. For impostors. For snake charmers in sheep's clothing. *(A beat.)* You don't know her. Baby. Twenty-five years, baby. What stories could that letter possibly weave by now? Made-up ones?

B. No.

A. Hopeful? *(A pause.)*

B. It's cold in here.

A. That's her shiver up your spine, is all. *(A pause.)* You think? *(A pause.)*

B. No.

A. Oh you child. Do you think I remember my first time? Barely. It was a cop. Just a friend of my sister's. And it was in the fall. And it was after a picnic. And his breath was cold as he peeled off my pants. *(A pause.)* What else? Well my mind just took care of the rest and buried it. That's what nature is supposed to do— Brush it on past and move on.

B. That's not the way it is for me.

A. Then tell me.

B. I'd rather not.

(A sits at the table. She touches B's arm.)

A. What could you both have between you two? You forgot her voice, didn't you? You did. She was yours twenty-five years ago, Joe. That's it, isn't it? Look at my hands. They're not spoons are they? None of our hands are spoons anymore. Not hers, Joe. We *all* look the same after a while, after an age passes and it's walked us by. We are not beaming anymore, no one has olive skin and no one's eyes open doors when they blink. We are *past* dancing in all of its forms. We are *past*. No one's sparkling up their father's stairs waiting for us to pull to the curb anymore. We are past. Don't you hear your peers scratch and shuffle and chatter about philosophy or politics or their *kids* at parties and on trains? *That's* our lives now, Joe. Look at me. Please. *(A brings B's hand to her face.)* My face is no more than all of our faces. Feel the grooves? Sunken seas that stream through our flesh and mark us identical souls forever and ever. No one escapes, my darling. See me? I'm your lover, now. No different from her. At *this* age. Which is *real*. Which is now. *(Re: the letter.)* There is no need for this anymore, can't you see? You have me.

B. I do.

A *(smiling)*. Aren't I better than a mirage which almost always dims into vast disappointment? A mirage? She's me, you know. The same face. You feel?

B. I have to go for a walk.

A *(turning away)*. Postman hates you. Sick of your needless, weary afterthoughts. World is weary of afterthoughts. And he'd wish you'd all learn that.

B *(stands)*. I have to go on a walk.

A *(stands. Pause)*. I'll order a pizza.

B. Do it. *(Nearing door.)* I'll pick it up.

A *(stops him at door)*. Joe. It snowed out today.

B *(surprised, looks out window)*. It did?

A. All week. Stay here.

B. I will. Later.

A *(approaches B)*. Later when? Today with me?

B. Today? Of course.

A *(very close now)*. What could you both have between you two? What?

B *(holding letter up)*. The postman... The postman makes it to the box at three.

(A snatches the letter with her teeth. She backs away, slowly. She opens it slowly, looking at B the whole time.)

A. An ancient tomb is opened, isn't it? Twenty-five years …what can history sing so well that keeps it alive so long? *(She opens the letter. Dozens of bright red rose petals fall from the card onto the floor. These petals must be more brilliantly colored than any we have ever seen. A flips the paper back and forth. It is all white— empty.)* What is this?

B. I don't know. *(A pause.)*

A *(examining it)*. No words…

(B takes it from A.)

B *(ashamed)*. It's love. *(A pause.)*

A. Fool.

B. I know.

A. You girl, you.

B. Yes.

A. In Fort Wayne. Where no native knows your name. *(A pause.)*

B. I know.

A. Then why?

(B bends to scoop up the rose petals. He puts every- thing back in the envelope.)

B. It's three. I just…must make it to the box. On time.

A. Write to me.

B. The pens are all out.

A. I'll check.

B. They are.

A. I'll buy more.

B. They'll dry. *(B reaches behind his ear for another pen and flicks it on the floor.)* Cheap. *(A long pause.)*

A. You…don't need pens.

B. That's right.

A. And you were such a good writer once. An English major! I remember all sorts of lines you could think—

B. Words mean nothing—after a while—for this.

A. You think? I remember when—

B. I have to go. *(B approaches door. He is behind A's back.)*

A. Postman. *(B stops.)* You ever wonder why they're so angry? Come to work with a lunch and a gun? They don't like to be fools anymore. It's a noble thing to be a messenger all your life, more so a messenger between two hearts. They're all our slaves for sure but the faith they must have in us to make their lives worthwhile and the pleasure— Being carriers of gold the other end expects? And waits for? And loves you for bringing the best news of the day? *(A beat.)* I'll tell him, Joe, what's inside of your card. What a useless prop it is. Needless waste of white. Postmen can't take it anymore. You can't do this to them! They need to feel of importance in their day. What sort of joke do you think these people are for you? *(B exits.)* Huh? I'll order a pizza and you think about it. Think. Say some things can't be said anymore or after a while? Ha! If it's worth delivering, you can do it for sure! I'll show you! It's easy! *(A sits. She writes. She tries three empty pens. Frustrated, she turns to hand B the card. He's gone. She stands and walks to the window. She looks outside at the snow. A moment. She checks her watch. She looks out the window again. A moment.)* Three o'clock.

END OF PLAY

DUMBO

(Down Under the Manhattan Bridge Overpass)

By
Wanda Strukus

DUMBO (Down Under the Manhattan Bridge Overpass) was first produced in 1997 at Actors and Playwrights Initiative Theater in Kalamazoo, Mich. It was a winner in the "Off-I-94" festival, under the co-sponsorship of Actors and Playwrights Initiative of Kalamazoo and the Chicago Alliance for Playwrights. The play was directed by Sandra Lupien, and featured James Moles and Derek Potts.

CHARACTERS

JOEY B.: 30s. Gangster and family man. Semi-polished.
EDDIE: 30s. Gangster. More-than-a-little roughed up.

SETTING: Manhattan Bridge. Brooklyn side.

TIME: The present. Dawn.

DUMBO
(Down Under the Manhattan Bridge Overpass)

AT THE CURTAIN: *JOEY, in a dark suit and tie, stands, leaning against a railing. Sound of a car driving up, a door opening, and a body hitting the ground with an audible thump and groan. The door slams and the car drives away. EDDIE enters stumbling, his hands cuffed behind his back. He falls. JOEY watches. After some difficulty, EDDIE rolls over and sees JOEY.*

EDDIE. Hey.

JOEY. Hey.

EDDIE *(pause)*. A little chilly out here.

JOEY. You cold?

EDDIE. Naw, I'm fine. Comfortable. A little nip in the air, that's all. A little edge.

JOEY. Feels pretty good.

EDDIE. Hell, yes. Fall. *(He sniffs.)* Mmmm. *(Pause.)* How's things?

JOEY. Oh. You know.

EDDIE Sure.

JOEY. How's things with you?

EDDIE. Never better. *(JOEY takes out his gun.)* How's your mother?

JOEY. Same. And yours?

EDDIE. Good. Real good.

JOEY. Good.

EDDIE. Gonna be a nice day.

    (JOEY clicks off the safety.)

JOEY. You never know.

EDDIE *(pause)*. You got a cigarette?

JOEY. Naw. I quit.

EDDIE. No.

JOEY. Yeah. Angela said I quit or she goes.

EDDIE. Where's she gonna go?

JOEY. Hey! Angie's a good-lookin' woman.

EDDIE. She's got rotten teeth, Joey.

JOEY. She got 'em fixed. And she did something to her hair. I don't know. She said they wrap it up in tinfoil. Cost me close to a hundred bucks. But she looks good.

EDDIE. You got a picture?

JOEY. Yeah, lemme pull out the photo album. Wanna see the videos? I got 'em in the trunk. Take a minute to set it up.

EDDIE. Evidence, Joey. All I been hearing the last five years is how you nearly killed your ma marrying some skinny, rotten-mouthed Swede and nothing but an ugly kid to show for it.

JOEY. She ain't a Swede.

EDDIE. Polock. Lemme see the picture. *(Pause.)* What? I know you got one. *(Pause.)* I'd feel better if I knew you weren't doing that shit to your mother.

(JOEY lowers his gun to take out the picture.)

JOEY. Angie and Joe Jr.

EDDIE *(whistles)*. Very nice. You go to one of those glamour studios?

JOEY. Naw. Took the kid down to Sears.

EDDIE. They do a good job.

JOEY. Very reasonable.

EDDIE. Well, they got high volume.

JOEY. Charged extra to put Angie in there. But what the hell. You tell me that ain't a beautiful woman and a beautiful kid.

EDDIE. I stand corrected, Joey. She really looks nice. And Joe Jr., too. Gotta watch his teeth though. If he's got his mother's mouth that's gonna cost you.

JOEY. Yeah, yeah.

(JOEY puts the photo away and trains the gun on EDDIE again.)

EDDIE. What are you giving me that look for? I know what that means. Is it bad?

JOEY. What?

EDDIE. What. My face.

JOEY. I gotta dump you in the river, Eddie. Don't matter what your face looks like.

EDDIE. Aw no, Joey.

JOEY. I'm sorry.

EDDIE. Look—

JOEY. No.

EDDIE. All you gotta do is toss me under the overpass. Nobody'll find me for a couple days. The weather's cooling off so I'll still look good for the wake.

JOEY. Can't, Eddie.

EDDIE. For my mother, Joey. You know I'd do it for you.

JOEY. I got orders.

EDDIE. You know what that water's like. All kinds of shit in there. Jesus, Joey, there won't be nothing left. You gonna look my mother in the eye while I got snails and shit chewing my nose off?

JOEY. Nope. No teeth.

EDDIE. What?

JOEY. Snails. Can't chew nothing. They just spray shit on you and you dissolve. Takes a while, though. Bluefish, now—that's what you gotta look out for. They're like what-ya-call-em. *(Pause.)* Piranhas.

EDDIE. You are a truly fucked individual.

JOEY. Jesus, Eddie. Lighten up. There's no bluefish in there. Last I heard.

EDDIE. You took a vow.

JOEY. On your feet.

EDDIE. By the time they pulled Lou Gambino out of the sound he was all the way out to Montauk.

JOEY. I ain't talking about Lou Gambino.

EDDIE. His own mother wouldn't look at him.

JOEY. That's 'cause he went out on a job and missed his Aunt Lucille's anniversary mass.

EDDIE. Naw, Joey.

JOEY. He didn't look so bad.

EDDIE. My mother said, "Joey, make sure they don't ever do that to my boy. Look at that face. His father's face." And you swore. You said, "I swear, Mrs. Palmieri, we'll keep him dry."

JOEY. She was distraught.

EDDIE. You swore in front of God and everybody.

JOEY. I can't do nothing about it.

EDDIE. They'll scoop me out with a sieve and pack me into one of those industrial-strength garbage bags, but they won't do it fast enough to keep me from dripping all over the place, the better part of the river running out my pockets, Joey, running out of my pockets and all over the shoes of my mother and your mother and all those people and if you think you are ever, ever gonna set foot in the neighborhood again, if you think

you're gonna set foot in Hastings again, then you ain't
    ever been there before.
JOEY. It ain't up to me.
EDDIE. Got the holidays coming up, too. Gonna be tough.
    You'll be taking Angie and Joe Jr. to Jersey for mid-
    night mass.
JOEY. Angie likes Jersey.
EDDIE. You'll be moving there. Lots of room for Joe Jr.
    to play. Make sure he gets his tetanus shot.
JOEY. Aw, shit.
EDDIE. I'm just saying. It's up to you.
JOEY. Why you gotta be such a bastard about this?
EDDIE. I'm doing it for you. I go down, I splash around a
    little bit. Then you tuck me in somewhere off to the
    side. By the time they find me, I'd be dry anyway. And
    nobody knows the difference. Except my ma. And your
    ma. Anybody asks, you say, "You know Eddie. He's a
    floater."
JOEY. Eddie the Floater.
EDDIE. He washes up all kinds of places. Right?
JOEY. Right.
EDDIE. Nobody's surprised. Nobody suspects. Except my
    ma, and that's good enough. No hard feelings.
JOEY. Yeah, okay. No hard feelings. I'll put you up on
    the bank.
EDDIE. I appreciate it, Joey. *(EDDIE struggles to his
    feet.)*
JOEY. I wouldn't do it for anyone but you. *(EDDIE starts
    walking away.)* Hey, where're you going?
EDDIE. Jesus, Joey. I know you got a bad back. I appreci-
    ate what you're doing. No reason for you to carry me
    down there when I'm still good to go.

JOEY. I don't mind.

EDDIE. I'd feel bad. Put your gun away. We're gonna have to slide down the side here.

JOEY. I'll be okay.

EDDIE. 'Til you step on a rat or something and blow the top of my head off.

JOEY. I don't fuck up on a job.

EDDIE. What about—

JOEY. Shut up.

EDDIE. Yeah, well, I don't need a haircut and you don't need to give me one. Put it away, for Christ's sake. I ain't got all morning.

JOEY. All right, all right. Let's go.

(EDDIE and JOEY climb over the side of bridge down to littered area on the bank of the river.)

EDDIE. You okay?

JOEY. Smells like shit.

EDDIE. I wouldn't touch anything I didn't have to.

JOEY. Yeah. You break it you buy.

EDDIE. Watch yourself, here. It's kinda sticky.

JOEY. Jesus.

EDDIE. You're a good guy, Joey. You know what's important.

JOEY. Yeah, right. Get in there and get wet. *(EDDIE starts wiggling his shoes off.)* What're you doing?

EDDIE. Taking my shoes off.

JOEY. What for?

EDDIE. I just got these.

JOEY. Leave 'em on.

EDDIE. I'm not fucking up a brand new pair of shoes. Look at that shine, eh?

JOEY. You leave 'em on or no deal.

EDDIE. I saved up for these special.

JOEY. You wade in there and get that river shit in your shoes. I want it in your socks and cuffs. Pockets. Fingernails. Get in there.

EDDIE. You take 'em, Joey.

JOEY. I don't want your goddamn shoes.

EDDIE. Aw, they're beautiful. Hardly worn.

JOEY. I got wide feet. Let's go.

EDDIE. Joey—

JOEY. You wade or you swim. Your choice.

EDDIE. I'm going. I'm going. *(EDDIE wades into the river and splashes around.)*

JOEY. Dig in there.

EDDIE. I don't wanna get stuck.

JOEY. I ain't gonna let you get stuck. Don't forget your hands.

EDDIE. This sucks.

JOEY. Whose idea?

EDDIE. Shut up.

JOEY. I can't remember. Whose idea was this?

EDDIE. Yeah yeah yeah.

JOEY. Dry 'em off in your hair.

EDDIE. Fuck you.

JOEY. If I throw a guy in the river, he's gonna have shit in his hair.

EDDIE. My ma ain't gonna like this.

JOEY. Yeah, yeah. Your father's hair. She's getting your face. She'll be happy.

EDDIE. Can I come out now?

JOEY. Did you get your pockets?

EDDIE. I got 'em.

JOEY. Okay.

(EDDIE comes out of the river.)

EDDIE. This is some kind of nasty shit. Left me in there much longer, I'd look like you.

JOEY. Can't have that. *(He takes out his handkerchief.)* Lemme fix you up.

EDDIE. Did you spit on that?

JOEY. Jesus, Eddie. No. Did I spit on it. What do I look like? Jesus. *(He wipes off EDDIE's face.)* There.

EDDIE. Look good?

JOEY. Yeah, you look good. *(He takes out his gun.)*

EDDIE. You want me to turn around?

JOEY. You don't gotta.

EDDIE. It'd be better.

JOEY. I know you wanna watch.

EDDIE. It's okay. *(He turns away from JOEY.)* Don't tell nobody.

JOEY. It don't matter to me.

EDDIE. You pretend it's somebody else.

JOEY. Fuck you I'm gonna pretend it's somebody else.

EDDIE. Hell, I don't care.

JOEY. Then shut up.

EDDIE. I appreciate what you done for me.

JOEY. Like I said.

EDDIE. I owe you.

JOEY. Sure.

EDDIE. Hey.

JOEY. What?

EDDIE. Keep an eye on that kid's teeth.

JOEY. I will.

EDDIE. Be seeing you.

JOEY. You bet. *(JOEY fires. LIGHTS out.)*

END OF PLAY

AN EARTHQUAKE

By
Lisa Soland

An Earthquake was first produced in 1992 at the Chandler Theatre in North Hollywood, Calif., by The Faculty Actor/Playwright Company as part of an evening of originals works entitled "Words, Words! Words!" It was directed by Charles Nelson Reilly, and featured Pepper Sweeney and Lisa Soland.

CHARACTERS

KATHY: A 25-year-old attractive, friendly young woman who has lived in this Los Angeles apartment complex for almost five years.

STEVEN: A "raw and natural" 29-year-old small-town man who has just moved to the city.

SETTING: In front of a small apartment complex in Los Angeles. The stage is bare except for a doorframe with a sign that reads "Apartments 1-10."

TIME: The morning.

AN EARTHQUAKE

AT THE CURTAIN: *There are rumbling sounds. LIGHTS come up on a trembling doorframe and swinging sign. A woman enters barefoot, wearing only an oversize T-shirt that reads, "Happy Birthday, Baby." She braces her body in the rocking doorframe and counts to herself. An excited young man, also barefoot, runs through the doorframe, wearing nothing but boxer shorts.*

HIM. Holy shit!

HER. Are you okay?

HIM. Yeah. Man alive! What a rocker!

HER. That was a big one. I could feel it right through my body! Twenty seconds max. I always count them out in my head while they're happening.

HIM. Shit. Incredible.

HER. Was that your first?

HIM. Yeah.

HER. Oh, that's great. I wish it were mine.

HIM. That's really something!

HER. Isn't it?

HIM. Yeah! I never thought it would be like that!

HER. They're pretty powerful.

HIM. The building's pretty solid though, huh?

HER. Oh, yeah. I've lived here four and a half years and it's pulled me through every one of them. I just wish there was some way you could tell when they were coming. Mrs. Penelope in apartment six used to have this cat named Shirley that would go nuts just before an earthquake but a pot fell on her head and that was that.

HIM. On Mrs. Penelope?

HER. Oh my God, no. The cat. *(Beat.)* Shirley.

HIM. Shirley.

HER. Yeah. Are you my new neighbor?

HIM. Yeah. Steven.

HER. Kathy. Nice to meet you.

(They shake hands.)

STEVEN. Nice shirt.

KATHY. Nice shorts.

STEVEN *(looking down)*. Oh God. I was sleeping.

KATHY. Me too.

STEVEN. Better than an alarm clock.

KATHY. I'm still shaking.

STEVEN. After four and a half years?

KATHY. Yup. I still shake. I sit straight up in bed and wait. I always do that. I wait and watch to see if it's going to get worse. Then I count, and when I get past ten, I run for the door brace.

STEVEN. Door brace? Is that what you're supposed to do? *(Examining the door brace.)*

KATHY. I don't know. They change their minds every year. Kinda like how many eggs you should eat in a week.

STEVEN. What's that down to?

KATHY. I don't care. I eat 'em when I want. I bet that was six.

STEVEN *(a bit lost)*. Eggs?

KATHY. No. Six on the Richter.

STEVEN. Richter.

KATHY. Richter. The scale. You know. *(Seeing that he doesn't, she explains.)* This guy Richter invented this scale-type instrument to measure the intensity of earthquakes and their probable location and then he named it after himself.

STEVEN. Richter.

KATHY. Yeah. That felt like over six. Over eighteen seconds, over six...

STEVEN *(finishing her sentence)*. Run for the door brace.

KATHY. Right.

STEVEN. Got it. *(Finding a crack in the wall of the apartment building.)* Hey, Kathy. It's cracking. Take a look at this.

KATHY. Oh no, no, no, no. That's an old one from my first earthquake—October first, two thousand and two. Four point five, Richter. Twelve and a half seconds max.

STEVEN. Max?

KATHY *(without a beat)*. What did Mel get you for?

STEVEN *(slightly lost)*. Rent?

KATHY. Yeah, rent. If you don't mind me asking.

STEVEN. No, that's fine. I'm paying six ninety-five a month.

KATHY. Jeez, he's slime.

STEVEN. I don't mind.

KATHY. Do you live alone?

STEVEN. Yeah.

KATHY. That's hard.

STEVEN. I do okay. You have a roommate?

KATHY *(beat)*. You know, I should go put something on.

STEVEN. That's okay.

KATHY. No, no. I'll just be a second.

(KATHY exits. STEVEN looks down at his attire and decides he better put something on as well. He exits. KATHY reenters, tying her robe and notices that STEVEN is gone. STEVEN reenters hopping, pulling up his jeans.)

BOTH:
(STEVEN. So, are you...?)
(KATHY. Did you just...?)
STEVEN. You go first.
KATHY. Oh. Did you just move to California or...?
STEVEN *(can't help himself)*. I liked the nightshirt better.
KATHY *(setting the boundary)*. So does my boyfriend.
STEVEN. Oh. You have a boyfriend?
KATHY. Yeah. *(Pointing to apartment.)* We've lived together here for three years now.
STEVEN. Oh.
KATHY. Off and on.
STEVEN. Great. That must be nice.
KATHY. Earthshaking.
STEVEN. I just moved out here from Cheyenne.
KATHY *(amazed)*. Cheyenne, Wyoming?
STEVEN. Yeah.
KATHY. I was born in Cheyenne!
STEVEN. No kidding!
KATHY. Yeah!
STEVEN. I wasn't!
KATHY. Oh. *(Beat.)* I've never met anyone from Cheyenne. Come to think of it, I've never met anyone from Wyoming. Why is that?
STEVEN. No reason to leave, I guess.
KATHY. Why did you?

STEVEN. I ran out of customers. I make Santa Fe furniture and everybody within fifty miles was sleeping on mine.

KATHY. Sleeping on your…what?

STEVEN. Santa Fe furniture.

KATHY. Oh.

STEVEN. I thought it might catch on out here.

KATHY. Oh, sure! It's a great idea. *(Beat.)* What's it look like?

STEVEN. Oh, kinda raw. Natural.

(They are standing very close.)

KATHY *(looking at him)*. Hmm. *(Stepping back.)*

STEVEN. What do you do?

KATHY. Oh, nothing. I just uh…I keep a journal.

STEVEN. Great.

KATHY. Twenty-five years ago yesterday.

STEVEN. What?

KATHY. I was born where you're from, twenty-five years ago yesterday.

STEVEN. Oh. Congratulations. You're over that "quarter-of-a-century hump."

KATHY. Yup. *(Beat.)* What's that?

STEVEN. Oh, you know. Those age humps everyone has to go over. 25, 30, 35, 40, 45…

KATHY. Oh. I feel fine. I guess I'm all humped out.

STEVEN. Too bad. *(Wincing at his remark, he tries to recover.)* Happy birthday.

KATHY. Thank you.

STEVEN. You're welcome.

KATHY. It's nice to hear that in person. All I got was a phone call from Missouri and this lousy T-shirt in the mail.

STEVEN. Hey, it looked great.

KATHY. That's nice to hear too, in person.

STEVEN. Are you still shaking?

KATHY. No, actually. I feel pretty good.

STEVEN. Me too. Wanna go get some breakfast?

KATHY *(quickly)*. I have a boyfriend.

STEVEN. No problem. Let's all three go. I'll grab my keys. *(He turns to go.)*

KATHY. He can't.

STEVEN. Okay—you and me then. *(He turns to go.)*

KATHY. He's out of town.

STEVEN. Okay. *(He turns to go.)*

KATHY. Rolla, Missouri. Doing *Oklahoma!* The musical.

STEVEN. They don't have earthquakes there, do they?

KATHY. No. They don't. Pisses me off.

STEVEN. Excuse me?

KATHY *(full of frustration, she tells it like it is)*. It's just that I've always wanted to make love during an earthquake and there I was, sitting alone—counting. It's dinner theatre, for God's sake. I told him not to leave. I told him he'd miss the season.

STEVEN. Season?

KATHY. Earthquake.

STEVEN. Oh. *(Beat.)* What a rotten thing to do.

KATHY. He's an actor. He can't help it.

STEVEN. I see. *(Pause.)* Well...are you hungry or not?

KATHY. Actually...yes. Yes, I am.

STEVEN. Great.

BOTH:

(STEVEN. I better go and...)

(KATHY. I have to go and...)

STEVEN. Change?

KATHY. Right. *(They laugh. KATHY extends hand to shake his.)* Waffles?

STEVEN. Waffles.

(They shake on it.)

KATHY. Great. Mel 'n Rosie's has fresh strawberries and they're right up the street on the corner of Melrose and Fuller...

(An aftershock occurs—we hear the same loud, rumbling and the door brace shakes along with the swinging sign.)

STEVEN. Holy shit!

(STEVEN runs for the door brace. KATHY begins to count and then moves into the door brace with him. They are rocking back and forth, facing each other.)

KATHY *(shouts out, explaining)*. Aftershock.

STEVEN. Right.

KATHY. Three and a half.

STEVEN *(now knowing the lingo)*. Richter.

KATHY. Ten seconds.

STEVEN. Max.

(KATHY dives into a kiss with a startled STEVEN, who does not resist. LIGHTS out. Rumbling swells.)

END OF PLAY

CRECHE

By
Monica Raymond

Creche was first produced at Boston Playwrights Platform in 2002. It was directed by Monica Raymond, and featured Jennifer Makholm and Kay Moriarty.

CHARACTERS

TRACY: Female, 17, slender, attractive, appears totally normal, carries a backpack.

CHAI: Female, 17, scrawny, pale, sad, an outsider, slightly alarming-looking.

SETTING: A nativity display in a raised circular island in the middle of a shopping mall, surrounded by a circular seating ledge. A larger-than-life-sized papier-mâché Mary presides over the center of the island, which is also the center of the stage. The display is in a folk-art style, nicely done with piled straw and papier-mâché farm animals—in no way garish or embarrassing. The infant Jesus is missing.

TIME: Christmas Eve, 5:00 p.m.

CRECHE

AT THE CURTAIN: *We hear strands of "It Came Upon a Midnight Clear." It plays for a moment, then fades. TRACY, her back to us, kneels on the ledge. CHAI enters.*

CHAI. You took baby Jesus.

TRACY. Oh God.

CHAI. I saw you take him.

TRACY. Who're you? Aren't you supposed to be shopping?

CHAI. I'm done with shopping. I bought my father an electric train car on eBay. It's a caboose. I hope he likes it. It cost me thirty dollars. I'm afraid it's fake, though. The real ones cost hundreds. And my sister's getting a skull and crossbones. When she decides where she wants it, I told her I'd pay. I told her I'd do it for her for nothing, but she wants to go to one of the real places.

TRACY *(irritable)*. Well, what're you doing at the mall, then?

CHAI. I like to hang out with Mary and baby Jesus. I took the T and a bus to get here.

TRACY. Where do you come from?

CHAI. The projects.

TRACY. I thought they didn't have projects anymore.

CHAI. They privatized 'em, so now they call 'em condos instead of projects. But they still got that shit linoleum, still have those weird foam ceilings with all the little holes in 'em...

TRACY *(sympathetic)*. Decor is important.

CHAI. Anyway, I like it here. It's peaceful.

TRACY. Peaceful? A mall? You've gotta be kidding. *(Pause.)* You should go to church.

CHAI. Nah, I don't like church. Some greasy-ass minister with BO shaking my hand. *(Afterthought.)* Church is dangerous! You read about those kids that got molested? It's worse than school. No thanks, I'll take this. *(Looks back at the creche.)* Only how'm I gonna hang out with baby Jesus now that you've stolen him?

TRACY *(testing)*. You gonna report me?

CHAI. I should. That's not very nice to take Jesus all for yourself. What about the other people who want to be with him?

TRACY. You some kind of Jesus freak?

CHAI. Nah. I have an uncle that is. Born again. I went 'n got saved 'n shit, but the next week they wanted you out on some street corner giving out pamphlets. I mean, forget it!

TRACY. Are you gonna? Report me?

CHAI *(shrugs)*. I'm not the police. *(Sigh.)* But you should give him back. I mean, on Christmas Eve...

TRACY *(opens backpack, pulls him out)*. Here's your baby Jesus. *(CHAI, ecstatic, embraces him, and stands on the seat to place him back in the manger. TRACY stops her.)* I got something better than baby Jesus.

CHAI *(still facing toward the display)*. There's nothing better'n baby— *(TRACY reaches into her backpack and pulls out a real newborn. CHAI turns.)* Oh—wow, that is better. I mean, it's a real one. A real little baby Jesus. *(CHAI and TRACY bend over the baby, cooing at his little fingers, toes. CHAI, to baby:)* Hey, cutie... how come he's so quiet?

TRACY. He's sleeping.

CHAI. No, he's not. Look, his eyes are open. Hey, cutie... he doesn't answer.

TRACY. What'd ya expect? He was just born.

CHAI. Really? Wow... *(To baby.)* Mushy um um whirr whirr mmmm... *(To TRACY.)* I expect, you know... *(She makes baby whimpers. Trying again, to baby.)* Mushy whirr whirr mm... What's the matter? Is he deaf?

TRACY *(embarrassed)*. I gave him, like, Robitussin.

CHAI. You did? Was he sick?

TRACY. No, he wasn't sick. I just didn't want him making a scene, that's all.

CHAI. Oh my God. *(Takes baby, begins rocking him vigorously. Through the following dialogue, she continues to rock him 'til he revives.)* What's his name?

TRACY. I call him Rudolph, on account of—see how he's got that shiny nose?

CHAI *(rocking him)*. Hey, Rudolph, how're you doing? *(Still shaking baby, looks up at TRACY.)* Is this your baby?

TRACY. Uh-huh.

CHAI. Did you just have this baby?

TRACY. Uh-huh. In the bathroom at CVS.

CHAI. You did? *(Wonder.)* I didn't even know CVS had a bathroom.

TRACY. A lot of people don't.

CHAI *(still shaking Rudolph)*. Wow, you look great! Did it—I mean—was it—

TRACY. It was moderately gross.

CHAI. Were you—alone?

TRACY. I couldn't very well ask Chris to come with me into the women's bathroom at CVS, could I?

CHAI. I guess not. So has he seen him yet? The baby's father?

TRACY. Chris is not the baby's father. The baby's father was Luke. *(Fondly.)* See, he's got Luke's eyes. Since then I was with Jorge, Wen-Ti, Dov, and now Chris.

CHAI. Wow—

TRACY. I got ADD. Attention deficit. It means you get bored easy. I don't like to stay with any one thing too long. *(Pause.)* As for Luke, I don't know where he is. So for all practical purposes, this baby has got no father.

CHAI. Just like baby Jesus. Did it hurt?

TRACY. Well, yeah, it did—but not too bad. Power yoga—I mean I really got those muscles toned. I didn't do it for that, but it turns out it helped. *(Taps CHAI.)* Leg lifts, crunches. Shoulder stand. Plough. They really help, let me tell you.

CHAI. Wow, well—congratulations! So am I the first to see this baby—I mean after you?

TRACY. I guess so.

CHAI. That's so magical! That makes me like—a god-mother or something. *(Flustered, puts out her hand.)* I don't even know your name.

TRACY *(uncomfortable)*. Tracy.

CHAI. My name's Chai.

TRACY. Isn't that some kind of tea?

CHAI. It's Indian tea. I was in Starbucks and I saw it on the package in these really mystical letters. Kind of like

Chinese letters, but of course it was in English. Chai. One word, like Madonna or something. Chai.

TRACY. You're lucky you didn't wind up Frappuccino.

CHAI *(hurt)*. That's not funny. *(To the baby.)* Whirr whirr mumble grr whirr. *(She hears a gurgle, and, reassured, hands him back to TRACY.)* I think he's going to be okay. *(Confiding, dreamy.)* You know what I really love? Fonts.

TRACY. What?

CHAI. Like in Microsoft Word, when you scroll and then there's all these fonts. Palatino. Garamond. That one would have to be a boy. Helvetica.

TRACY. What?

CHAI. I thought they would make nice names for kids. Pica. Pica's not a font, but—it would make a nice name for a baby girl, don't you think? I'd like to be a graphic designer. If I don't become a drug addict first.

TRACY *(not all that interested)*. You do drugs?

CHAI. Yeah. Well, I can't afford real drugs. So I mostly do just—like Tylenol. *(TRACY laughs, then they both laugh.)* A graphic designer. I mean what I'd really like to be is a welfare mother. But you can't—

TRACY *(panicky)*. Don't say that, don't say that.

CHAI. Why?

TRACY. That's like wanting to be—a Beatle or, like, dial your telephone. Those things don't exist anymore.

CHAI. I know, I know, I said—

TRACY *(abstracted)*. No, you be a graphic designer. That's nice 'n—steady. *(TRACY lays the baby in the straw in the manger where baby Jesus lay.)*

CHAI. Oh, now I see why you took baby Jesus away. You wanted Rudolph to get some of that extra-special Jesus energy. That's so—

(TRACY turns away from the baby.)

TRACY. I gotta go. Bye.

CHAI. Do you want me to wait? With him? 'Til you get back?

TRACY. Yeah. Sure. You can wait. *(Takes a step away, thinks the better of it, turns back.)*

CHAI. Well, how long—do you think—you'll be? Because it's Christmas Eve, and—

TRACY. You don't have to wait.

CHAI. No, that's OK. I want to.

TRACY. I'm not coming back.

CHAI. Don't you—want him?

TRACY. Nah.

CHAI. You don't want—Rudolph?

TRACY. Nah. I'm not a baby person.

CHAI. Maybe you should've thought of that before—

TRACY. Oh don't turn all Christian Coalition on me— come on! I was straight with you, didn't want to leave you here freakin' out, babbling to the cops about some girl named Tracy—

CHAI. But you could give him up for adoption—in a hospital—it would all be legal—

TRACY. Yeah, right. But the thing is, see, this never happened. See, you do the adoption thing and thirty years later, he's on "Oprah" blah blah I wanna find my birth parents blah blah the trauma I'm adopted 'n all that shit. I don't want that. This way he's not adopted. He's just found in a manger. No father, no mother. Just— *miracle babe.* OK, this is a nice neighborhood. You got quality people. Someone's bound to come and find him and give him—a good life, y'know, Legos and Dad shooting hoops. That's not me. I got ADD. Attention deficit. I can't stay interested in things for more'n a short period of time. See, I'm going into my senior year. I got to do the test prep, apply Wesleyan, maybe Brown. Maybe I won't get in, but I gotta try. Sing the senior show—my voice is professional quality. Major—Fine Arts, International Relations—maybe a double major. Junior year abroad...Paris, maybe Amsterdam. Maybe Paris *and* Amsterdam. Then I'm gonna get a job at—well, not the dot.coms, they're out, but whatever is like what the dot.coms used to be when I graduate. My cousin worked at this place where they used to pay for the whole company to play paintball. Once a month. They'd go out to this big field in the country and *(mimes shooting an imaginary paint gun) key-yew!* And I'm going to have an apartment with these really shiny wood floors and lots of white wicker. Open plan. Decor is important. *(Confidentially.)* And I'm gonna fuck my boss! You've gotta have perky little tits for that, you can't, y'know—droop. And I'm only gonna date guys—unless they're my boss—who, first of all he's gotta be really cute, fit, works out. And he's gotta have a really good job—but then he's gotta have something really unique—like, he's kinky and he has a dungeon in his basement. With all this apparatus. Or a wine cellar. Or a speedboat or a yacht or something. Something to keep me from being bored out of my gourd. OK, that's me. I'm a planner. I know what I want. A baby right now is just not part of that. I gotta go, my parents have this thing on Christmas Eve and they really freak if you're late.

CHAI. But why didn't you—

TRACY. See the thing is I'm anorexic, so I'm always missing periods anyway. So by the time I realized, it was kinda late.

CHAI *(heavy)*. Yeah.

TRACY *(heavy)*. Yeah.

CHAI. He's not, like, malnourished, is he?

TRACY. He looks okay. I eat pretty good. For an anorexic.

CHAI. Your parents?

TRACY. They were just happy I was putting on weight.

CHAI. Wow. *(Pause.)* I mean—could they take him?

TRACY. Come on. I mean, look at me. I know these aren't the best values. I wouldn't give them a second chance. *(CHAI reaches into the creche and picks up Rudolph. She holds him out to TRACY.)* Yeah, he's cute, isn't he? I was almost tempted. But you gotta do what you gotta do. *(Pause.)* I'd hate to be old and looking back one day and think I could've been a publicist, if I hadn't had this kid! OK, I see what you're thinking. You're thinking you're going to take this baby home with you. And save him. You'll be a big savior. Well, you just put Rudolph back in that manger. Rudolph is not growing up in a project! Rudolph is going to go home with one of these families who can't have kids of their own 'cause they've waited too long, and is just dying for a nice little white baby boy for Christmas!

CHAI *(in agony)*. But what if they close—

TRACY. They're not closing for hours. People are gonna be shopping right up to the last minute. *(Pause.)* I'm a planner. Put Rudolph back in the manger. Oh ye of little faith. *(TRACY moves to exit. From the edge of the stage, she turns back.)* I'm not *totally fucked.* It's not like I left him in a Dumpster! *(TRACY exits. A pause.)*

CHAI *(sings softly to the baby).*

Rudolph the red-nosed reindeer,

Had a very shiny nose…

(She continues to hum and sing softly to the child as she holds him.)

CHAI *(to herself).* Garamond. It would have to be Garamond. *(The baby begins to whimper.)* Hey, Big Boy—it's gonna be all right.

(CHAI pats him. She seems about to walk away with him. She's not sure what to do. Finally, she puts him tenderly back down in the manger. He cries lustily. CHAI exits. The baby continues to cry loudly as the LIGHTS go down or the curtain falls.)

END OF PLAY

SHORT-TERM AFFAIRS

By
Donna Spector

Short-Term Affairs was first produced in 2001 by Actors on the Verge in New York City. In 2003, it was a finalist in the Actors Theatre of Louisville National Ten-Minute Play Contest and was a winner in the Palm Springs National Short Play Fest.

CHARACTERS

MARK FANBERG: Age 34.
DENISE DELANEY: Age 32.

SETTING: The Bureau of Short-Term Affairs. A stark office in a mid-town Manhattan building. A small table with a telephone and two chairs.

TIME: The present.

SHORT-TERM AFFAIRS

AT THE CURTAIN: *DENISE is seated at a table. She is talking on a small pink phone.*

DENISE. No, I'm sorry. You must have misunderstood our advertisement.

(MARK enters.)

MARK. Hello. I'm looking...

DENISE *(puts her hand over the mouthpiece)*. Sorry. I'll just be a moment. *(Back to phone.)* Listen, if you're looking for something "real," whatever that means, you've got the wrong number. *(She slams down phone.)* Yes?

MARK. Yes, I, uh, I'm looking for a...

DENISE. Oh, let me guess. You're looking for the perfect woman to fall in love with, get married, have 2.5 children, a springer spaniel, some cast-iron lawn ornaments—deer and cute little dwarfs painted in bright Christmas colors—a ranch-style house in the suburbs...

MARK. Well, actually...

DENISE. And you want to grow old together and take long walks on the beach, and when you become senile and incontinent, you want her to take care of you.

MARK. No. I must be in the wrong place.

DENISE. Oh. Sorry. It's been an unnerving day. So what are you looking for?

MARK. A relatively brief affair. Six months to a year. Fun and exciting, but no kidding ourselves that it's going to last. That sort of thing.

DENISE. Really? You're sure this is what you want?

MARK. Yes. I've tried other dating services, but they're always trying to match perfect people, and when I go out with a woman, she starts talking love after a few weeks, and she uses words like "commitment," and I break out in hives, and I feel this *panic*, so I thought your ad sounded more, uh, realistic.

DENISE. You're an emotional coward?

MARK. I suppose so. Yes.

DENISE. Good. That's important. We specialize in emotional cowardice and/or disillusionment.

MARK. I've never opened up enough to be hurt or disillusioned.

DENISE. That's fine. You have hurt women, of course?

MARK. Yes. Though I prefer not to.

DENISE. That's good. We're not looking for cads. Just decent people who understand the brevity of attraction.

MARK. Yes. The transitory nature of all things.

DENISE. We're born alone and we die alone. And all in between is ephemeral.

MARK. *Yes!* A mere façade. And true communication between people is impossible.

DENISE. *Yes.* Because if I say I was bitten by a dog this morning, you might see a German shepherd, when actually it was...

MARK. ...a small but vicious schnauzer.

DENISE. That's...odd. Just what I was going to say.

MARK. I knew it! It was as though I was taking down dictation right from...your brain.

DENISE. Yes. I felt that too, I... *(Beat.)* But down to business. Let me explain our process. First, I take detailed notes about you. Then I go through our files and find someone so obviously wrong for you that you will immediately feel attracted...

MARK. Good so far.

DENISE. I'm glad. This attraction and attendant excitement will be based, of course, on your knowledge...

MARK. ...that she's so wrong for me that we would never speak of love or commitment.

DENISE. Yes. You do understand. You will both know that all you're in this for is...

MARK. ...fun.

DENISE. Yes. Fun. *(Beat.)* You do seem to be an ideal candidate. Now, our fee is $100 per short-term affair. Is that too much for you?

MARK. No. It would be worth it to know...

DENISE. ...that you were free of entanglement.

MARK. Exactly.

DENISE. Good. Let me get down some vital statistics. *(She takes a notepad and pen.)* First and last name?

MARK. Mark Fanberg.

DENISE. Age?

MARK. Thirty-four.

DENISE. You don't look that old. Where are you from?

MARK. I was born in Chicago, but I grew up in New York.

DENISE. Yes, your accent.

MARK. We live in New York. How can you detect an accent?

DENISE. I'm from Los Angeles.

MARK. I thought you had a California accent.

DENISE. Californians have no regional accent. We speak American Standard.

MARK. American Standard is a fallacy. All accents are regional. Did you major in linguistics?

DENISE. Yes. At U.C.L.A. *(Beat.)* And your education?

MARK. M.A. in philosophy from Cornell.

DENISE. Very nice. Occupation?

MARK. I sell health insurance.

DENISE. Really. That's a waste of a good education.

MARK. What are you doing with your education?

DENISE. I'm glad to be helping people to find others who are wrong for them and thereby avoid the necessity of…

MARK. …growing up.

DENISE. Actually, I was going to say: the inevitability of heartbreak. Which is both painful and…

MARK. …irrelevant in the larger scheme of things.

DENISE. Yes. When one faces…

MARK. Death. Nothingness.

DENISE. Yes. *(Beat.)* Would you please quit finishing my sentences?

MARK. Annoying, isn't it?

DENISE. That's the understatement of the millennium.

MARK. Right.

DENISE. Something you said a moment ago. There's a red light flashing in my brain. Do you think growing up is synonymous with being open to love and commitment?

MARK. No. It just slipped out.

DENISE. Don't you think love and commitment are myths?

MARK. Of course.

DENISE. That old "Till death do us part" business. How can you know what you'll feel in five years? Or a month? Even tomorrow? God, people are so stupid, promising everything, when they don't even know the moment they're in.

MARK. You let someone invade your space, and then they can abandon you.

DENISE. And then you're really hurt, and it takes you ages to get over it and get on with life.

MARK. Right.

DENISE. Right. *(A deep breath. Then, slightly hostile.)* So. What are your interests?

MARK. Films, music, folk dancing...

DENISE. Folk dancing? Isn't that for old people?

MARK. Hah! Shows how little you know. People of all ages folk dance.

DENISE. I see. *(She writes on notepad.)* What sort of music do you like?

MARK. World music—Asian, African, Indian, Balinese gamelan music, uh, Balkan folk music...

DENISE *(writes)*. You don't like jazz?

MARK. I find jazz boring.

DENISE. Boring? How could you find jazz boring?

MARK. It's too "in" right now.

DENISE. I see. You're cultivating a rebel image.

MARK. I'm not cultivating an image at all. I like what I like.

DENISE. What do you do for light reading? Aristotle? Nietzsche? Wittgenstein?

MARK. Not at all. At the moment I'm reading Boswell's *Life of Johnson.*

DENISE. You have odd tastes for a person your age.

MARK. You're pretty damn judgmental.

DENISE. You have a problem with that? You think I shouldn't be a human being with opinions, just because I'm gathering information on you? I should like everything you like?

MARK. I did think you'd be more objective. After all, I'm a prospective client.

DENISE. Oh, really? "Prospective"? You're backing out, then?

MARK. What are you talking about? I haven't paid anything yet.

DENISE. I see. It always comes down to money, doesn't it?

MARK. *No.* I said $100 was *fine.* It's *fine.*

DENISE. When you go to a restaurant, you add up everything down to the penny, don't you? And if your date's swordfish was two dollars more than your salmon, you charge her for it, and if she's thirteen cents short because she doesn't happen to carry as much money around as you do, you hold a grudge 'til she pays you that thirteen cents.

MARK. Why would I worry about thirteen cents? If it was fifty cents it might bug me, but *thirteen?* Get real.

DENISE. Please. Don't be so touchy.

MARK. Who's *touchy?* Just take notes. I don't have all night.

DENISE *(controlling her anger).* Neither do I. *(Beat.)* What sort of films do you like?

MARK. I'm afraid to tell you.

DENISE. Go ahead. I won't say a word. *(Beat.)* Well? I'm waiting. Pencil poised.

MARK. I like thrillers.

DENISE. *What?*

MARK. You see? I shouldn't have told you.

DENISE. No, it's fine. *Thrillers? God.* I didn't mean that. Why shouldn't you like thrillers?

MARK. I feel like a worm under a microscope. You like to do this to men, don't you? Get them to reveal themselves, and as soon as they open up, you pull out the old Girl Scout knife.

DENISE. Not at all. This is my job. *(Beat.)* Let's talk about sex.

MARK. No.

DENISE. We must.

MARK. That's too personal. I'm not telling you anything.

DENISE. How can I find the wrong person for you if I don't know your preferences?

MARK. *Okay. I like* sex. With the right person.

DENISE. The *right* person?

MARK. The *wrong* person then. If I'm attracted to her.

DENISE. Frequency? Positions?

MARK. You don't have to know that.

DENISE. I do.

MARK. Other people tell you things like that?

DENISE. Of course. Isn't sex the basis of attractions to the wrong people?

MARK. I suppose.

DENISE. How often do you like to have sex?

MARK. I could do it every night if I'm really attracted.

DENISE. Every night? At your age?

MARK. You think a thirty-four-year-old male can't have sex every night?

DENISE. I'm sure it's *possible. (Beat.)* Fantasies?

MARK. God. *(Beat.)* Okay. I'm into hospital scenes. Doctor-nurse, doctor-patient...

DENISE. And you're always the doctor? Domination stuff?

MARK. I like to be the one in control. I know it's not politically correct, but...

DENISE. I knew it. You're the gynecologist. The helpless woman is on the table, her feet up in those metal stirrups, no nurse in the room, or maybe there is a nurse in the room, and she's a voyeur?

MARK. Everything is white: walls, floor, doctor's coat, and there's a bright light which makes what goes on even more alluring because it should be a dark room...

DENISE. There are machines whirring, which makes the whole process even more scientific?

MARK. No possibility of love.

DENISE. Just pure sex in a forbidden setting?

MARK. Yes.

DENISE. You're disgusting.

MARK. So are you. *(Beat.)* Why don't we go for a drink?

DENISE. Are you out of your mind?

MARK. There's a cute little bistro around the corner.

DENISE. Chez Fred? I wouldn't be caught dead there. Those phony Toulouse-Lautrec posters and candles...

MARK. Okay. How about the ugly deli down the street?

DENISE. Their coffee is at least three days old. The bagels are petrified.

MARK. How about my place then?

DENISE. Where do you live?

MARK. The Village. West Fourth. *(Beat.)* We could pick up some sushi.

DENISE. I hate sushi. It's dangerous. I might get worms. Or die.

MARK. You could slip on the soap in your bathtub, crack your head on the tiles and die.

DENISE. That's ridiculous.

MARK. It's the number-one killer in America.

DENISE. You're either an idiot or a liar.

MARK. I always tell the truth. *(Beat.)* You'd look much better if you'd let your hair hang loose.

DENISE. Thanks for the fashion tip. Do you always wear brown shoes with blue pants?

MARK. Do you always wear orange lipstick?

DENISE. Have you considered hair implants for your premature bald spot?

MARK. You'd look better in a skirt.

DENISE. You'd look better with a close shave.

MARK. God, you are so wrong for me! I'm really getting turned on.

DENISE. You don't even know my name.

MARK. I don't care.

DENISE. It's Denise. And you owe me $100.

MARK. *What?*

DENISE. This will be the first short-term affair our service is providing.

MARK. It might be just one night.

DENISE. That's short.

MARK. I'm not paying $100 for one night.

DENISE. All right. For you, $99.95.

MARK. You should be a stand-up comic.

DENISE. I've thought of it.

MARK. Don't think too long. *(Beat.)* Are you attracted to me?

DENISE. Yes. I've never met anyone so irritating. Even the hairs on my arms are annoyed.

MARK. Just the hairs on your arms? Well, let me tell you, you make the hairs on my back crawl.

DENISE. You have hairs on your back? God!

MARK. So you hate men with hairs on their backs? I might've known.

DENISE. You know, when you first came in here, we were so simpatico I thought you might be right for me, but boy, was I wrong about how wrong you are!

MARK. Then we make a deal. This is a six-month affair. I want my money's worth.

DENISE. Damn it! *(Beat.)* All right. This is September 16. That means... *(She counts on her fingers.)* ...we break up on March 16.

MARK. No tears, no recriminations. Right?

DENISE. Right. Are you clear we are not going to have any true emotional intimacy in this...arrangement?

MARK. Absolutely. No real involvement.

DENISE. Good. I don't want any misunderstandings.

MARK. Damn it! Quit repeating yourself. No intimacy. I understand completely.

DENISE. Good. And you owe me a nickel.

MARK. What are you talking about?

DENISE. I've changed my mind. No special deals. It's one hundred dollars flat.

MARK. Welcher!

DENISE. Scrooge!

MARK. Chiseler!

DENISE. Tightwad!

MARK. You have great bedroom eyes.

DENISE. Don't you say anything nice to me! I won't have it!

MARK. You watch yourself with me too.

DENISE. Fine.

MARK. Fine.

DENISE *(grabs him)*. Let's get started.

(They kiss as LIGHTS fade.)

END OF PLAY

RUMPLE SCHMUMPLE

By
Megan Gogerty

Rumple Schmumple was a finalist in the 2003 Kennedy Center/ACTF National Ten-Minute Play Festival and premiered at Dad's Garage Theatre Company in Atlanta, Ga. It was directed by Sean Daniels, and featured Alison Hastings and Geoff Uterhardt. It also received a Write Angle Productions Ten-Minute Play Award in 2003.

CHARACTERS

QUEEN: A queen.
RUMPLESTILTSKIN: A funny-looking little man.

SETTING: A royal nursery room in a tall tower.

TIME: A long time ago.

RUMPLE SCHMUMPLE

AT THE CURTAIN: *The QUEEN is guessing.*

QUEEN. Are you Carl?

RUMPLESTILTSKIN. No.

QUEEN. Shifty?

RUMPLESTILTSKIN. No.

QUEEN. Needle Nose Pliers?

RUMPLESTILTSKIN. No.

QUEEN. Philomena?

RUMPLESTILTSKIN. No.

QUEEN. Randy?

RUMPLESTILTSKIN. No.

QUEEN. Jean-Luc Picard of the Starship Enterprise?

RUMPLESTILTSKIN. No.

QUEEN. Rumplestiltskin?

RUMPLESTILTSKIN. What?

QUEEN. Forget it, that's a dumb one. Betharina?

RUMPLESTILTSKIN. No.

QUEEN. Bethlehem?

RUMPLESTILTSKIN. No.

QUEEN. Bethanphetamine?

RUMPLESTILTSKIN. No.

QUEEN. Gee, this is hard. Give me a hint.

RUMPLESTILTSKIN. No.

QUEEN. Come on.

RUMPLESTILTSKIN. Forget it.

QUEEN. Okay, fine. I give up. Here. *(Hands the baby over to RUMPLESTILTSKIN.)* She needs feeding every two hours. I've already pumped, so she's set for the next day or so, but then you'll have to switch to formula. Cloth diapers give her a rash, so I use disposable. I know, it's hard on the environment, but tough rocks, I have a life, you know?

RUMPLESTILTSKIN. Uh...

QUEEN. Be sure to give her a good burping after meals too. Spit-up is inevitable, so if I were you, I'd invest in some good washable knitwear.

RUMPLESTILTSKIN. Wait.

QUEEN. She can't go anywhere without her blankie, or she makes the most ear-splitting noise. Also, she's a biter.

RUMPLESTILTSKIN. Wait! Don't you want to guess some more?

QUEEN. No, I told you, I give up. Take her talking Elmo doll. She's not that attached to it, but it drives me crazy, so you might as well.

RUMPLESTILTSKIN. You're supposed to keep guessing, remember? I spin straw into gold, you promise first-born baby, I give you name-guessing loophole. That was the agreement.

QUEEN. What's it been, three days? I know when I'm licked. Here's the bottle sanitizer, and her pacifier. It's shaped like a lady's nipple!

RUMPLESTILTSKIN. Slow down. Let's think about this.

QUEEN. She's got some books that make animal noises somewhere...

RUMPLESTILTSKIN. You don't want to do this.

QUEEN. Yes, I do. Fair's fair.

RUMPLESTILTSKIN. No, it isn't. This is your firstborn baby.

QUEEN. I'll have another.

RUMPLESTILTSKIN. No, you won't.

QUEEN. Are you questioning my right to reproduce?

RUMPLESTILTSKIN. That's not what I meant.

QUEEN. Keep your laws off my body!

RUMPLESTILTSKIN. I just meant, this baby is special to you. She's irreplaceable.

QUEEN. You know what else is irreplaceable? Eight hours of sleep at night. Can't wait.

RUMPLESTILTSKIN. What kind of mother are you?

QUEEN. Look. I was young, I made some rash decisions. You're providing me an opportunity to make things right. Not that I have to justify my actions to you. And how dare you pass judgment on my mothering.

RUMPLESTILTSKIN. I am going to eat your baby. I am going to take her, hang her from a tree, skin her, and cook her. Then I am going to eat her. Her cries of pain will echo throughout these hills and only add delicious ambiance to my cooking and eating of her. And you are telling me this is okay with you?

QUEEN. Well, it's not my first choice. But what are you gonna do?

RUMPLESTILTSKIN. You fight! You—you keep guess-ing!

QUEEN. Hey, maybe you haven't noticed, but His Majesty is like, eighty thousand years old. Somebody has to keep an eye on the economy. *(Shift.)* Is it so wrong to want to establish my career before I get tied down with raising kids? Don't I owe it to my kids to be emo-tionally balanced as a person before I bring them into this world? Isn't it better for my kids that way? Maybe not this kid.

RUMPLESTILTSKIN. What about your biological clock?

QUEEN. You don't know the first thing about my clock.

RUMPLESTILTSKIN. Statistics show—

QUEEN. I know what the statistics show.

RUMPLESTILTSKIN. You'll be forty and pining for your baby. Lost and miserable.

QUEEN. Are you insinuating that I can't be happy if I don't have a child?

RUMPLESTILTSKIN. You have a child!

QUEEN. My child, my clock, my choice. Now take the little darling and get out.

RUMPLESTILTSKIN. You know what? You really did guess my name. Earlier. You guessed it, and I pretended you didn't.

QUEEN. Oh. This is so sad.

RUMPLESTILTSKIN. I'm serious.

QUEEN. Really, this is pathetic. The lengths you will go... Does fatherhood scare you that badly?

RUMPLESTILTSKIN. I'm not going to be the father! I'm going to be the eater! I mean I'm not. You're confusing me.

QUEEN. I know having a child is a terrible adjustment. Let me give you some advice. Go outside, light a small fire—

RUMPLESTILTSKIN. It's raining.

QUEEN. Light a small fire in the rain, center yourself, wrap my little pumpkin in some aluminum foil, throw her in the coals there, and think about the future.

RUMPLESTILTSKIN. My name really is Rumplestiltskin!

QUEEN. Whatever we have to tell ourselves. Now, do you have everything? You can call me if there's something I've forgotten.

RUMPLESTILTSKIN. Forget it. I won't take her.

QUEEN. Yes, you will.

RUMPLESTILTSKIN. You're crazy, I'm not dealing with you. I demand to see your supervisor.

QUEEN. I'm the queen.

RUMPLESTILTSKIN. The king, then.

QUEEN. You think the king is my supervisor?

RUMPLESTILTSKIN. Oh, dear Lord.

QUEEN. What kind of backwater chauvinism—

RUMPLESTILTSKIN. Stop it! Enough! You're going to make me— *(Beat. A thought.)* You're bluffing.

QUEEN. What?

RUMPLESTILTSKIN. This is a ruse. You're trying to trick me.

QUEEN. I don't know what you're talking about.

RUMPLESTILTSKIN. You're trying to get me to leave the baby here.

QUEEN. No, I'm not.

RUMPLESTILTSKIN. Oh, ho! And I almost fell for it, too. Sneaky! Very sneaky. But not sneaky enough!

QUEEN. Whatever. Are you going?

RUMPLESTILTSKIN. I am going. And I am taking your baby.

QUEEN. Fine. *(Beat.)*

RUMPLESTILTSKIN. Here I go.

QUEEN. Okay.

RUMPLESTILTSKIN. I'm going to eat her up.

QUEEN. Can't wait. *(Beat.)*

RUMPLESTILTSKIN. You're bluffing. I know you're bluffing.

QUEEN. Look, you don't believe me? Give me the baby.

RUMPLESTILTSKIN. Aha!

QUEEN. I'll cook her.

RUMPLESTILTSKIN. Come again?

QUEEN. I'll make you a nice take-out meal. How do you like her? Barbequed? Broiled? It's been a while since I've been in the kitchen.

RUMPLESTILTSKIN *(aghast)*. You're unbelievable!

QUEEN. Oh, you can cook her because you're some baby-eating demon creature, but because I'm her mother, I can't?

RUMPLESTILTSKIN. Finally, you're making sense.

QUEEN *(sighs)*. Such a double standard. Give me that baby.

RUMPLESTILTSKIN. I will not.

QUEEN. Don't be such a priss. Give it.

RUMPLESTILTSKIN. No.

QUEEN. Come on.

RUMPLESTILTSKIN. Get your hands off!

QUEEN. Let me cook my baby!

RUMPLESTILTSKIN. Under no circumstances.

QUEEN. First you want me to keep her, now you won't give her to me.

RUMPLESTILTSKIN. I don't trust you to take care of her.

QUEEN. Like you'd do such a great job.

RUMPLESTILTSKIN. Better than you!

QUEEN. Ha, ha, ha! Delusions of grandeur from such a tiny man.

RUMPLESTILTSKIN. I could be a very good parent.

QUEEN. You and what army? Being a parent requires skills and finesse. You gotta bring home the bacon *and* fry it up in a pan.

RUMPLESTILTSKIN. You think you're better than me? Okay. Prove it. Prove you're a good mother, and I'll give you the baby.

QUEEN. Who do you think you are? I don't have to submit to your authority or anybody else's.

RUMPLESTILTSKIN. Fine. I'll just take her home with me, where I'll dress her in frilly pink dresses—

QUEEN. Fine.

RUMPLESTILTSKIN. —and make her play with Barbies.

QUEEN *(horrified gasp)*. You wouldn't dare!

RUMPLESTILTSKIN. I'll saddle her with some nice body-image problems. "I hate math, let's go shopping!"

QUEEN. That is too cruel, even for you! How could you stoop so low?

RUMPLESTILTSKIN. Face it, lady. I'm wicked. Now start singin', or the kid gets a subscription to *Cosmo*.

QUEEN. Okay, okay, okay! I love my baby. I wanna kiss her little face off.

RUMPLESTILTSKIN. Not helping!

QUEEN. She's the greatest, she's the best!

RUMPLESTILTSKIN. More...

QUEEN. She is my sun and my moon, and I'd die a thousand deaths if any harm were to befall my child!

RUMPLESTILTSKIN *(grudgingly hands over the baby)*. That's better.

QUEEN. Pig.

RUMPLESTILTSKIN. You know, it's women like you that make it so we can't trust you. You get into these messes and then go looking for handouts from magical creatures. Let this be a lesson to you, young lady! Don't mess with the magic man, because I am strong and invincible and know no weakness! *(Disappears. Reappears.)* I'm keeping the pacifier. *(Disappears.)*

END OF PLAY

STUFFED

By
Jeanette D. Farr

Stuffed was first performed at the University of Nevada, Las Vegas, in the Paul Harris Theater in 1999. It was directed by Anthony Persanti, and featured Andrew Kaempfer and Traci Allanson.

CHARACTERS

BUBBA-BLUE: In his 30s to 40s. A large, menacing figure but soft as a bubble.

AUDREY-LEE: A little spitfire on the verge of puberty.

SETTING: A garage. It's where Bubba lives. There is a cot, hotplate and crates which he has made into a workbench. The "prized possession" is a large stuffed owl that should have a place of distinction.

TIME: The 1950s. A hot, summer evening at sunset.

STUFFED

AT THE CURTAIN: *BUBBA-BLUE is trying to drive a nail into a board by hitting it with an old rusty coffee can. In frustration, BUBBA-BLUE strikes the nail harder and harder with the coffee can. As the rhythm increases, AUDREY-LEE enters out of breath. She stops and looks back from where she came. She carries a burlap sack. She approaches BUBBA-BLUE and watches for a while. He catches AUDREY LEE's eye. He pounds the nail softer, then stops.*

BUBBA-BLUE. I don't have time to get made fun of to-day.
AUDREY-LEE. Not this time.
BUBBA-BLUE. Whatever it is—it don't matter—
AUDREY-LEE. I'm here on business.
(AUDREY-LEE walks over, opens the burlap sack and shows him what's inside)
BUBBA-BLUE. So?
AUDREY-LEE. I'm willin' to pay.
BUBBA-BLUE. I don't know what you mean.
AUDREY-LEE. Twenty-seven cents…
BUBBA-BLUE. Go home.
AUDREY-LEE. Three of them cents is wheat pennies.
BUBBA-BLUE. Don't you have a home?
AUDREY-LEE. I can get you more…come Friday.
BUBBA-BLUE. Or somewheres to be besides here?
AUDREY-LEE. …or if I find pop bottles…I can—
BUBBA-BLUE. Get lost!

AUDREY-LEE. Take in the pop bottles. *(Pause.)* I brought you a whole box of Tasty-cakes. I know it must be a long time since you had somethin' sweet. They make all kinds now. Not just filled in the middle with cream. But lemon kind and berry kind.
(He takes the box of Tasty-cakes and eats three in a row. She watches him and smiles.)
BUBBA-BLUE. Bury it.
(Her smile disappears.)
AUDREY-LEE. Uh, uh.
BUBBA-BLUE. It's gonna start to stink up the place.
AUDREY-LEE. You can fix it.
BUBBA-BLUE. You think you know somethin' and you don't.
AUDREY-LEE. I know you like Tasty-cakes the way you scarfed 'em down the way you did. I know everyone thought you was weird 'cause you ate raw meat once. I know your mama thought you was sick in the head and sent you away for a long, long time and while you was there you learned…
BUBBA-BLUE. That wasn't me.
AUDREY-LEE. Tellin' lies again, Bubba-Blue?
BUBBA-BLUE. Don't call me that.
AUDREY-LEE. I also know that's what they called you.
(She sings—children's rhyme style.)
    Buh-buh-Blue
    What he do.
    Stuffed his Mama
    With a rus-ty shoe.
BUBBA-BLUE. That's what's a lie!

AUDREY-LEE. True as your belly there. Mama says that's why you live in this here garage 'cause you can't afford to live nowhere else.

BUBBA-BLUE. Just plain Bubba.

AUDREY-LEE. And I heard from some other folks...

BUBBA-BLUE. *Well you shouldn't oughta believe everythin' you hear!* 'Cause when people talk about stuff they don't know nothin' about it makes 'em look stupid. I never talk nothin' about nobody 'cause I mind my own business...

AUDREY-LEE. But I *am* here on business.

BUBBA-BLUE *(looks her dead in the eye).* I don't bother nobody. Don't talk to nobody and I likes it that way. You and your spittle of pals yellin' things at me all the time—

AUDREY-LEE. They ain't my pals. Mama won't let me play. Says I need to be a young lady.

BUBBA-BLUE. Well...young ladies don't come where they ain't invited.

AUDREY-LEE. But—

BUBBA-BLUE. *Go!*

AUDREY-LEE. But—I—I heard you'd be able to fix my...fix... *(AUDREY appears to be in tears.)*

BUBBA-BLUE. No...don't. Quit your snivlin', now. *(She cries louder.)* Give it here. *(She hands him the bag and smiles. He looks inside:)* There ain't much left of it, is there. I tell you what. Why don't you leave it with me.

AUDREY-LEE. No.

BUBBA-BLUE. I'll figure out what to do with it.

AUDREY-LEE. And have you just go an' bury it? Uh, uh. I wanna stay and watch.

BUBBA-BLUE. You shouldn't be here.

AUDREY-LEE. I ain't scared.

BUBBA-BLUE. Well maybe you should be.

AUDREY-LEE. Little girls get scared. I ain't little no more.

BUBBA-BLUE. You're little enough.

AUDREY-LEE. Mama said I'm gonna be a woman soon.

BUBBA-BLUE. That's even worse.

AUDREY-LEE. She says my whole insides will change.

BUBBA-BLUE. You can't stay.

AUDREY-LEE. Why?

BUBBA-BLUE. 'Cause...I...well... It just isn't right for a young lady to...

AUDREY-LEE. Tryin' to keep your ears clean?

BUBBA-BLUE. What?

AUDREY-LEE. That's what Mama says for "stayin' outa trouble."

BUBBA-BLUE. You just can't. That's why.

AUDREY-LEE. You're still followin' all the rules they had.

BUBBA-BLUE. Rules?

AUDREY-LEE. All the rules at the hospital.

BUBBA-BLUE. Quit tellin' tales, girl.

AUDREY-LEE. Like tellin' you what to eat, when to eat, how to walk, when to talk, when to piss, how to piss.

BUBBA-BLUE. Watch your mouth...

AUDREY-LEE. That you couldn't say the word "piss" and that you could only do certain things in there as "trades" like makin' baskets and clay pots and stuffin' animals...

BUBBA-BLUE. You better quit—

AUDREY-LEE. Which they had a fancy word for... tax-i-der-my. 'Cause that's what they do in hospitals is use them fancy words...isn't that right, Bubba-Blue?

BUBBA-BLUE. You can't believe everythin' you hear.

AUDREY-LEE. I don't know what the big fuss is. Stuffin' animals is not as scary as they all say.

BUBBA-BLUE. They—they who?

AUDREY-LEE. People in town.

BUBBA-BLUE. I told you—you shouldn't believe...

AUDREY-LEE. Anyone who does tax-i-dermy gotta have a screw loose. That by the light of the big full moon you find anything you can that's livin' and breathin' to stuff—'cause even though you been out for a while, you still hungry for it—always was...

BUBBA-BLUE. You better quit!

AUDREY-LEE. What do them animals say to you before they die, eh, Bubba?

BUBBA-BLUE. Quiet now!

AUDREY-LEE. I thought it was really creepy at first—an animal when it's stuffed. Mama says they learned you how to stuff animals so the animals could see what you do. Glazed eyes always open. You can't sneak up on them that way.

BUBBA-BLUE. *Fine! (He takes the burlap sack and shakes it at her.)* First you drain all the blood...

AUDREY-LEE. The what?

BUBBA-BLUE. Then you have to take all the innards out...

AUDREY-LEE. The blood? Is there that much?

BUBBA-BLUE. If it's been dead for a while it starts to stink a bit. But if it hasn't, you can almost hear it scream.

AUDREY-LEE. That so?

BUBBA-BLUE. Then you can take just about anything you can find. Leaves, sticks, couch-cushion fluff... and...

AUDREY-LEE. What if your ma won't let you.

BUBBA-BLUE. Stuff.

AUDREY-LEE. But what if they're the good couch cushions from the nice white couch that's covered with plastic that your ma won't let you sit on even if you have your best undies in the whole wide world on!

BUBBA-BLUE. Undies.

AUDREY-LEE. And she won't even let you get near it 'cause she's afraid you're gonna drool on it or something 'cause that's what the plastic's for...

BUBBA-BLUE. I don't—

AUDREY-LEE. And the only thing she lets on that fluffy white couch is the fluffy white kitty cat who she loves more than anythin' else in the world...

BUBBA-BLUE *(looking in bag)*. Is this...? Oh...

AUDREY-LEE. I could tell her it was an accident. That I just found it like that.

BUBBA-BLUE. Listen here.

AUDREY-LEE. That's what you did, isn't that right, Bubba-Blue? You told them it was an accident?

BUBBA-BLUE. You gotta fix this one on your own...

AUDREY-LEE. And they believed you. You told them you loved your mama and you didn't know how it happened. That she just stopped breathin' on her own. *(Pause.)*

BUBBA-BLUE. Don't know where you heard that, missy.

AUDREY-LEE. I didn't hear it from no one. I just knew. *(Pause.)* That part's true, isn't it, Bubba?

BUBBA-BLUE. Do you wanna learn? *(Pause.)*

AUDREY-LEE. Right now all I want is my cat fixed.

BUBBA-BLUE. I'm not gonna show you more than once what to do. I don't waste my time on just anyone.

AUDREY-LEE. Mama says I got…

BUBBA-BLUE. Fuck your mama!

AUDREY-LEE. …lots of potential. *(Pause.)*

BUBBA-BLUE. Yes. Yes you do. *(Pause.)*

AUDREY-LEE. That's one thing that makes us alike—you and me. Mean mamas.

BUBBA-BLUE. I guess.

AUDREY-LEE. I would've done the same. If I was you, I mean.

BUBBA-BLUE. Why don't you find us some leaves.

(AUDREY-LEE, suddenly with a burst of energy, gets ready to leave the garage. She sings to herself a different children's song.)

AUDREY-LEE.
Buh-buh Blue.
What he do.
Stuffed Mama's kitty
So it looks brand new.

(She stops.) People will stop, Bubba-Blue. Talkin' I mean. Pretty soon you'll be hearin' nothin' but good things. People won't be talkin' about you and your mama anymore.

BUBBA-BLUE. Don't believe everythin' you hear.

AUDREY-LEE. I'll tell 'em. Tell 'em all the good things you're doin' here.

BUBBA-BLUE. What?

AUDREY-LEE. How you and me—we spent some time together, and you're not such a bad person after all like people say.

BUBBA-BLUE. You…you can't say nothin'.

AUDREY-LEE. Mama's gonna wonder what happened… and I can't tell her it was me. She'd send me away. Think I had a screw loose.

BUBBA-BLUE. No. I won't. You can't go back.

AUDREY-LEE. Not with a cat that looks like that. She loved that cat more than anything else in the world. And a stuffed cat is better than no cat at all. *(She picks up a pillow.)* Hey. Hey…we can use this, can't we, Bubba? Can't we?

BUBBA-BLUE. Yes.

AUDREY-LEE. You said that cushion fluff would work and this here pillow is just as good.

BUBBA-BLUE. That's right.

AUDREY-LEE *(handing him the pillow)*. Here. See? I'm learnin', aren't I? I suppose we can get some marbles for the eyes if worse comes to worse. *(AUDREY-LEE goes to the bag and looks inside. BUBBA holds the pillow tight.)* And when we're done…

BUBBA-BLUE. We can say it was an accident.

(AUDREY-LEE reaches into the bag. BUBBA-BLUE clutches the pillow with both hands as LIGHTS fade to BLACK.)

END OF PLAY

DUMPSTER DAN

By
Christopher Wall

Dumpster Dan premiered at the First Look Theatre Company's Festival of New Works in 2003, sponsored by New York University. It was directed by Nancy Robillard, and featured Craig Lenti and James Brill. It also won the SlamBoston! Ten-Minute Play Competition, sponsored by Another Country Productions.

CHARACTERS

DAN: High-school freshman.
DAN'S FATHER: 40s.

SETTING: Two mats represent Dumpsters on opposite sides of an alley. A milk crate is used as a chair throughout. Dan's Dumpster is empty. His father's Dumpster contains a baseball cap, clipboard, glasses, books, beat-up suit jackets, tie (already knotted), towel and a toy ray gun.

TIME: The present.

DUMPSTER DAN

AT THE CURTAIN: *DAN sulks in his Dumpster. FATHER sits in another Dumpster across the alley. He tries to get DAN's attention.*

FATHER. Hungry? *(No response.)* Not hungry? *(No response.)* Alive? *(DAN turns farther away and sulks. His FATHER gives up. To the AUDIENCE.)* I was at the kitchen table. Looking at all the stuff we'd accumulated over the years. Mounds of—! Piles of—! I could hardly find the darned sink and get a drink of water. *(Pause.)* At some point you have to make a decision and take control of your life. So that's what I did. I decided to get rid of it all, everything I owned, and live off the land.

DAN. Which was hard to do, 'cause we live in a *city*.

FATHER. Good point. That started me thinking. *(Scratches his chin.)* I love thinking. *(Scratches some more.)* I came up with an inspired solution: urban resource reclamation.

(DAN can't resist. He gets out of his Dumpster. Leading question.)

DAN. What's that, in layman's terms?

FATHER. You subsist on stuff people throw away.

DAN. Which means?

FATHER. You climb into metal containers and wade around 'til you—'til you— Fine. Have it your way.

(Together.)

DAN. Dumpster diving.

FATHER. Dumpster diving.

DAN *(to the AUDIENCE)*. Dad didn't stop there. He got rid of our furniture and quit his job, but we still had our apartment. 'Til one day he came home and said—

FATHER *(as if waking from a nap)*. I fell asleep behind the A&P on an egg crate. Best sleep I've had in years. Hmm. *(Scratches his chin.)*

DAN. Please. No more thinking!

FATHER. I passed my old partner on his way to the office. He was hunched over, weighed down by all the *things* he had to maintain. I got a better night's sleep than he did. What other proof do we need? *(Pats DAN playfully.)* I'll give the keys to the first person I see. Ha ha! Can't wait to see the expression on their face! *(FATHER starts off.)*

DAN. Wait! What about my books and clothes and—and *stuff?*

FATHER. You'll find better stuff out there.

DAN. Mom would never let you get away with this!

FATHER. Dan! *(A flash of anger. He calms himself.)* It's you and me now, all right? Trust me. *(He pats DAN on the arm.)* You'll feel better once we're out of here.
(DAN huffs as his FATHER goes to his Dumpster and reads.)

DAN *(to the AUDIENCE)*. After a few weeks, Dad began to change. He stopped drinking. His hygiene improved.

FATHER. That makes one of us.

DAN. He read five books a week. We had the best conversations. There was even talk of him entering the Boston Marathon. *(DAN climbs on the milk crate outside his dad's Dumpster.)* As for me, it took a while to get the hang of it.

(FATHER puts out his arm to spot him.)

FATHER. Come on, Dano.

DAN. What if something's sharp?

FATHER. I checked.

DAN. What if something's moving?

FATHER. I checked. I'm right here. Nothing will happen to you.

(DAN jumps in and goes through the trash. He finds a ray gun.)

DAN. Wow! It's in mint condition.

(He plays with it, excited. FATHER laughs.)

FATHER. I'm right. God, I love being right! You know, Dan, we're defying history. Returning to man's original, glorious state. We'll forage a few hours a day, then have time to engage in higher activities. Culture. Poetry. Family values.

(FATHER reads. DAN plays nearby.)

DAN *(to the AUDIENCE)*. I don't know how I kept it a secret at school. *(Beat.)* Yes I do. I have no friends. Actually, I have two, but they aren't let's-hang-out-at-your-house-I- want-to-know-you kind of friends. It was pretty nice, while it lasted.

FATHER *(aside)*. Do we have to do the next part?

DAN. You started it. You can't stop now.

FATHER. I don't like thinking about it.

(FATHER curls up in his Dumpster.)

DAN *(to the AUDIENCE)*. I was showering at a hydrant before school when the garbage truck came early. And Dad was still sleeping. You can guess what happened.

(DAN beeps and puts his arms out, imitating a garbage truck with front-loading prongs. FATHER wakes with a start.)

FATHER. What's going on? *(As DAN picks up his arms, FATHER tilts, lifting the mat so the trash slides too.)* Hey! Put me down! *(DAN's arms rise above him. FATHER tries to hang on.)* Somebody! Please! Help! *(DAN's arms are behind his head. FATHER pulls the mat over on top of himself and doesn't move. DAN looks at him with concern. FATHER limps off.)*

DAN. Dad? *(To the AUDIENCE.)* I was in the waiting room twelve hours. News teams arrived with the ambulance. A picture of dad on a stretcher aired on every network. With an orange rind on his head. And my two friends, who watch gobs of TV, aren't you-live-in-a-Dumpster-but-we-can-still-hang-out kind of friends. And those stupid newscasters kept sticking a microphone in my face asking where my mom was! *(Pause.)* I wanted to tell them that my mom was—that she— *(Pause.)* She always knew what to say. *(DAN rearranges his father's Dumpster, ranting.)* Why'd I end up with you, huh!? It's not fair!... Get rid of my stuff, move out and oversleep and almost get yourself killed and—and— *(He grunts in utter despair and frustration.)* You better die, 'cause I don't want to see you again!

(He grabs his things, climbs on the milk crate and jumps into the other Dumpster. He arranges his things. FATHER limps on.)

FATHER. Dan? Where you been? I thought you'd visit me at the hospital.

DAN. I left when I saw it wasn't fatal.

FATHER. Thanks. *(Pause.)* I see you moved across the alley.

DAN. It's as far as I could carry my stuff, all right? Go away! *(FATHER sighs and goes to his Dumpster. To the audience.)* And to think the only normal thing I had left was high school! *(Snorts at his own joke, then stops. It's not funny.)* I always avoided getting picked on. I'm short. Big kids looked right over me. But now they hunted me like small game.

(FATHER puts on the baseball cap and plays an older classmate. He pushes DAN to the ground.)

FATHER. That CD you got me was scratched.

DAN. It was thrown out for a reason.

FATHER. Get me another. You find a gold chain for my girlfriend?

DAN. I tried. They're hard to find. *(FATHER twists DAN's leg in a wrestling move.)* Ouch! How about something bigger? A teddy bear? She'd like a teddy bear.

FATHER. How do you know? You talk to her?

DAN. No. I'd never do that. Ouch! *(Looking around. Desperate.)* Dad?

FATHER *(snickering)*. He's busy, Dumpster Dan. In another alley. *(He pulls DAN toward a Dumpster.)* It's the cafeteria Dumpster for you.

DAN. No! *(Grimacing.)* The milk reeks. They served Sloppy Joes today. *(FATHER pushes him into the Dumpster. DAN dries off with the towel. To the AUDIENCE.)* You might have prayed if you were me. But I appealed to a higher authority… *(He goes to his FATHER, who wears glasses and a jacket and sits on a crate doing paperwork.)* Principal Lawson, it's getting worse. My English teacher made me take my chair out in the hall 'cause I stunk up class and—and— *(Beat.)* Will you look up from your paperwork?

FATHER *(sniffing)*. Step back, please.

DAN. I'll sue. Under the Americans with Disabilities Act. My dad's a disability!

FATHER. I hear he's a brilliant man. Kind of a New Age philosopher king. Maybe he's on to something. *(Returns to his paperwork.)* Why don't you try? I don't see you trying. *(Pause.)*

DAN. Why won't you listen to me? *(DAN storms off.)*

FATHER. Dan? *(He watches DAN go, concerned. To the AUDIENCE.)* I watched Dan sulk around the alley and wondered what his mother would have done to get him back. *(Beat.)* I couldn't believe it. I'd gotten rid of everything we owned together and I was still thinking about her. *(Pause.)* I tried to get a job.

(DAN, as the employer, in tie and jacket, sits on the crate and reviews an application.)

DAN. There's a break in your employment record.

FATHER. I was finding myself.

DAN. Did it work?

FATHER. Yes. But I lost my son in the process. *(FATHER slaps his knee and laughs.)*

DAN. That's not funny.

FATHER. No. It's not.

DAN. Give me your contact information in case something opens up.

FATHER. I don't have any.

DAN. No address or phone number? *(He tosses the clipboard away.)* Come back when you won't waste my time.

(DAN takes off the jacket. FATHER moves the crate across the stage.)

FATHER *(to the AUDIENCE)*. It was the same thing getting an apartment.

(DAN sits on the crate with a folder and application.)

DAN. Occupation?

FATHER. No one will hire me 'til I have a place to live.

DAN. You can't rent a place 'til you have income.

FATHER. I've already seen ten brokers. This is discrimination!

DAN *(ripping the application)*. Most people don't give up their job and home at the same time. It's discrimination against dumb people.

FATHER. Thanks.

DAN. Just trying to help.

(DAN sits in his Dumpster, his head down.)

FATHER *(to the AUDIENCE)*. I was at the kitchen table. And everywhere I looked there were mounds of—piles of—things we'd bought together. I found her fingerprints everywhere. On the cabinets, the doors. I thought I'd stop missing her out here. *(Pause.)* Dan? I'm sorry. I'd take it all back if I could, but it looks like we're stuck for now—

DAN. Go away.

FATHER. And since we're in the same neighborhood and could both use a friend... *(Pause.)* I'm not doing very well. I'm scared to go to sleep sometimes. At my age. Can you believe it?

DAN. You just—go think of her over there, and I'll think of her over here, and that's the way it's going to be.

FATHER. Okay. I'll be— Well, you know where I'll be.

(FATHER sits in his Dumpster. To the AUDIENCE.) I

tried to sleep. But every time I closed my eyes I felt the world tilt sideways and was dragged up in the air and was sure death was waiting for me. So I sat. And stared at the streetlights reflecting off the haze. And about two in the morning I heard something. This haunting sound reverberated across the alley, off the walls of my Dumpster, and out over the city. It was the sound of a boy crying. *(He goes to DAN, who cries silently, and puts his arm around him.)* I climbed in and held him. And for a few hours we were just two people huddling together, waiting for morning. *(To DAN.)* Hush now. Hush.

DAN. I like this part.

FATHER. I know.

DAN. I never thanked you for it.

FATHER. I know. *(Pause. Nodding toward his Dumpster.)* Have you thought of moving back? *(Pause. DAN shakes his head "no.")* That's all right. It's all right.

(FATHER rocks him quietly.)

END OF PLAY

ROCKS IN THE BED

By
Kathleen Warnock

Rocks in the Bed was first produced in 2003 by En Avant Playwrights at Hunter College in New York City. It was directed by Peter Bloch, and featured Joanne Joseph, Chance Muehleck and Campbell Bridges.

CHARACTERS

MRS. PERRY (Maisie): A very old woman.
A YOUNG MAN (Wally): In his 30s.
PHOTOGRAPHER (Cliff): In his early 30s.

SETTING: A cramped bedroom in the first-floor apartment of an old house in Greenwich Village, New York City. It is distinguished chiefly by the fact that there are small, round white rocks everywhere: on the bed, on the bureau, on the bedside table, on the floor. In the corners.

TIME: Some years ago. Late morning.

ROCKS IN THE BED

AT THE CURTAIN: *MRS. PERRY enters, slow, but businesslike. She leads two young men, one with a camera, one with a notepad.*

MRS. PERRY. ...he lasted a long time, he did. Not one of those quick and easy ones: like an execution or fall down the stairs break your neck. Not long overall, I mean in a lifetime...a year out of seventy, but a long time if you're there every day.

A YOUNG MAN. And you were here for all of it?

MRS. PERRY. Scrubbing the steps outside, all those visitors tracking in mud. Cooking soup, washing him when he couldn't make it to the terlet by himself. I didn't sign up for that! But the man had no family. Friends... he had friends, if you call 'em that, all the day and the night. Lot of poets. I never would have let him have a room if I knew he was a poet.

A YOUNG MAN. What did he tell you he was?

MRS. PERRY. He didn't. But with his hands, you know. They were all rough, and he didn't say much, and he didn't talk like an educated man. I thought he worked in a factory, maybe on the docks. He paid the rent. If he had something to drink, it was the way a working man drinks, he made it to work on Mondays. He paid his rent on Fridays before he hit the bars.

A YOUNG MAN. So you had no idea who he was?

MRS. PERRY. A man lives with you twenty years, you get a very good idea who he was.

A YOUNG MAN. I mean his work.

MRS. PERRY. The poems. I been given copies of the books. You people. Students, writers, you come by here and tell me the stuff I didn't know. Didn't need to know. Didn't have to know.

PHOTOGRAPHER. Wally, what kind of shots are you looking for?

A YOUNG MAN. How's the light?

PHOTOGRAPHER. Not good. But I don't want to use a flash.

A YOUNG MAN. Yeah. I agree. Natural light.

MRS. PERRY. No flash. Makes my eyes hurt. Washes out the faces in the pictures.

A YOUNG MAN. People take a lot of pictures here?

MRS. PERRY. Oh yes. Some take 'em for themselves. I'm in a book, too. The man sent it to me.

A YOUNG MAN. What does it mean to you?

MRS. PERRY. A picture of me in a book? Means he gave me some money to use it. Means I see myself on the postcard stands in some of those fancy bookstores. I get the postcards from the people who come here.

PHOTOGRAPHER. I know the photo you're talking about. You're holding a picture, and standing behind the bed. It's very good.

MRS. PERRY. You know the photo…

PHOTOGRAPHER. …but I don't know you. I know. But I like it as a record. Of a time. Of a person. I like the mystery of it.

A YOUNG MAN. Some mystery.

MRS. PERRY. Mystery to some. Pain in the ass to others, pardon my French.

PHOTOGRAPHER. Do you ever think of taking it down? Of throwing the rocks away?

MRS. PERRY. No. It's kind of a conversation piece, isn't it? I don't mind doing it. But the city's after me, the developers. They want to buy me out or throw me out. But this is my house. The hysterical society came by and said something about it's a landmark...but you have to pay people to make your place hysterical.

A YOUNG MAN. I imagine you could get quite a lot of money from developers.

MRS. PERRY. It's my house. I say who stays, who goes.

A YOUNG MAN. He stayed. He stayed for twenty years.

MRS. PERRY. He was a good tenant. Reliable. I liked having a man around.

A YOUNG MAN. Was he your lover?

MRS. PERRY. Keep a civil tongue in your head, young man. I'll throw you down the front steps.

PHOTOGRAPHER. Wally...

MRS. PERRY. I was married for forty-six years. My husband's grandfather built this house, he was a sea captain. By the time my husband came along, the money was gone, and all they had was the house. My husband went to sea, and I kept house. We let the rooms to steady, single men and women who didn't entertain. I earned my living by the sweat of my brow, young man, and in those days, when you were married, you took it serious, and you stayed married!

A YOUNG MAN. Not everyone.

MRS. PERRY. Oh, I'm not talking your high-society types...the man about town and the *deb*-u-tant...when you were *poor* you stayed married. *(Pause.)* He wasn't that good-looking a man anyways. Sometimes he went with a girl for a little while, but he really wasn't interested in gallivanting or being married. He came home. Spent a lot of time in his room, writing and smoking. That's what did him in.

THE YOUNG MAN. The writing?

MRS. PERRY. The smoking.

PHOTOGRAPHER. Was that why you moved him down here?

MRS. PERRY. You got that right! Me and my legs couldn't make it up three flights when he got sick. He didn't ask me to bring his food. He was very polite. Didn't complain. But I figured if no one took care of him, he'd end up in a charity ward, none of his friends was gonna spring for a doctor or a fancy sanitarium.

THE YOUNG MAN. He had family.

MRS. PERRY. I know. I know that.

THE YOUNG MAN. He told you?

MRS. PERRY. Some he told me, some I figured from what he left out.

PHOTOGRAPHER. The family, you know. Had money.

MRS. PERRY. There seemed to be some bad blood.

THE YOUNG MAN. Thinner than water.

MRS. PERRY. What's that?

THE YOUNG MAN. As opposed to thicker than water.

PHOTOGRAPHER. Wally, you're being a jerk.

THE YOUNG MAN. Shut up, Cliff.

MRS. PERRY. He had a son.

THE YOUNG MAN. He had a son. He left the son.

MRS. PERRY. He felt bad about that.

PHOTOGRAPHER. Wally, ask what you want to ask.

MRS. PERRY. Are you two young men related? You bear a resemblance.

PHOTOGRAPHER. We're brothers.

THE YOUNG MAN. Same mother.

MRS. PERRY. You're his boy.

THE YOUNG MAN. By birth.

MRS. PERRY. Can't say as I see much in common.

THE YOUNG MAN. No. No. No. Nothing in common.

PHOTOGRAPHER. You didn't have to come, Wally.

THE YOUNG MAN. I don't know what I expected. Rocks. Damned rocks.

MRS. PERRY. Watch your mouth, young man!

PHOTOGRAPHER. Why the rocks?

MRS. PERRY. It's a Jewish custom, so I'm told. When you visit the grave of the deceased, you leave a pebble, to show you visited.

THE YOUNG MAN. He wasn't Jewish.

MRS. PERRY. But some of his friends was. The city took the body right away. He didn't want a funeral. Made arrangements to be cremated. No memorial, no words over the grave. The one guy, Izzy Noel, they called him, just busted into tears when he got here and heard about it, and the bed with no one in it. Old Izzy, he ran out and picked up a rock from a pile where they was paving the street, brought it back. I said, don't you put a rock on my coverlet. But he said, it's to show respect. It got out of hand right away…all the others came. His friends, his drinking buddies. Some people I didn't know in suits and ties. Editors, lawyers. The friends had piles of rocks, and they'd give one to everyone who came in. Now it's…well…it's a room full of rocks. The tourists come. Make a big production of putting one on, some of them all weeping and wailing, and reciting his poems.

PHOTOGRAPHER. Did you put one on?

MRS. PERRY. Of course I did. For respect.

THE YOUNG MAN. I have no respect for him.

MRS. PERRY. I think he wanted to…he was going to get in touch. When he knew the jig was up.

THE YOUNG MAN. Why didn't he?

MRS. PERRY. He thought about it a lot, and decided that leaving you alone was going to hurt you less.

THE YOUNG MAN. I wouldn't have seen him. Or I *would* have. I would have come and told him off.

MRS. PERRY. Probably would have killed him. Well, sooner.

THE YOUNG MAN. I always thought…I'd get the chance.

MRS. PERRY. So did he.

THE YOUNG MAN. I don't remember him. I didn't know him.

MRS. PERRY. I knew him some. Towards the end, he cried sometimes. You know, he was an awful strong man, but he just got weaker and weaker. And once I found him, the tears running down his face, and he said: I only have so much strength, and I don't want to waste it trying to keep from crying. I think death is worth crying about.

THE YOUNG MAN. I didn't wish him dead.

MRS. PERRY. I don't think you did. He was very sorry to be dying. I think he thought there'd be time to get back to you.

THE YOUNG MAN. I would have liked to ask him things…

MRS. PERRY. He asked where you were.

THE YOUNG MAN. I would have come.

MRS. PERRY. I would have called if I knew where you were. Who you were.

THE YOUNG MAN. What did he want?

MRS. PERRY. Well, he didn't want to die. He was pretty clear on that. But when there wasn't any choice, he wished he had his family. He had his poems, and his books, but he said, Maisie: I'd trade it all to die at home in bed with my family around me. I think I'm going to be a long time lonely after this, and I want to say goodbye to them. I told him I could give him the home and the bed, but not the other. I asked him if he wanted me to call anyone. He said tomorrow, yes, Maisie, I think tomorrow. Well, that time there wasn't a tomorrow.

THE YOUNG MAN. I would have been there.

MRS. PERRY. He died at four in the morning. I knew it was his time. I turned the light on. I said to him, no one should have to die in the dark. He couldn't talk anymore. He had the death rattle. I sat by him. I gave him a little water. At least someone was there when he went. I told him it was all right to go. It was what I could do.

THE YOUNG MAN. It wasn't all right. It was never all right for him to go.

MRS. PERRY. If you had been there, you would have let him go.

THE YOUNG MAN. I was never there.

MRS. PERRY. I'm sorry for your trouble, young man. It must be hard to miss a man so completely.

PHOTOGRAPHER. You want to go, Wally?

THE YOUNG MAN. Right here? He died in this bed?

MRS. PERRY. I changed the sheets, made it up again.

THE YOUNG MAN. I should have known him.

MRS. PERRY. Young man, that wasn't your fault. It was his, and he was sorry.

PHOTOGRAPHER. Wally, you have a family.

MRS. PERRY. Seems like you have a good brother.

THE YOUNG MAN. And a good mother. And a good father.

MRS. PERRY. Can you live with that, Wally?

THE YOUNG MAN. I guess I have to, don't I? There's nothing I can do about it.

(MRS. PERRY reaches into the pocket of her house dress, pulls out a rock.)

MRS. PERRY. Sometimes, when they come, they don't have a rock. So I keep some around.

(She holds out the rock to the YOUNG MAN, who hesitates. PHOTOGRAPHER reaches for it.)

PHOTOGRAPHER. May I?

(MRS. PERRY gives it to him).

THE YOUNG MAN. Why, Cliff?

PHOTOGRAPHER. For respect.

THE YOUNG MAN. Respect for who?

PHOTOGRAPHER. For my brother's father. If not for him, I wouldn't have you.

(He places the rock on the bed. His brother watches.)

MRS. PERRY. I have another one.

PHOTOGRAPHER. May I? *(She gives it to him. He puts the rock next to his brother's.)* I think we can go now. Thank you for your courtesy, Mrs. Perry.

MRS. PERRY. He would have been pleased that you came.

THE YOUNG MAN. Do you think I needed to know him?

MRS. PERRY. Maybe that's what you need to find out. If you want to come back, I'll be here.

END OF PLAY

BODHISATTVA BY LAGOON

By
Cass Brayton

Bodhisattva by Lagoon was first performed in 2004 by Actors Theatre in Santa Rosa, Calif., as part of "Quickies: A Festival of Short New Plays." It was directed by Celeste Thomas, and featured Carol MacRae, Karl Mossberger, Maria Giordano and Tim Earls.

CHARACTERS

The play may be performed either by a single actor, or by two men and two women.

WOMAN : Female, elderly.
GUY : Male, 30s.
GIRL: Female, early 20s.
QUEEN: Male, 40s.

SETTING: The setting of the play can be fairly minimal. Sets and/or lighting could suggest a location in a hidden corner of a large urban park. Characters are not talking directly to each other. They share the space of the stage but inhabit it separately. The degree to which they are aware of each other is a choice to be made by the director and actors.

TIME: The present.

BODHISATTVA (bow-dee-SA-tva) – A being who postpones entering nirvana (the final stage of enlightenment) in order to remain in this world to reduce the suffering of others.

BODHISATTVA BY LAGOON

WOMAN.
　Lotta trouble today.
　Things were settling down, yeah,
　to a nice quiet smooth kind of calm
　down here by the water,
　what I call my lake,
　even if it is the color
　of the green pea soup
　my mother used to make.
　The calm went all to hell
　with the trouble that come this morning.
　I ain't the one that found it.
　No sir, I was nowhere near that
　floating body,
　nowhere near it.
　But they come asking me all manner of questions,
　suggesting I might've somehow
　had something to do with what they found.
　And I just told them straight up,
　the wages of sin…
　I don't know nothing,
　nothing—
　and I don't want to know nothing.
　They said we know you saw more
　than you're letting on,
　and that much is true.
　That is true.

GUY.
    I told him right out.
    When it came to boosting grub
    he was useless as an extra tit on a cow.
    "That's me" he said. "Udderly useless."
    Udderly useless.
    You could never stay mad at the guy.
    His problem was he's too pretty.
    Walk in a store with him
    and right off the bat
    they'd be shadowing us.
    One time he got caught at a check-out
    with tofu dogs stashed down his pants.
    Tofu dogs!
    Now I ask you,
    was it really worth the trouble?
    I had to fake like I was having a seizure
    so he could skip out
    'fore they called the fuzz.
    We hooked up later
    and he gave me one of those
    fuckin' tofu dogs
    —wasn't half bad—
    and he pulled out this other thing
    he got away with—
    a frisbee.
    A stupid fuckin' frisbee.
    But it was the color of grass.
    So I say,
    "Who the fuck steals a green frisbee
    for fuck sake?
    You'll lose it soon as it hits the ground."
    He says "It's not green. It's loden."
    "Who the fuck cares," I said.

"You're still gonna lose it."
That's the thing about him.
he never thinks a—
never thought ahead.
As a con? Udderly useless.

GIRL.
O-o-o-ou, he was one crazy fucker, man,
one cra-zee fucker.
Hell-bent on having a good ole time
no matter how bad things seemed to get.
He'd come by and say,
"Girl, you get your ass in gear,
we're goin' dancing."
And I'd say "Ah shit, man,
I'm too wasted. Come back tomorrow."
And he said "Nuh-unh-unh.
That's a day never ever ever comes.
The moon's out tonight and
I gotta see you dancing your dance
down by the lagoon
out in the moonlight."
Then he said, "Let's get dolled up."
And he brought out some nail polish.
Emerald topaz.
And he took my hand
and he painted my nails
and then he blew on them
to get them dry.
His breath felt warm, so warm,
like my hand was being kissed
by an angel from God.

QUEEN.
   I'm not going to be living out here forever.
   No, really!
   I'm only passing through.
   Queens and foliage do not mix.
   I mean, look at these plants.
   Where's the shimmer?
   He's the one who got me out here.
   I was on the streets at the time.
   It's a long story, but the point is
   these vouchers didn't come through
   and the people I supposedly could count on...
   Then I met him at my storage locker,
   we got to talking and he told me he had this spot.
   Out here, he said,
   at least the ground's covered with vines and leaves
   to make a cushion under the tent.
   A tent—
   something I hadn't seen the inside of
   since I got kicked out of the Boy Scouts for...
   Well that's another story.
   You get the picture.
   He called it our little campground,
   pretended we were on some grand tour
   of the national monuments.
   —Well I guess.
   It's a bizarre place to live,
   but I had pretty much run out of options.

WOMAN.
   I told those cops.
   I don't know nothing about no body.
   It's not even on my side of the water.
   Can't they figure that much out?

They just kept sayin' they're gonna run me in.
Go ahead, I told 'em. You go right ahead.
I wouldn't mind a night passed
in a warm room
on a real mattress in a real bed,
even if it's thin as a slice of Sally Ann ham.
Just bein' off of the ground…
off the ground…
They told me beat it
and don't be getting any ideas
about coming back to settle in
'cause this place is off limits.
The park's closed at night.
Like that ain't a joke and a half.
One of them cops, the bald one,
he told me "Really, Mama, it ain't safe here."
Tell me something I don't know, Kojak.
Now that they zipped up the bag
and carried him off to find his maker,
they won't be coming round here no more.
Maybe a body can get some peace.

GUY.
He could be a sick fuck sometimes
and I told him so,
right to his face.
Here's the deal.
There's a little scene that happens out here
every afternoon.
A bunch of cars drive up.
All these single guys get out,
good shape, nice clothes.
They go for a walk here in the bushes.
I don't like it

But—hey—live and let live.
I go find myself a log to lie on,
somewhere far from the trails,
some tree that came down in a storm.
I wait 'til they do what they gotta do.
But not him.
No, sir.
He went looking for it.
Wanted in on the action.
I warned him.
Told him it's unnatural.
He said, "Man,
it's the most natural thing in the world."
Said we're all monkeys who come from the forest.
I told him these guys are trouble.
He said, yeah, that's what he wanted.
That's when I told him he's a sick fuck.
But he just laughed.

GIRL.
To him, living out here like this,
it wasn't a jungle, man.
It was the Garden of Eden.
One day he came and found me
down where I was panhandling.
Like he was meeting me after work or something,
just to walk me back to this dump.
I was bummed, man,
I mean, who wouldn't be?
Scrounging all day for a few lousy quarters?
I wanted to be somewhere else—
wished I was anywhere else.
When we got to the park
we walked by this hill

and it was a wash of wildflowers.
The colors, man, the purple, and gold,
in the middle of all those bushes,
it just made your eyes pop.
He started picking them and
made this chain of flowers
and put it around my head.
Told me I was one of the blessed ones.
That's when I found out
he thought about some day being a monk.
He talked about the color of the poppies,
how it wasn't really gold, it was saffron.
How he'd get to dress up in robes that color.
It's the only time I heard him say anything
about the future.
The only time he let on
there might be somewhere else
he wanted to be, too.

QUEEN.
He was just a kid,
barely in the spring of his years.
That's why I called him Sprout.
He never realized how much you get away with
when you're young like that.
Didn't know how often
you're dodging bullets.
How you live in a state of grace
with all that life erupting inside you,
a volcano pulsing and bursting
to force its way out.
He didn't need to be living out here.
I told him he should turn a few tricks
to come up with some scratch,

pull in the greenbacks like normal people do.
He tried it, he said,
but couldn't take the look in their eyes
when it came time to collect.
"So don't look," I told him. "Don't look."
"How would you get inside them?" he asked.
Why would you want to, I'd like to know?

WOMAN.
And it is prophesied:
A mighty rain shall pour forth,
the skies shall open
and the Earth shall be cleansed
the wicked washed away
and the garden shall be whole once more.
The most humble shall become exalted
and the righteous shall flourish
again in the land. *(Pause.)*
And the innocent who dwell among the evil
likewise shall they be washed away.

GUY.
He mighta felt his time was up.
'Cause last month for no reason at all
he dragged me down to some place,
community center, something.
They have some deal cooked up
where they give away cameras.
All you gotta do is take pictures.
Nothing special,
just pictures of where you live,
who you know,
shit like that.

No posing or nothing,
just everyday stuff.
What a waste of film, I thought.
And to me, it didn't feel right
getting a camera for nothing
without having to boost it.

WOMAN.
I was sitting reading the scripture
when this young man came up to me.
He was eating sunflower seeds
and he asked if I wanted some.
I seen him around with those nasty boys
so I said I got no need to be taking food
from a sinner.
He asked does faith play a role in my life?
I held up my Good Book.
He pointed up at this big old tree
and said,
"You see the vine wrapped around that trunk?"
"'Course I do."
"Well I'm that vine," he said,
"and that tree?
That tree is lifting me out of the mud
up to the light,
up where the birds fly high."
Then he put down the bag of seeds and walked away.
But I saw him sneak a look over his shoulder
to see if I was watching
and he waved at me.

QUEEN.
   "Are you ashamed of me?" I asked him?
   It's the only time I saw him flustered.
   I didn't bring it up at the time it happened,
   which was not long after
   we first made our acquaintance.
   We were on one of our evening promenades,
   taking in the sights out on the street.
   Just talking, you know,
   getting to know each other,
   feeling each other out.
   One of his friends runs into us.
   Literally runs into us.
   We're just walking down the street
   and he comes barreling out of a store
   guzzling a drink of some kind
   —you know—oblivious.
   Slams right into us.
   He's someone I'd seen around.
   Kinda cute, kinda dumb.
   Always an appealing combination.
   He'd kind of avoided me in the past, I thought.
   What's his problem?
   But there we were
   right in each other's face.
   I elbowed Sprout.
   "Introduce your friend."
   And he did.
   Then we continued on
   but I could tell he kind of blushed,
   embarrassed that the oblivious guy
   saw the two of us together.
   A few days later,
   when we were fighting about something

I brought it up.
He denied it, but I called him on it.
'Cause it's one thing a queen can just feel,
like a waitress knows a tipper,
like a hooker knows a cop,
like a cheerleader knows the score.
He copped to it,
said it's only because he didn't know me yet,
that he felt like he was
introducing his mother.
At least I didn't remind him of his father.
He said he felt ashamed,
that he'd never treat me
that way again.
Or anyone else.
Promise.
He'd always think the best.
I like the way contrition
can turn someone into a little cherub.
So I blew out the candle
and let him make it up to me.

GIRL.
He gave me this bracelet.
Told me these are prayer beads.
Then he showed me how to sit quiet
to calm my nerves
and just take some time
to think about my life.
He said think of it like taking a step
outside yourself
so when you come back,
you're really, really there.
We did it together

maybe a couple of times a week.
He said, "If you start looking around,
you'll find all kinds of other people who do this—
all over the place—
so you'll never have to feel alone."
I hope he's right about that
'cause I feel awful lonesome right now.

GUY.
So he made me sign up for the camera
and start taking pictures.
When I went and showed 'em what I did
I thought they'd take the damn thing back,
but, they didn't...
They're gonna put 'em in a show. *(Pause.)*
The shot I'm really glad I got
is the one I took of him.
The sucker's all blurry
'cause he never stood still
long enough for me to take the fuckin' shot.
He was playing with that stupid frisbee,
jumping like he had wings and could fly.
So it's all just a wash of color,
but his long hair's snapping in the wind
and you can tell he's laughin'
and it looks like him
just the way he was, mostly.

QUEEN.
There's no point in even saying it
but it's just not fair.
He goes off to find a little pleasure—
or give a little pleasure—

and for no reason at all
ends up floating face down
in some scum-filled pond.
This world makes no sense.
And this queen ends up alone
in a tent in the park.
I ask you:
Does such a world make sense?

WOMAN *(eats some sunflower seeds)*.
I saw that green flying-saucer toy
floating in the lake.
That's when I knew...
If I had any tears left in me
I might want to cry for that boy.
I got to believe there's a reason,
some reason such a sad thing could take place.
But I can't find one.
I can't find no reason on God's green Earth
why a boy like that should be taken away.
They already got enough angels in heaven.
Don't they?
It's us down here,
us who needs them the most.

(She eats some sunflower seeds and scatters some for the birds. LIGHTS fade to black.)

END OF PLAY

CONVERTING

By
Catherine Filloux

Converting premiered in 1995 at Women's Project & Productions in New York City. It was directed by Anne D'Zmura, and featured Bill McGuire and John Daggett.

CHARACTERS

HARRY: Old and shaking.
FRED: Old and shaking.

SETTING: Central Park.

TIME: The present.

CONVERTING

AT THE CURTAIN: *HARRY and FRED sit in Central Park. A flash of fluorescent light streaks across the stage.*

HARRY. Now, that roller-skating. You're young, you could do that...

FRED. Oh, sure. I could do that.

HARRY. Why don't you? I don't mind. I'll just sit here and watch. If you want, go ahead and take a turn around with all of them, with their fluorescent clothing. Please, it would give me pleasure to know someone is having fun.

FRED. Well, maybe I will.

HARRY. Go. It will be light for hours.

FRED. Are you sure? I hate to leave you alone.

HARRY. Oh, come on. You're young, you should enjoy yourself.

FRED. And you? You shouldn't enjoy yourself?

HARRY. The young should enjoy themselves. The old should watch.

FRED. Well, you're right, I am in rather good physical shape.

HARRY. It's from all that pingpong you do.

FRED. Yes, you do develop a strong, supple arm. *(FRED flexes his arm, admiring its sinew.)*

HARRY. Is the sex still as good?

FRED. Oh, sure.

HARRY. Even with Jan gone, and all?

FRED. Oh, yeah!

HARRY. Ah, youth!

FRED. Well, yes. I'm just lucky, I guess.

HARRY. I envy you your energy, your vitality.

(FRED breathes with difficulty, touching his heart.)

FRED. Oh, of course...vitality.

HARRY. Go ahead, go get some of those roller skates.

FRED. In a second.

HARRY. Is the sun getting to you?

FRED. No.

HARRY. It's coming down a bit hard, shall we move into the shade?

FRED. In a second.

HARRY. Tell me, the writing? On its way to Broadway yet?

FRED. ...On...its...way, sure. Agent...confident.

HARRY. Oh, well that's good. I wish I could write. I dictate, but I can't transcribe. That movie I wrote for Paul Newman, he still wants to make it. They're still in discussions with DreamWorks.

FRED. Huh...

HARRY. But *you,* you have your life in front of you. You're worth another few plays. And they'll probably be your best, you devil. *(FRED grunts. He is nearly laying on the bench now.)* Taking a little nap? That's what I envy most I think. The way you all can sleep. Anytime, anyplace. I resign myself now to an hour or two a night. The rest of the time I'm *thinking* about sleeping. But you, you can even sleep during the day. Don't let me bother you, go ahead and get some shuteye. Then you can go rent the skates.

FRED. Blades.

HARRY. What?

FRED. Bl-Blades.

HARRY *(laughing loudly). Band-aids! Don't be a chicken. Didn't you used to be a wrestler?*

FRED. Yes.

HARRY. Skating is nothing compared to wrestling.

FRED. It's not called skating. It's "rollerblading."

HARRY. You even know the lingo, you bastard. Count me out, I can't keep up. *(Another flash of fluorescent light streaks across the stage.)* Why the fluorescent colors? Just tell me that. They all wear those hideous fluorescent colors. It's so damned hard on the eyes. I shouldn't be bothering you, you're sleeping. Go ahead, you're young. Sleep! *(FRED struggles to take his wallet out of his pants pocket.)* Well, good for you. How much do you think it'll set you back to rent the equipment? That's one place where I'm lucky, I tell you. You spend a lot less money when you're old. Nothing to spend it on. *(FRED hands his driver's license to HARRY.)* Oh, no, you should take this along with you, for identification, in case you get in an accident. These skates are very dangerous. You see it on the news. Broken bones. Take the driver's license with you, you never know.

FRED. Look at it.

HARRY. What did you say?

FRED. Look at it.

HARRY. I'm looking at it, so what? A photograph of you looking so young it makes me want to vomit.

FRED. Read it.

HARRY. Read it? I'd rather read *Mein Kampf.* This is boring literature, my friend. Go ahead and I'll sit here and watch the birds. And the fluorescent colors. Oh, they hurt my eyes. Those colors should be banned for the sake of *old people.*

FRED. Read the date.

HARRY. The date? Oh come on, you're young! You get up early, you go down to the DMV on Worth Street, isn't that it? Worth? White? Wright? My memory. You are so fortunate. All the street names start to sound the same. You go down to whatever the hell the name of that stupid street that starts with W. Is it W? And you wait in line. So it's a two-hour wait, you bring a book and you get the damn license renewed.

FRED. Birth...date.

HARRY *(loudly). Birds...hate? Hah! You hate birds? Just wait, birds will look better and better. You'll know that soon you're going up there with them. They'll become your best friends, just wait and see...*

FRED. Read...the...birth...date.

HARRY. Read the birth date. 1911.

FRED. Right.

HARRY. 1911? This isn't your ID. Why did you get a fake ID, you bastard? What kind of racket are you involved in? A side career, I can't believe it. I can barely get my shredded wheat into my bowl, forget pouring the milk.

FRED. It's not a fake ID. I was born in 1911.

HARRY *(hooting). I was born in 1912!!*

FRED. I know.

HARRY. *You lied to me!*

FRED. I know.

HARRY. *You said you were born in 1914!*

FRED. I know.

HARRY. You said you were two years younger than me. That day we met in the Marxist Writers Group you said you were two years younger. *Two years younger than me!*

FRED. I lied.

HARRY. You *son of a bitch.*

FRED. Right.

HARRY. *You <u>son</u> of a bitch.*

(FRED now has his hand permanently on his heart.)

FRED. I was lying about my age, Harry. I had to tell everyone the same thing so I wouldn't get confused. Plus, how was I supposed to know we were going to become such good friends?

HARRY. *You're older than me!*

FRED. That's what I'm trying to tell you.

HARRY. *I'm younger than you!*

FRED. You're getting the picture.

(HARRY hands back the driver's license.)

HARRY. It's a *terrible* picture. *(HARRY jumps up from the bench and does a delighted dance.)* You're older than me, you little shit! I'm younger than you. I can't tell you how good that makes me feel. You're keeled over on that bench like you're ready to croak…

FRED. A minute ago, I was getting some shuteye.

HARRY. *Don't tell me to shut up, big guy. (Dancing.)* Don't try to rob me of the few years I have left. I'm young and I love it. And to think just a little while ago you weren't suggesting *I* try rollerblading. Oh, no! Here you knew you were on your deathbed and you played along, pretending you were the youthful wrestler. *I could cream you at pingpong!*

FRED. It was getting to me.

Converting 271

HARRY. What?

FRED. The pressure.

HARRY. What pressure?

FRED. The pressure of trying to be young for you, Harry. You see me as this Roman god. This ideal athlete, with the perfect body and the perfect mind. It was taking me entire days to get ready for our visits. The facial creams, the obligatory workout, the painkillers, not to mention everything I had to withhold. The fibrillation, like a bird fluttering in my heart, making me so scared I can barely breathe, and the medicine that's supposed to convert the beat back to the right beat, but you wait and wait, Harry, listening to your heart, waiting for the change that doesn't come. Do you know what it's like? Waiting for your heart to convert? And the writing, Harry. I've been writing *for you* for years, so I would live up to your expectations. I've been trying to be young, but I can't rollerblade. That is where I draw the line. I thought to myself, can I possibly go over to the Boat Basin and rent those goddamn sadistic instruments of torture just so Harry will think I am who he thinks I am? And I just couldn't. I couldn't get up from the bench. I was sitting here thinking if I was really young I would buy a jersey in one of those damn fluorescent colors you're always talking about, just to impress you, and then the fluttering started again and it was all too much, I couldn't keep it up one second longer...I had to tell you about my heart...

HARRY. Your heart is *old,* my friend. *(Swaggering.)* Maybe I'll take a gander down to the Basin and get some blades. Take a little jaunt around. Will you be okay here with the birds and the bright colors to keep you company, old friend?

FRED. Sure, go ahead. I'll stay here and watch.

HARRY. I always looked at your skin and wondered what kept it so youthful. Facial creams?

FRED. Hundreds of dollars worth.

HARRY. A year?

FRED. A month.

HARRY. That's crazy. Look at my skin. It doesn't look that different from yours in the end and I spent *nothing*. Did I tell you DreamWorks is putting the Newman film in production? I'm still on the map, old friend. I'm still on the map and I'm about to start something new. I've been dictating but I *can* transcribe with the best of them, I *will transcribe...*

(HARRY marches off. FRED sits on the bench. A flash of fluorescent light streaks by. FRED feels something inside his chest.)

FRED. Oh, my God! *(FRED waits a moment, listening to his heart.) I'm converting! Oh, my God, where is Harry when I need him? (Jumping up and down.) I'm converting! My heart is converting back to its original beat. (Getting down on his knees.)* Oh, thank God. Thank God. Please don't let it ever do that again.

(HARRY reenters, shuffling. He holds his forehead. A bit of blood leaks from a wound.)

HARRY. Fred?... You're praying?

FRED. I converted, Harry. I converted.

HARRY. To what, old friend? Isn't it a little late?

FRED. What happened to your head?

HARRY. I got knocked down by a diabolical roller skater. She *blinded* me with her *bright* shirt...

FRED. Come sit down.

(They sit.)

HARRY. ...Maybe next time.

FRED. Sure. Why not?

HARRY. ...When you said the sex was good...could you elaborate?

FRED. I was lying.

HARRY. ...You said you wanted to tell me about your heart?

FRED. Breaking.

HARRY. Because of the flutters?

FRED. Separate.

HARRY. Lonely?

FRED. Beyond.

HARRY. Fred?

FRED. Yes? *(HARRY's hand shakes a lot as he takes out his wallet and shows FRED his driver's license. FRED's hand shakes a lot as he looks at it.)* Son of a bitch. 1911. You're my age. *(Assessing HARRY.)* You would never know it... Extremely deceiving.

(A flash of fluorescent light bathes them.)

HARRY. It's coming down a bit hard. Shall we move into the shade?

(Shade slowly moves across them, until we are in darkness.)

END OF PLAY

DEFROSTING

By
Domenick Vincent Danza

Defrosting premiered in 2002 at Chicago Dramatists as part of the Ten-Minute Workshop festival. It was directed by Tania Richard, and featured Casey Hayes and Robert Koon.

CHARACTERS

HUGH: Mid-30s, average height, thin, wiry, high-strung.
LOUIE: Mid-30s, tall, heavyset, easygoing.

SETTING: A kitchen and dinette in an apartment. There is a kitchen table and chairs, and an empty spot where the refrigerator should be. An exit UR leads to the rest of the apartment. An exit UL leads to the back porch.

TIME: The present, summer. A Sunday evening.

DEFROSTING

AT THE CURTAIN: *HUGH is frantically preparing food in the microwave. There is a knock on the door.*

HUGH. It's open.

LOUIE. *(enters from UR).* Hey Hugh.

HUGH. Hey Lou.

(Dog barks.)

LOUIE. Where's the dog?

HUGH. Outside.

LOUIE *(looks out back door UL).* Hey, Dewie. *(To HUGH.)* What's the refrigerator doing on the porch?

HUGH. That's why I invited you.

LOUIE. I thought you invited me for dinner.

HUGH. I did.

LOUIE. Who else is coming over?

HUGH. No one.

LOUIE. Why so much food?

HUGH. The freezer needed to be defrosted.

LOUIE. So you put it out on the porch?

HUGH. No. I chopped at it with a hammer and a screwdriver.

LOUIE. And...

HUGH. I broke something in it and Freon came shooting out.

LOUIE. So you carried it out to the porch.

HUGH. No. The firemen did.

LOUIE *(laughing).* You called the fire department?

HUGH. No. I looked in the yellow pages for an emergency phone number because the Freon smelled bad and I didn't know if it was toxic. The operator connected me to the fire department and they sent over four burley men to check it out.

LOUIE. Is Freon toxic?

HUGH. No, but they said it would be safer if they put it out on the porch.

LOUIE. So they did.

HUGH. Yeah. Veggie Burger? *(LOUIE takes one and sits.)* Take more.

LOUIE. No thanks.

HUGH. Lean Cuisine?

LOUIE. What kind?

HUGH. Turkey.

LOUIE. I like the chicken.

HUGH. Sorry. All out.

LOUIE. Any lettuce or tomato? Veggie Burgers are gross without lettuce and tomato.

HUGH. No.

LOUIE. Ketchup?

HUGH. Mustard.

LOUIE. Maybe I'll have the Lean Cuisine.

HUGH. Sure. Iced tea or beer?

LOUIE. Beer.

HUGH. Here you go.

LOUIE. It's warm. *(Beat: HUGH gives LOUIE a sarcastic look.)* Oh yeah. Maybe I'll have the tea. Notice I didn't say "iced."

HUGH. You're catching on.

LOUIE. Why didn't you just put everything in a cooler?

HUGH. Don't have one.

LOUIE. Let's go buy one.

HUGH. Too late.

LOUIE. Oh, so it's an "invite someone over to eat the food from the refrigerator before you throw it out" dinner.

HUGH. Yup.

(Pause: They eat.)

LOUIE. Are you going to talk about it?

HUGH. What?

LOUIE. The nightmarish, stressful, funny funk you're in that made you attack the freezer with a hammer and screwdriver.

HUGH. It's been forever since I defrosted that fucking thing. I should have blown it off again today. There's something to be said for procrastination. *(Beat.)* Tell me what's been going on in your life that would make my day not seem so bad.

LOUIE. What makes you think my life is so bad.

HUGH. Because you're Louie and I haven't seen you since we swapped horror stories from last winter's snowstorm.

LOUIE. The boys were staying with me for the past month.

HUGH. How come? Did your ex-wife need a break?

LOUIE. She had a hysterectomy.

HUGH. Well, that's good news.

LOUIE. Tell me.

HUGH. Was she sick?

LOUIE. I don't know. We didn't talk about it.

HUGH. Why didn't you bring the boys by?

LOUIE. Why, so we could all breathe in Freon and die together? Do you have any chips?

HUGH. Yeah, but don't eat them. They're not perishable. Fish fillet?

LOUIE. What kind?

HUGH. Gordon's Baked-à-la-Something.

LOUIE. Ooh, good. I hope there's dessert.

HUGH. Cheesecake, melted strawberries, soupy ice cream and warm milk.

LOUIE. Mmmm! Something to look forward to.

HUGH. How are the boys?

LOUIE. Good. Real good. I was Super-Dad. Working, cooking, renting movies. My house needs a new roof.

HUGH. Huh?

LOUIE. A new roof. You know all that rain we had last week.

HUGH. Yeah.

LOUIE. Well water was coming in everywhere. Down the walls. Through the light fixtures.

HUGH. All of a sudden?

LOUIE. As soon as it started to rain. We had that dry spell for a couple of months. Then...

HUGH. ...forty days and forty nights...

LOUIE. ...of nothing but rain. After everything dried out I went up into the crawlspace to check it out. I pushed open the trapdoor and I saw the light of day. Now I'm not a professional or anything, but I could tell there was a problem. $3,000 worth of damage.

HUGH. Oh my God! My refrigerator story doesn't seem so bad now. Thanks.

LOUIE. Screw you.

(Dog barks.)

HUGH. How do you want your eggs?

LOUIE. Scrambled.

HUGH. What caused the problem in the roof?

LOUIE. Apparently it was a problem since the winter or fall. Water got in somehow during the snowstorm and rotted away the wood.

HUGH. At least you didn't attack your roof with a hammer and a screwdriver.

LOUIE. I also didn't call the fire department.

HUGH. What else should I have done? I panicked. I'm all alone here. I didn't want to come home to find the dog dead in the kitchen from Freon ex-fixiation.

LOUIE. Is that why he's outside?

HUGH. He's keeping an all-night vigil with the refrigerator.

LOUIE. Separation anxiety.

HUGH. A pit-bull trait. *(Beat.)* Toast?

LOUIE. The bread is not perishable.

HUGH. No, but the butter is.

LOUIE. I'll take that beer.

HUGH. Warm?

LOUIE. Yeah.

HUGH. Did you have a good time with the boys?

LOUIE. Yeah. Ryan's at that age where he's starting to talk back. Smart mouth. Thinks he knows more than me, you know? Brandon keeps him in line.

HUGH. Your parents watch them when you were at work?

LOUIE. Yeah. Any cheese for the eggs?

HUGH. Actually, yes.

LOUIE. We went to Chuck E. Cheese three times. Something about jumping into a barrel of plastic, colorful balls that just makes average pizza a hell of a lot better.

HUGH. You did *not* jump in the balls?

LOUIE. No. I meant from their point of view. Getting them ready for bed is activity enough for me. Since it's summer vacation they want to stay up late. They think I don't hear them playing in their room after lights out.

HUGH. Well they do know more than you.

LOUIE. Right. Oh yeah, I have a job interview next week. More money, less commuting time. The worst thing is that I can't afford anything anymore. Now $3,000 to repair the roof.

(Dog barks.)

HUGH. Cheddar, swiss or provolone?

LOUIE. Yes, please.

HUGH *(beat)*. I know what you mean. My landlord is probably going to have me pay for a new refrigerator.

LOUIE. Just hack him with a hammer and screwdriver.

HUGH. Are you going to have to take out a loan to fix the roof?

LOUIE. From my retirement fund. Maybe I'll win the lottery.

HUGH. Sometimes I think it would be easier to just die in my sleep.

LOUIE. You should have inhaled the Freon while you had the chance.

HUGH. Does it come in pill form? *(They laugh. Dog barks.)* It's great hearing you talk about the boys. They're terrific. And as hard as everything is, at least you have them. Something to look forward to instead of more of the same. It's really amazing how much they change each time I see them. I can see you in them. In little ways. For me it's just the same thing every day. I just want to know when it's going to let up. Then I pop a hole in the refrigerator while trying to do something productive and it's just the last straw, you know. I feel so dead inside. Just disconnected and useless. Shit I can't even defrost the freezer without fucking up. *(Dog barks.)* Dewie shut the fuck up before I come out there and kick the living shit out of you! *(Beat.)* Hot dog?

LOUIE. I can't eat anymore.

HUGH. Me neither.

LOUIE *(beat)*. You're not serious about that dying in your sleep thing, are you?

HUGH. Not anymore.

LOUIE. What do you mean?

HUGH. Nothing's been going right. I know that's a pretty blanket generalization to put over everything, but it's just the way it's been. *(Beat.)* The other night I came home, walked the dog, then sat on the bed and took my sneakers off. I just sat for a minute feeling unbelievably defeated. The dog was totally hyper. Jumping on the bed. Jumping off the bed. Taking my shoes. Grabbing at my socks. He got on the bed and rolled on his back wanting me to scratch his belly. I looked at him and said, "What's with you? You sit around all day doing nothing. You get all excited when I finally get home. I take you out for a walk. You pee. We come in. I spend the rest of the evening practically ignoring you. Your life is more boring and useless than mine and yet you're so happy all the time. How do you do it? What do you have to look forward to?" He looked right at me and said, "Life itself."

LOUIE. You talk to your dog.

HUGH. Yes.

LOUIE. And he talks back?

HUGH. On a good day. *(Begins to look through the garbage.)*

LOUIE. Sounds like he's got it more together than you do.

HUGH. Thank God someone does.

LOUIE. What are you doing?

HUGH. Getting a cigarette.

LOUIE. In the garbage?

HUGH. I threw out a half a pack last night.

LOUIE. Why?

HUGH. I sort of quit a few weeks ago.

LOUIE. And you have an emergency stash in the garbage.

HUGH. No. I'm allowed to smoke on Saturday night. It makes it easier. Last night I threw away what I didn't finish.

LOUIE *(pause)*. Let 'em stay there.

HUGH. Can't find 'em anyway.

LOUIE *(pause)*. How about dessert?

HUGH. You said you were full.

LOUIE. Soupy ice cream's nothing to joke about. What flavor?

HUGH. Vanilla.

LOUIE. On top of the cheesecake...

HUGH *(pause)*. ...with strawberries.

(LOUIE gets up to help HUGH get dessert. LIGHTS fade as dog barks.)

END OF PLAY

THE LATE AFTERNOON (AROUND 3:45 OR SO) BEFORE CHRISTMAS

By
Brett Neveu

The Late Afternoon (Around 3:45 or So) Before Christmas premiered in 2001 at The MehaDome Theatre at Frankie J's on Broadway in Chicago. It was produced by C'est Destine as part of "A Triple XXXmas Special: 3 Xmas Plays, 3 Playwrights, 3 Directors." The play was directed by Clint Corley, and featured Don Blair and Matthew W. Roth.

CHARACTERS

RICHARD BARTLET: In his 30s.
SANTA CLAUS: Older (yet ageless…)

SETTING: Santa's office. There is a chair and a desk. Another chair sits opposite.

TIME: The present.

THE LATE AFTERNOON (AROUND 3:45 OR SO) BEFORE CHRISTMAS

AT THE CURTAIN: *SANTA CLAUS, dressed as SANTA would be dressed, sits in the chair behind the desk. He has a coffee cup, a pen and a manila folder. He sips his coffee a few times. A pause. RICHARD BARTLET enters. He wears a festive sweater and khaki pants. RICHARD stands for a moment looking at SANTA. He walks to SANTA and attempts to sit on his lap.*

SANTA. No, no.

RICHARD. Oh. I'm sorry. *(RICHARD stands, embarrassed. A beat.)*

SANTA *(gesturing to chair)*. Please sit down.

RICHARD. I'm sorry.

SANTA. Sit down please.

RICHARD. No problem.

(RICHARD sits down in the chair opposite the desk. A pause. SANTA looks at the name on the folder.)

SANTA. Richard Bartlet?

RICHARD. Yes.

SANTA. Of Bloomington?

RICHARD. Yes.

SANTA. What is your address?

RICHARD. 303 Harling Street.

SANTA. Did you move?

RICHARD. Oh. Yes. Last April.

SANTA. Your previous address?

RICHARD. 1618 Menker. Road.

SANTA. Okay.

RICHARD. Menker Road.

(SANTA opens the folder for a brief second. He quickly closes it and puts it back on the desk.)

SANTA. What do you want?

RICHARD. What do I want?

SANTA. For Christmas. What do you want?

RICHARD. Oh. I'm sorry. I thought you meant, "what did I want from you?"

SANTA. That is what I mean.

RICHARD. No, I thought you meant that I wanted something. That I had a complaint or something.

SANTA. That's not what I meant.

RICHARD. I know that. Right. I'm sorry.

SANTA. That's not what I meant.

RICHARD. Okay. I guess I would like a new jacket.

SANTA. Let's back up for a moment.

RICHARD. Okay.

SANTA. You've been naughty.

RICHARD. I have?

SANTA. Don't joke.

RICHARD. I *may* have been naughty, I don't quite remember the specifics—

SANTA. We should talk about you being naughty before we continue.

RICHARD. Oh.

SANTA. You knew what could possibly happen at the time when you were being naughty, didn't you?

RICHARD. The incident you may perhaps be referring to happened this past summer, so, in my defense, Christmas seemed quite far away.

SANTA. It's not like things change here, Richard. Naughty is still naughty no matter what the circumstances.

RICHARD. I understand that.

SANTA. Warm weather is no excuse.

RICHARD. I understand.

SANTA. Do you think I'm some sort of rube?

RICHARD. I don't think you're a rube, Santa.

SANTA. Santa?

RICHARD. Um. Santa *Claus*.

SANTA. I don't mean to be a hardliner, here. It's not as if you don't know what's going on in your own life. It's not that you don't know if the situation you are in is "naughty" or if it's "nice." It's not even a judgment call. It's merely common sense.

RICHARD. Some things fall into a gray area.

SANTA. No they don't. Don't try to get me into a semantics discussion. You certainly know the difference, no matter the seeming confusion. There is no gray area.

RICHARD. This incident I believe you're referring to wasn't actually that naughty. Parts of it were naughty, I admit, but some other parts of the incident were quite nice.

SANTA. I'm not in the business of dissecting "incidents." I don't have time to go over every part of a person's actions and say, "Well, this part was half nice, and this part over here is leaning toward naughty, so I'll go ahead and give it a seventy-thirty split towards 'nice.'" That's not how things work.

RICHARD. Yes, but, if you were in my shoes—

SANTA. How long have you been coming to see me, Richard?

RICHARD. How long? Off and on, I guess, about thirty years.

SANTA. And in that entire time, have I ever said, "You know, what you did this past year was, in reality, both naughty and nice, a big giant mixture of both, so listen, I'll give you something *close* to what you want instead of what you really asked for."

RICHARD. No. You've never said that.

SANTA. I say, "Naughty" or I say, "Nice."

RICHARD. That's true.

SANTA. You either get what you want for Christmas, Richard, or you get nothing at all. *(Pause.)* I know it can be a difficult thing to understand. You try your best all year long, then you come in here and then tomorrow morning I happen to decide "naughty" and then you have to live with the consequences.

RICHARD. It's not hard to understand, it's just unfair.

SANTA. What was that?

RICHARD. I said that it was unfair.

SANTA. It's unfair?

RICHARD. It's mostly unfair. All I'm asking for from you is a new jacket, nothing too fancy, just a modest jacket, and you hold "naughty" over my head.

SANTA. Richard—

RICHARD. You don't seem to understand my position.

SANTA. I do understand your position. I understand it better than you, I think.

RICHARD. That doesn't make any sense! You can't know my position better than me!

SANTA. There's no reason to shout.

RICHARD. I'm sorry.

SANTA. I am not going to tolerate shouting.

RICHARD. I am sorry I shouted.

SANTA. You shouldn't shout. *(SANTA opens the manila folder and makes a quick mark inside. He shuts the folder. A pause.)*

RICHARD. Does that count for this year or for next?

SANTA. You are lucky that it counts for this year.

RICHARD. So you've decided that I'm naughty then?

SANTA. You know I can't discuss my decision—

RICHARD. So I guess maybe I should just go ahead and say what I *really* think since it looks like it doesn't make a difference either way.

SANTA. It does make a difference—

RICHARD. It sure sounds like you've decided that I'm naughty.

SANTA. No, I haven't decided anything just yet. I am only currently discussing with you the situation which happened this past summer, and now, I suppose, this business from a few moments ago when you began shouting—

RICHARD. Listen, I'm sorry I shouted. I was just concerned that I had perhaps done something *so* naughty that it would overshadow the entire year for me. I did do a few nice things, too, you know.

SANTA. Yes you did, that's true.

RICHARD. At least I tried to do some nice things. And even when there were things I did that I knew were naughty, I later tried to do nice things to make up for them. For example, I put a garden in the back of the house. That was nice. Did you see me doing that?

SANTA. I did.

RICHARD. What did you think?

SANTA. You did a very nice job.

RICHARD. I even tried to grow some herbs. Did you notice the herbs?

SANTA. Yes.

RICHARD. I was planning on cutting them and drying them. I never got around to doing that.

SANTA. Good intentions count.

RICHARD. They do?

SANTA. Certainly.

RICHARD. I had lots of good intentions over this past year.

SANTA. Let me define good intentions for you, Richard. You must have began something with good intentions, then not having completed the task, you must have felt *guilt* afterwards. I count that as a good intention.

RICHARD. This past year I thought about lots of good things and had lots of guilt because I didn't do them.

SANTA. Thinking about things and doing things halfway are two different concepts. One counts as "nice," and one is plain old laziness.

RICHARD. Laziness? I was never lazy.

SANTA. You were lazy some of the time.

RICHARD. Everyone is lazy.

SANTA. That is why I don't keep track of "lazy."

RICHARD. Then maybe I should just be lazy all year with a few nice things thrown in to tip the balance.

SANTA. Are you being sarcastic?

RICHARD. Maybe that will be my new plan for next year, whatcha think?

SANTA. Fine. You should try that out.

RICHARD. It would certainly keep me out of trouble with you.

SANTA. It might at that.

RICHARD. If I just sat on the couch all day and then around December 1st I helped an old lady with her groceries or something, that would certainly tip the balance towards "nice."

SANTA. You bet, that sounds like a fine plan.

RICHARD. I'll do that, then.

SANTA. Keep this in mind, Richard, however— In the summertime, when you are relaxing by the pool, in your new "lazy" lifestyle, don't be tempted again to do something naughty because Christmas "seems so far away."

RICHARD. Go ahead, throw it back in my face, that's fine.

SANTA. "Great naughtiness is destined to repeat itself."

RICHARD. Who said that?

SANTA. I did.

RICHARD. So you believe I'll be naughty again?

SANTA. I'm just taking your past into account. When I was looking over your folder before you came in, I noticed a few reoccurring naughty incidents over the years.

RICHARD. Can I see that folder to find out what those incidents are?

SANTA. Some of the worst naughty incidents occurred three or four times in the course of *the same* year.

RICHARD. Can I see that information you have?

SANTA. You know what incidents I'm referring to.

RICHARD. No, not all of them.

SANTA. Yes you do.

RICHARD. The ones I tend to repeat I would like to know more about.

SANTA. This folder is for office use only.

RICHARD. Obviously I must not know those repeated actions are naughty, or I wouldn't go on repeating them.

SANTA. I think if you thought about it carefully, you would figure out which naughty incidents I'm referring to.

RICHARD. Can't you just give me a copy of that naughty-incident list? It would be much easier. *(A long pause.)*

SANTA. Was there anything else you wanted?

RICHARD. I wanted?

SANTA. Besides a modest jacket.

RICHARD. It doesn't have to be modest.

SANTA. I understand.

RICHARD. Well, then, how about a new stereo?

SANTA. What?

RICHARD. Yeah. I want a new stereo.

SANTA. You've got to be joking.

RICHARD. Well, I figure since I'm so naughty that I might as well say "sky's the limit." I'd love a new car, also.

SANTA. Stop it. This is insulting.

RICHARD. I promise I'll be really good.

SANTA. You should really stop talking like that.

RICHARD. I'm sorry.

SANTA. More of your sarcasm will definitely not win me over.

RICHARD. I know. I really didn't mean to talk like that.

SANTA. It doesn't help things for you, or your need of a new jacket, all that sarcasm, it doesn't help your cause at all. *(A pause.)*

RICHARD. What have you decided?

SANTA. You know you won't know my decision until tomorrow morning.

RICHARD. I was hoping you could give me your decision this afternoon.

SANTA. You were incorrect.

RICHARD. I know I'm naughty. I knew it coming in the door.

SANTA. You don't know everything, Richard.

RICHARD. I know myself. I know the things I've done. I know I'm not perfect.

SANTA. I'm not asking for perfection, I'm just asking for "nice."

RICHARD. Sure.

SANTA. So you'll know my decision first thing in the morning.

RICHARD. I'm sorry, Santa.

SANTA. Santa *Claus*.

RICHARD. Santa *Claus*. I just get so worked up over this stuff. I can't sleep and my mind keeps going over everything again and again.

SANTA. It's okay.

RICHARD. Well. Thanks for seeing me.

SANTA. Of course. You know I always have an open door. You can come by anytime. If you have any problems we can work them out together. No matter what time of year it is.

RICHARD. I'll remember that.

SANTA. Just give me a heads up first so I can have them pull your file for me. There's a lot of Richard Bartlets out there, and I want to make sure I'm talking to the right one. I wouldn't want to blame you for something you didn't do or give you credit for a good deed that you had nothing to do with.

RICHARD. How many Richard Bartlets are there?

SANTA. I'd have to look it up, but there's quite a few.

RICHARD. Well, it was very nice talking to you.

SANTA. Yes it was.

RICHARD. Hopefully, I'll see you tonight.

SANTA. Well, either way, you won't "see" me. You might hear me, though! *(Laughs.)*

RICHARD. Right! Reindeer paws! *(Laughs, sings.)* "Up on the Housetop, Reindeer Paws." *(SANTA appears confused as RICHARD makes pawing motions and laughs. A pause.)* If you want, there'll be some cookies and a soda by the telephone in the kitchen for you.

SANTA. Really?

RICHARD. Yeah, well, I had some friends over a few nights ago, and I have a few leftover cookies. If you want any they'll be there by the telephone.

SANTA. That's great. I really appreciate it.

RICHARD. They're sugar cookies.

SANTA. That's great.

RICHARD. Okay. Well, thanks.

(RICHARD extends his hand. SANTA stands and shakes it.)

SANTA. Thanks for coming in, Richard.

RICHARD. No, no—thank *you*.

SANTA. Have a good afternoon.

RICHARD. "And to all, a good…afternoon!" *(Laughs.)*

SANTA. Yes. Goodbye.

(RICHARD stops laughing. Pause. RICHARD exits. SANTA sits. He puts away RICHARD's folder and pulls out another. He sips his coffee and looks toward the area RICHARD entered from. Fade to black.)

END OF PLAY

LILLIAN GOES TO THE MIRROR

By
Cherisse Montgomery

Lillian Goes to the Mirror premiered in 2004 at the Mae West Fest in Seattle, Wash. It was directed by Judy Jacobs, and featured Crystal Eney and Erik Eagleson.

CHARACTERS

LILLIAN: Early 30s. Wears blazer, glasses, skirt and loafers. Beneath her button-down blouse is a black bra stuffed with white tissue.

DAN: Early 30s. Dressed comfortably.

SETTING: The stage is divided into three areas: the poetry-reading area, where the unseen audience is female; Lillian's changing area; and Lillian and Dan's kitchen. The changing area consists of house shoes, a coat tree, and a robe with a ponytail holder in the pocket. Hanging near the coat tree is a full-length mirror. The kitchen is represented by a table and two chairs. They will pantomime preparing and eating their breakfast using no food, silverware or plates. The only other prop is a metal spatula.

TIME: The poetry reading is in the present. The kitchen scene with Dan takes place in memory. The changing area blends both past and present.

LILLIAN GOES TO THE MIRROR

AT THE CURTAIN: *LIGHTS up on LILLIAN who walks from the audience to the stage. She preens a bit before reaching the stage, perhaps smoothing her skirt and checking her hair. Applause, wolf calls, and murmurings are heard from the audience.*

LILLIAN. This one I call "Amazons Gone Wild." *(Pause.)*
We have waited for the Moon who guides
our waters, our yolkblood, and the hunt.

Under her light and by the fire, she
blesses the knife and my pound of flesh.

The women welcome my new body
with gifts of pine cones and skyward howls.

They say my brunette train of hair will
cover the persistent scar, but still,

it is strange to be forever marked
by an absence.

(Sound of applause. Then the clatter of a falling chair. LIGHTS up on DAN who scrambles to pick up the chair then continues cooking breakfast. LILLIAN notices but tries not to react.)

LILLIAN *(to AUDIENCE)*. This poem is based on the traditions of the ancient Amazons who, in ritual, severed their left breasts. Unlike traditional women, Amazons wavered between male and female gender identities. Warriors with long hair, a single breast, and blades of steel.

DAN. Out of bed, Lily! Beauty sleep is no substitute for breakfast.

LILLIAN *(to AUDIENCE)*. But, there must have been an unhappy few, who felt empty, lacking, and were haunted by memories of when they were whole and beautiful...

DAN. C'mon, beautiful! I didn't slave in this kitchen for nothing.

LILLIAN *(to DAN)*. You are not welcome here. I have washed my hands and memories clean of you.

DAN. You aren't gonna make me eat all this by myself, are you?

LILLIAN. I have forgotten you. Height, your brand of shampoo, eye color, your crooked bottom tooth.

DAN. C'mon, Lily, like a big girl.

LILLIAN. I don't want to.

DAN. Don't let your eggs get cold. Last two.

(LILLIAN walks to the changing area.)

LILLIAN. I just bought a dozen this week. *(LILLIAN begins exchanging her blazer for the robe, her glasses for the ponytail holder, and her loafers for house shoes.)*

DAN. Forgot to use butter the first few times. We'll have to buy more.

LILLIAN. Are you burning them now?

DAN. No, that would be the sausage. Out of that, too.

LILLIAN. I could've cooked this morning.

DAN. I wanted to do it this time. *(LILLIAN primps in the mirror then enters the kitchen.)* You look pretty this morning. No... *(Examines her face.)* Lovely. Definite upgrade since yesterday. How do you manage?

LILLIAN. I—you, too.

DAN. I look lovely?

LILLIAN. Handsome. I meant to say handsome. *(Heads to the cupboard.)* Napkins. We don't have any napkins.

DAN *(cuts her off)*. I'll do it. I'll do it all this morning.

LILLIAN. The grease makes—

DAN. A greasy mess, I know. *(Pulls her chair out.)* Allow me to direct you to your chair. *(Illustrates.)* Two sausage patties. Lightly toasted wheat bread. And eggs, sunny-side up just the way you like them.

LILLIAN. Thank you.

DAN. Mama Dan called this morning.

LILLIAN. Oh?

DAN. Wants to know when we're going to stop playing house and actually do it. She's not getting any younger. *(He notices LILLIAN is not eating. Illustrates.)* You should be eating. See, like this.

LILLIAN. I guess I'm not very hungry this morning.

DAN. Try and eat as much as you can. You need the strength as much as anybody. *(Beat.)*

LILLIAN. Do you want my eggs?

DAN. What's wrong with the eggs?

LILLIAN. Nothing. I'm just not in the mood—

DAN. Lots of protein in eggs.

LILLIAN. I know about protein.

DAN. Then...I guess I don't understand.

LILLIAN. They're quivering. They look afraid.

DAN. Funny, they look sunny-side up to me.

LILLIAN. Dan, they look like... *(DAN walks over to her side.)* Can you see it?

(DAN scrapes the eggs onto his plate.)

DAN. Too much cholesterol anyway.

LILLIAN. Everything else looks very appetizing. The sausage is...

DAN. Very dark.

LILLIAN. Black. And wonderfully crispy.

DAN. A recipe I picked up from an old Cajun I know.

(LILLIAN searches the table.)

LILLIAN *(rising)*. Jelly—

DAN. Allow me. *(DAN rises and grabs the jelly.)*

LILLIAN. How much time do we have?

DAN. Appointment's in an hour.

LILLIAN. One final hour...

DAN. Have any dreams last night?

LILLIAN *(spreading jelly)*. Not that I remember.

DAN. Keeps you informed of your state of mind. Yesterday, on the Discovery Channel, they had this doctor—well, if you can call him that, a "dream" doctor—

LILLIAN. Dan, you realize, if it spreads—

DAN. Don't think like that.

LILLIAN. They might have to—

DAN. They won't.

LILLIAN. But, if it is true—

DAN. Lillian—

LILLIAN. Could you still love me if—

DAN. Hey... *(He kisses her.)*

LILLIAN. I'll hold you to that.

DAN. Remember the wedding? Dressed all in white, coming down the aisle on your father's arm. Remember how scared you were, Lily?

LILLIAN. I remember, Dan.

DAN. Here... *(He grabs the spatula and drags her to one end of the kitchen. He hands her the spatula.)*

LILLIAN. We don't have time for this, do we?

DAN. Just take the spatula. Stay there. *(He walks to the opposite end of the kitchen.)*

LILLIAN. The grease is dripping on my hand, Dan. And, on the floor.

DAN. Remember—

LILLIAN. We'll have to mop.

DAN. Remember how great you looked. Immaculate in all that white lace. Nobody could see me for you.
(She begins walking slowly toward him.)

LILLIAN. It was the train that made that possible. Too long.

DAN. I meant before that.

LILLIAN. You want to know what I remember: falling face down at the foot of the altar. Father Henry dropping the Bible on my head. A bloody lip.

DAN. People fall all the time. And just like the rest of them, you stood up, fit yourself back together, and went on with the ceremony. You looked beautiful...like some sort of modern-day Cinderella.
(She arrives at his side.)

LILLIAN. Dan?

DAN. Say "I do." Say it like you did two years ago. It kind of quivered out of you.

LILLIAN. There are alternatives. Holistic remedies.

DAN. Holistic, that means teas and crystals and mucho dinero out the yin yang.

LILLIAN. It means no operation. *(Beat.)*

DAN. I couldn't ask that.

(She hands him the spatula.)

LILLIAN. I should go get dressed.

DAN. But I didn't get to kiss the bride.

(They kiss, this time more brief and contrived. LILLIAN pulls back.)

LILLIAN. I still have time for a quick shower.

(LILLIAN enters the changing area and begins putting on her original costume. DAN cleans the kitchen, wipes off the table, etc.)

DAN. Do you know what you're wearing?

LILLIAN. Khakis.

DAN. What shirt?

LILLIAN. Do you think I'm so frazzled that I can't dress myself?

DAN. Wear the white one. White goes with everything.

LILLIAN. Which?

DAN. You know, short sleeves, ribbed cotton.

LILLIAN. Oh, the v-neck…

(LILLIAN checks her reflection in the mirror. DAN sits at the kitchen table, gazing off.)

DAN. You look pretty in that shirt. Third date, remember? Sushi…I think we had sushi. *(Beat.)*

LILLIAN. I think I'll go by myself to the doctor—

DAN. That's fine.

LILLIAN. There's really nothing for you to do there… you'd probably go insane in the estrogen ward—

DAN. It's fine, Lillian, really. You go. I'll stay here.

(LIGHTS out on DAN. LILLIAN enters the poetry-reading. During the following speech, LILLIAN slowly peels away blouse, tissue paper and bra.)

LILLIAN.

And maybe...one of these marred Amazons wanders off alone to the river and is awed by a familiar face on an altered body.

She had been told that beauty lies in ringlets and headbands, the Maybelline face, push-up bra, and guitar-curved figure.

She stares at her reflection for hours and realizes that Narcissus must have been an Amazon because nothing could be more beautiful...

(LILLIAN reveals chest of a woman who has had a mastectomy.)

...she makes liars of the dictionary writers who thought they knew what it meant to be a woman.

And the memories worried her no longer.

(She bows.)

END OF PLAY

GRUNIONS

By
Barbara Lindsay

Grunions premiered at Theater/Theatre in Hollywood, Calif., in 1988 as part of the Golden West Playwright's "Epiphany Plays." It was directed by Richard J. Nierenberg, and featured Joan-Carrol Banks and Sanford Clark. It was a finalist in the 1989 Actors Theatre of Louisville National Ten-Minute Play Contest.

CHARACTERS

AUGIE:

CARLA:

} A married couple

SETTING: A beach along the California coast.

TIME: The present. Late at night.

GRUNIONS

AT THE CURTAIN: *AUGIE and CARLA are there. There is a refreshing unabashedness about AUGIE, while CARLA, on the other hand, is more tightly wound.*

AUGIE. What time is it? They're supposed to run around midnight. This is great, isn't it? Look at this night we've got here. Couldn't be better. Actually, I wanted to go a little farther up the coast, get away from the lights and the people, but I was afraid we'd miss it. How you doing?

CARLA. Fine.

AUGIE. Is that...? No. Is that just foam? I can't even tell. Although if you can't tell, it probably isn't them. It'll probably be unmistakable, don't you think? How you doing? Oh no, you know what I did? I forgot my flashlight. How could I be so stupid? I should have brought my flashlight.

CARLA. What flashlight?

AUGIE. The flashlight. The silver one. There's only one, isn't there?

CARLA. That's not your flashlight.

AUGIE. Whose is it?

CARLA. It's ours. It's mine, too.

AUGIE. Well sure.

CARLA. You kept saying "my flashlight" as if it's somehow just yours. How's that supposed to make me feel?

AUGIE. No, of course, our flashlight, yours and mine. *Mi* flashlight *es su* flashlight. Naturally. How could we not think to bring it? Hope the moon stays out. I wonder, do they always run during a full moon? I can't remember if it was full last year. Remember?

CARLA. Yes.

AUGIE. Are you cold? Do you want my jacket? We should have brought the blanket. Our blanket. This is great, isn't it? I didn't even think to bring a six-pack. A six-pack would be just the ticket right about now. I can't believe I forgot. I'm like a kid. It's amazing I got out of the house with my fly zipped. Oh. *(He zips his fly.)* I wonder if they can hear me talk or feel the vibrations in the sand when we move around.

CARLA. I'm cold.

AUGIE. You want my jacket?

CARLA. It's after eleven. Let's go home.

AUGIE. Are you kidding? We'd miss it. We just got here. What's the point of coming down if we just turn around and go home?

CARLA. There is no point in coming down here.

AUGIE. Right.

CARLA. That's my point.

AUGIE. That's my point, too.

CARLA. So let's go.

AUGIE. No no, that's not my point. My point is that there's no point in coming down here if we just leave. Don't you want to see it?

CARLA. Not particularly.

AUGIE. Why not?

CARLA. I just don't. It's stupid.

AUGIE. Honey, this is a natural phenomenon. I mean, it only happens once a year. This is a great opportunity. Think of the people in Kansas. They'd have to get plane tickets and hotel reservations to see this. We're just forty minutes away. It's too good to pass up.

CARLA. Pass up what? These little fish swim onto the beach, flop around, and swim away. And then they die.

AUGIE. Yeah, but that moment on the beach is the highlight of their little lives. All that flopping around is laying eggs, or, what do you...spawning or mating, something like that. This is the big night for these guys. Life's last orgy.

CARLA. What are you so excited about? This isn't a moon landing we're talking about here. It's fish. It's fish nobody even eats.

AUGIE. Yeah they do.

CARLA. Oh, Augie.

AUGIE. Okay, but it's fish who do something none of the other fish do. Like the swallows returning to Capistrano, or the lemmings throwing themselves off the cliffs, like that. There's mystery here, and magic, a little bit of the unexplainable. I don't see how you can not be interested.

CARLA. I'm just not.

AUGIE. For real?

CARLA. Yes.

AUGIE. I don't get it. The first time we came here to see it, you said it was the best night of your life. And last year, I remember distinctly, you were so excited to get here, you stubbed your toe rushing me out the door and didn't even notice until we were in the car.

CARLA. Last year, you will also remember, our shoes got wet, I got sand in my panties, we had a big fight over nothing, you got a sore throat, and we did not see the grunions.

AUGIE. We weren't in a good spot.

CARLA. We didn't see them the first time, either.

AUGIE. We just weren't in a good spot. This is a much better spot. I've got good instincts for these things. Look there, what's that? Is that...? Is that...? No, that's seaweed, isn't it. Oh man, this is great. I wouldn't miss this for anything. I mean, think about this. I know you're not interested, but just think about this for a minute. Out there someplace, there's this huge mass of silver fish heading this way. They don't know why. We don't know why. It wasn't a decision, they didn't take a vote, no one sent them an invitation or a map. Just some little instinctual time-release firecracker went off in their bodies, and all as one, they turned and formed a line as long as the California coast, and started swimming. They're swimming right now, as if that's the only thing that matters. It's single-mindedness with no mind, urgency that's pure urge. They don't know what drives them; they don't give it a name or ask it a question. They just turn as one and start the swim that brings them here, to this place where we stand, for a massive celebration of sex and death. Look at this, I'm giving myself goose bumps. All my hairs are popping up.

CARLA. That's the wind.

AUGIE. Well, so, what do you think?

CARLA. About what?

AUGIE. What I was saying.

CARLA. It's ridiculous.

AUGIE. It certainly is not. It's slightly exaggerated scientific fact.

CARLA. It's PR. Somebody sold you a bill of goods that this wonderful event is going to take place on the beach.

AUGIE. I'm not the only one. Look at all these people.

CARLA. Sure, everybody is told the same story. It keeps us all excited, keeps us coming back for more, keeps us thinking that life is going to start any minute now, if we can just find the right spot, get in on the action.

AUGIE. Are we talking about the same thing?

CARLA. Well I'm sorry, but it's still just fish to me.

AUGIE. Carla, can I ask you something? Don't take this wrong, but are you having your period?

CARLA. Goddamn it, Augie, don't ask me that! You always ask me that. I hate it when you ask me that. It's insulting.

AUGIE. Well what's bugging you?

CARLA. We just have different ideas of what this evening is supposed to look like.

AUGIE. There's nothing to it. We come down here, the grunion arrive, they do their little fish business, we go "ooh, ahh, look at the fish," they go home, we go home.

CARLA. For heaven's sake, grow up. We are not going to see the grunions.

AUGIE. Why not?

CARLA. We never do. Do we? Have we ever?

AUGIE. We've missed them twice. That's not "ever."

CARLA. Twice is every time we've tried. That's "ever."

AUGIE. We'll see them this year.

CARLA. No we won't. It's pointless. It's like waiting up to see Santa Claus. I feel as though my whole life is going to be spent standing on the beach with my eyes wide open and my hands clasped expectantly, waiting for fish to show up. And the fish won't show up.

AUGIE. I thought you wanted to see it.

CARLA. You don't understand anything I'm saying.

AUGIE. No, of course not.

CARLA. I did want to see it. I always do. I keep thinking this time will be the time and it never is.

AUGIE. It's just fish. Nothing to get traumatized over.

CARLA. For heaven's sake, this is not about fish!

AUGIE. I've been trying to work this backwards, but I can't seem to pinpoint that moment when we took a turn for the worse. You were fine during the phone call from Marge. Dinner was okay. Doing the dishes was no problem. Let's see, I took a shower, you watched the news. You said, "The grunion are running tonight," and I said, "Great, let's go. I feel lucky tonight." Okay, so I'm putting on my jacket, putting out the animals, we're getting the car out of the garage...

CARLA. Do you remember the first time we came to see it? It was about four years ago, right after we got married. We thought I was pregnant, and we had a bottle of champagne, but no glasses. You asked me to dance, so we took off our shoes, and you popped the cork. And while we were dancing, you said the softest, most intimate things to me, right into my ear, so that I could feel them as much as hear them. And I remember thinking, "This is it. At last, at last, I'm as happy as I'm supposed to be."

AUGIE. Wait a minute, I've got it.

CARLA. Dancing barefoot in the sand, drinking champagne from the bottle.

AUGIE. It was in the car, right? Driving past the Knickerbocker Liquor Locker. You said, "Let's get some champagne" and I said, "Time's a'wasting," or something like that. Right? Of course, I see it now. You want this to be like the other time, right? That's it, right?

CARLA. I would rather not remember some things. I would rather not hope for some things.

AUGIE. Okay, right, I got it, sure, of course, listen, you want to dance?

CARLA. No.

AUGIE. You want me to go get some champagne?

CARLA. No.

AUGIE. Take off our shoes?

CARLA. No, no.

AUGIE. Well what? You want me to breathe in your ear?

CARLA. No.

AUGIE. You want to get married again?

CARLA. No.

AUGIE. What? What? You want a divorce?

CARLA. No.

AUGIE. A vacation?

CARLA. No.

AUGIE. A new carpet? A poodle? A back rub? Ice cream? A suicide pact? What? What? Carla, what the hell do you want?

CARLA. I want something to turn out the way it's supposed to!

AUGIE. Well welcome to the human race! You think this is what I had in mind? You think when I proposed I had this great fantasy going that four years down the road we would come to the beach and yell at each other over fish? Do you think I knew that there would be times when you'd look at me like I'm a used Kleenex, or that I'd look at you and think "Holy hell, when's the next flight to Alaska?" No, no, I'm just like you; I thought it was going to be all peaches and roses and sand in our toes and wind in our hair, and the fish will always come and the bills will pay themselves and we'll have three fat, rosy kids, and ha ha, baby, the joke's on us. 'Cause you know what you get, Carla? Do you know what you get? This!

CARLA. This what? What is this? This isn't even anything.

AUGIE. Yes it is.

CARLA. Oh right, sure, this is standing on the beach. This is waiting, this is fighting.

AUGIE. Right.

CARLA. But this isn't anything like I thought anything would be like.

AUGIE. No, I know, me neither.

CARLA. This is just this. I mean, it includes a lot and everything, but it's not, you know, something else. Do you have any idea what I'm trying to say?

AUGIE. I'm doing the best I can.

CARLA. I know that, Augie, really I do. I know you meant this to be special and nice, and it's the full moon and the sand and all, but I just couldn't help thinking about being somewhere else.

AUGIE. Maybe if you were with somebody else, too.

CARLA. I didn't say that.

AUGIE. No, I know, but still. I know I don't make you happy.

CARLA. For heaven's sake, whatever I'm doing, I'd rather be doing it with you.

AUGIE. Yeah?

CARLA. Well don't be ridiculous. Don't you know that? You're the one who probably wishes you were with somebody else. Somebody who knew how to enjoy herself and didn't take everything so hard.

AUGIE. Actually, now that you mention it, no, I don't.

CARLA. Okay, fine, so we're in the wrong spot, but we're with the right person.

AUGIE. I don't know. Seemed like a good spot to me. I mean, look at the view you've got of the moon from here.

CARLA. Yes, I noticed that. It looks pretty on the water, doesn't it? Big old white moon.
(He puts his jacket around her shoulders, then finds something in his pocket.)

AUGIE. Well look what we've got here. *(He holds up a stick of gum.)*

CARLA. Augie, you brought refreshments.

AUGIE. It's not champagne.

CARLA. Well then, I guess we don't need glasses.
(They each chew half the stick of gum.)

AUGIE. Are you still cold? Do you want to go home?

CARLA. No, I'm beginning to think you might be right. I think this may be the spot after all. *(They watch the waves.)* Augie, I'm sorry.

AUGIE. Shh. If we're very quiet, the fish might come.

CARLA. Or not.

AUGIE. Or not.

END OF PLAY

TRIO

By
Mark Smith-Soto

Trio (originally entitled **Deal With This: Trio From the Holocaust Museum**) was first produced by Theatre Orange of the Arts Center of Carrboro/Chapel Hill as one of the winners of the 2003 "Ten by Ten in the Triangle" Competition. It was directed by Thomas (TeKay) King, and featured David Byron Hudson, Donald Shenton and Larry Evans.

CHARACTERS

SOLDIER: In his early 20s. Thin, dark, nervous.
CAPTAIN: In his late 30s. A precise and controlled man.
PRISONER: In his 40s. Thin, dark, intense.

SETTING: A Nazi camp. The theatrical space should be filled with an impressionistic use of light and sound, the shadow of barbed wire, background echoes of metallic voices and muffled grief. The specific details do not matter, just the nightmare sense that pervades those awful moments when our humanity is tested beyond its limits, and even God seems to turn His face away.

TIME: 1941...2001... Anytime.

TRIO

AT THE CURTAIN: *Shadows and light.*

SOLDIER.
  Why me? Was it merely an accident
  he found me alone for a moment, I stooping
  to hike up my boot, he the last of the group
  to leave the room? Or had he planned ahead:
  this is the one, he's my best shot? I caught
  him staring at me twice, and twice I held
  his eye to teach him how to give, to force
  my will like when a boy must train a dog
  to stay. He must have misunderstood, I
  don't know what he imagined he saw,
  maybe pity for the blonde and her two girls,
  I did speak gently to them before I
  felt his eyes on me, almost forgot for
  a moment why they and I were here. Didn't
  really forget, who could, but fell into
  a place inside myself where these faces
  repeated like words that somehow mattered...
  What were they saying? Nothing my own wife
  and daughters said, as I got up from breakfast
  months ago, hanging in play from my belt
  and holster, kissing my neck goodbye at the door.
  That was the language of home; now a different
  language ordered things along...

PRISONER.
  ...And so I watched

him check the bodies one by one, touching us
as little as possible and pushing us on,
afraid to feel the muscle and the bone
move under clothes already turning rags.
I saw him talk too much so his lip would
not tremble, I noted the way his eye
lingered on the woman ahead of me,
her voice soft in her girls' ears explaining
that the trip would go on for just a while longer,
that they were almost there...

SOLDIER.
    ...I moved them by
and passed on to the next, and this was him:
a shapeless jacket torn at the lapels,
stony eyes behind those dirt-smeared glasses,
and had the thought, not much lost here,
and shoved him to the left. But later then,
my watch almost over, his face appears,
me hunched over my boot, he hunched over
his words, hands together like they were glued,
mouth moving softly, quickly, whispering
his pleases, shooting looks like a frightened bird...

PRISONER.
    ...They hate it when
you beg; it makes them feel. I'd seen it before,
could count on that recoiling fear to fall
all over me and make the world stop.
It is important that you understand.
Death was the only freedom that could matter
to a man who'd stood and watched from somewhere
outside his skin, his sister picked up by

the arm and flung against a wall. The stain
of that sound ran down my throat into the pit
of my body, and the look she turned on me
stuck and hardened; I was a stone myself.
She screamed and ran at the man who took her
to the next room and made her quiet at last,
but very slowly...

SOLDIER.

Some sixty years have passed, and still I see
him crouched in front of me, his dark intense
smell in my face, his sudden body scaring me
to my feet so I almost fell. They know
how to shrink their shoulders and beg in that
aggressive way— I don't know what he saw
in my face, why choose me to wheedle with
his yellow eyes?

CAPTAIN.

All wrong, the way he lost all pride.
scrambling to his feet like a frightened dog,
the way he held his head stiff listening
to the Jew jabbering away, face gone
blank, dry mouth ajar. Even from the other
side of the yard, through the open window,
I could see him breathing hard, could feel him
tremble in his uniform, saw how he
was listening. I almost yelled, but felt
compelled to let them show me what could happen
between the two of them, the way any nakedness
demands to be watched. The little scene did not
last long, I held my breath and thought
he's going to help the creature to escape,

treason was smeared all over his face, he let
the Jew touch him on the knee, the arm, both
of them dark and thin, two brothers on a teeter-totter,
one up, one down, the balance hung exactly
in the air, I held my breath ready to run in.

PRISONER.
    My sister was gone then. And where was I?
    Not asleep, not mad but hideously awake
    and sane beyond the reach of tears or words.
    The impossible was always hard for me,
    the god of numbers hidden in a book,
    the prayer of goodness children lay their heads on.
    But who imagined evil could be as simple
    as a man's freckled hands and wrists, that belts,
    buckles and boots could snap together into
    a human shape? Through the window I saw
    the captain light a cigarette and glance
    our way, holding himself back from coming
    to speed things up, behavior unworthy of
    a man like him. If anything went wrong
    he'd set things right. This was my chance;
    and I was ready then.

SOLDIER.
    No one else around for a moment, that too
    was clever, so I'd not be shamed into
    making an example of him, to give me time
    to think if there could be a way. Of course
    I knew the hole in the fence behind the shack
    we used was big enough to squirrel out,
    he could be gone before the noticing,
    if I had been the fool he thought I was.

CAPTAIN.
> A stupid man.
> There was no need to use
> such force, only fear reacts that way. Things need
> to proceed at an ordained speed, neither
> faster nor slower than called for; the barrel
> in the ribs would have been enough to send
> the beggar squawking back to the place in line
> assigned to him; how irritating to have him
> killed just then, a typographical mistake
> in a report that spoils it all. I could
> barely keep my hands off the trembling fool,
> a slap to the face to knock him back to self,
> but that would have required explanation!
> How even begin to explain what was
> expected? Some things can't be taught. Elegance
> cannot be taught, economy of means,
> the beauty of conclusions rightly timed—
> that was not the face of a man to understand
> such things.

SOLDIER.
> This I didn't think, but felt it in my throat:
> Out of a thousand, why let this one go?
> Body after body after body, the unbroken
> procession of them circling the compound
> like a noose, the crying, the whispers, the reasonable
> responses that stank of common sense. What did
> he expect, that I would turn and say "Everybody
> stop, there's been a terrible mistake,
> everyone gather up your things, here are
> your babies and your wallets, now just go home"?
> There was no way! The smallest crack would shatter

the dam, the flood would drown us where we stood
in our obedient uniforms...

PRISONER.
No more processions for me, the trip was done.
I bent as if to fix my shoe, and almost laughed
to see him do the same, timing only
a minor god could have arranged. We were
alone. I came up to him softly and stood by him;
he reared up as if I had kicked him, grasped
his rifle, yelled. I think he yelled, I was
not listening. Down on my knees I tugged
at his arm, his leg, and looking up slowly
poured into my eyes everything I'd seen
that day, that week, that year that blinded heaven.
I spoke. My words astonished me; they came
to my lips quivering with a kind of love,
as if begging not for me but for his sake:
Let yourself go.

SOLDIER.
The moment before I lifted up my rifle
by its barrel to bring the butt down on
his face, he saw the uselessness, the light
rushed from his cheeks, he raised his chin, he made
no noise except to huff and hit the ground.
That taught him not to show his teeth and gums,
not to pull on the leg of a man's pants.

CAPTAIN.
I should have slapped him hard—I would
feel better about it all now. Instead I have
a hollow in my chest that brings

the moment back, one body on the ground,
begging arm still outstretched, the other body
gone stiff with fear as if turned to salt.
I'd seen it clearly from across the yard,
the moment when it came into his head
to let just this one go, to turn his face
and let him run. My hand was on my gun
for both of them, the Judas and the Jew,
I was tensed and ready and—why deny it?—
eager to do what must be done.

PRISONER.
No beggar ever begged so well. They moved me
to tears, the words I spoke as if to God,
kneeling on the dirty floor, looking into
that dark thin face that could not look away.
Was that a tear building in his eye?
More than I got from God. I was afraid then
for the first time, afraid he'd look around
and say Go, go, go, for God's sake go. He
hadn't seen the captain watching, we were alone,
and who would know if he let one escape?
I held my breath and felt a flicker of
some strange happiness, as if I'd seen something
I'd never hoped to see. The next moment
his face crumbled, I saw it give like a great
cracking of ice, and knew I'd get my way.
The rifle rose with all the anger and fear
that I could wish. And I was sad for him
just then, not sad for me. I lifted my chin,
and whispered to myself: brother set me free.

SOLDIER.

I lifted up the gun and brought it down,
it only happened once, I thought my heart
would stop. But it did not.

CAPTAIN.

And then it was over. I was two seconds late,
arrived to see the weakling sway and gasp
and bring his rifle down against the other's
face. When I looked up from the corpse I saw
the idiot eyes were dull, no signs of mind
inside that useless skull. He never flinched.
I might have imagined it but it almost seemed
he turned himself to receive the force full on.
It finished him at once, that single blow,
the shattered nose-bone shrapnelled to the brain.
And that was all. My hand was on my gun,
ready for the treason when it came, and when
it did not come, I had to hold the bullets
in my gut. To keep such feelings in,
to hold my voice to a pitch appropriate
for underlings, to turn and leave the trash
for what it is and join my friends for a smoke
outside—this is the use of power at its best,
hurt as it must sometimes, hurt as it must.

SOLDIER.

I was luckier that day than I realized,
the captain had been watching through the window.
Even as it was he was not happy. Had
he seen me hesitate, seen me wonder
for a moment where I was, wonder
who was this man begging at my feet,

who was I to be begged at in this way,
a twenty-year-old man dressed in an elegant
shirt, in thick, tight pants, bringing all my
force to bear on an offered face? He came
over then and checked the shape there on
the ground. I had killed the lucky man.
The captain stared at me, hand still
at the pistol on his waist. *Deal with this*,
he said, and walked away. Some sixty
years ago those words began their journey,
they are forever arriving in my head.

END OF PLAY

CHEATING DEATH

By
Frank Higgins

Cheating Death was first presented in 2003 by Atlantis Playmakers in Billerica, Mass. It was directed by Adam Perlman, and featured Carlos Zalduondo, Gwynne Flanagan and Will McGregor.

CHARACTERS

CAROL: A woman approaching middle age.
DEATH: A young, handsome man.
HERB: Carol's husband.

SETTING: The bedroom of Carol and Herb.

TIME: The present.

CHEATING DEATH

AT THE CURTAIN: *CAROL and HERB are sleeping in their bed. The dark, shrouded figure of DEATH enters with his staff.*

DEATH. Carol. Carol Milberger.

CAROL. Honey?

DEATH. Wake up, Carol.

CAROL. What time is it?

DEATH. Later than you think.

CAROL. No, it's not even light yet. We've still got time. Let me rub your neck... C'mon, you know it helps you. *(DEATH hesitates, then sits on the bed. She rubs DEATH's neck.)* You worry too much. So they hired a younger guy at the office; he doesn't know *half* what you know. You know *people*. You're in the people business. The boss knows that; you'll last forever, 'til death do us part.

DEATH. Carol, I've come for you.

CAROL. Oh honey, it's okay.

DEATH. Open your eyes.

(She sees him, and notices her husband still snores beside her.)

CAROL. Herb! Herb, wake up!

DEATH. He won't be joining us.

CAROL. Take what you want; take anything but get out! There's nothing valuable in here anyway.

DEATH. Not true.

CAROL. So that's what you want? You've come to the wrong place, buddy. *(She takes out a can of pepper spray and a stun gun.)* Get out of here right now and I won't hurt you— I warned you. *(She sprays him in the face; DEATH does not react. CAROL steels herself and charges. She stabs at him with the stun gun. DEATH makes no effort to defend himself, and the electric charges have no effect. She drops the stun gun and takes a karate stance. She hacks away; DEATH stands mute and passive. CAROL is finally exhausted. She claps her hands twice and the LIGHTS come on.)* What the... All right, get up, Herb. Joke's over. *(She shoves her husband who continues to snore.)*

DEATH. It's no joke.

CAROL. Right. My birthday was *yesterday*. Who do you work for? Singing telegrams? Well no tip for you— And *you* stop pretending you're sleeping.

DEATH. He can't hear us.

CAROL. That was some act you put on; pretending to be so worried about the young guy at the office, pretending you had to take a sleeping pill. Well it's not funny, and it's not funny you took the batteries from my stun gun. *(She touches her husband in the rump with the stun gun and he reacts and we hear the SNAP of electricity.)* Oh my God! Herb! Oh baby!— Call nine-one-one.

DEATH. He'll be all right. He's not on my to-do list.

CAROL. ...Oh God...this is real.

DEATH. Yes.

CAROL. No. I'm dreaming! I'm hallucinating! Drugs in college: bad *bad!*

DEATH. Prepare yourself.

CAROL. No! No!! I'll—I'll play you for it. I'll play you for my life. I saw that movie; you play chess, right?

DEATH. This is reality, Carol.

CAROL. No!!! You think I'm going to get on my knees, don't you? You think I'm going to beg you.

DEATH. It's happened.

CAROL. Well I'm *not*. Death is just a doorway. So how does this work? You touch me with your staff, I die?

DEATH. Works for me.

CAROL. I'm ready. Beam me up.

DEATH. This won't hurt.

(As DEATH reaches, she grabs his arm and whips it behind him. She pulls back his hood to reveal a young man.)

CAROL. Josh? Josh, what are you doing here?!

DEATH. You're good.

CAROL. My first boyfriend—how *dare* you? You stop calling and then you just show up after twenty-five years? Well I'm married, and even if I weren't, I am so *over* you— God, you haven't aged at all. This face. No crow's feet. How do you keep yourself young?

DEATH. How do you think, Carol?

CAROL. What, still single?— You had me going for a minute there. *(To HERB.)* And how did you even know to call Josh? I never men— You're *not* Josh, are you? But you can look like Josh when he was young?

DEATH. Whatever helps.

CAROL. So this really *is* real. Is Josh dead?

DEATH. He's an *accountant.* But he's fine.

CAROL. Why me? Why *now*? I'm *never* sick; I get mammograms, I eat right. How do *I* die? I'm *not* going. I'll give you whatever you want.

DEATH. Don't need anything.

CAROL. My soul. You can have my soul, right? But I get another forty years? And then you'll take my soul at the *end* of that time, but I still get the forty years?

DEATH. You're confusing me with that other guy.

CAROL. Death, Satan, it's the same!

DEATH. No.

CAROL. Please. Isn't there *anything* I can do? Isn't there anything I've done—good deeds, *something* that can give me another few years?

DEATH. …You asked about Josh.

CAROL. Can you take him instead?

DEATH. No. But what you said: "So this really is real. Is Josh dead?" At your worst moment, you thought of somebody else. Nice.

CAROL. So can you cut me some slack for that?

DEATH. I guess I do need *something.*

CAROL. So we're just haggling details now, right?

DEATH. Good muscle tone. I want it.

CAROL. I give you my muscle tone you'll let me live? God, I'll end up looking like my mother.

DEATH. Is that worse than death?

CAROL. You haven't seen her. Okay, take the muscle tone from the bottom of my arms.

DEATH. More. *(He points to her breasts.)*

CAROL. No mastectomy.

DEATH. Agreed. But the direction.

CAROL. No! I don't want them pointing south!

DEATH. Southwest.

CAROL. Not southwest.

DEATH. I need southwest.

CAROL. No southwest!

DEATH. How will it look if they don't point southwest?

CAROL. Good!

DEATH. No. Every other woman your age is south, or southwest, but you're west? Nobody will think they're real if they're west. You gotta give me some compass points.

CAROL. ...West southwest.

DEATH. West southwest?

CAROL. Less west than due west but still west.

DEATH. ...West, southwest. *(He gestures and it's done.)* What else?

CAROL. You've got enough.

DEATH. I gave you west southwest, you give me something.

CAROL. No teeth.

DEATH. Don't want 'em.

CAROL. No body parts.

DEATH. Didn't ask.

CAROL. Wait, hysterectomy.

DEATH. What would I do with a used uterus?

CAROL. Then what?

DEATH. ...Your laughter.

CAROL. You're serious?

DEATH. And not just any laughter. Your *girlish* laughter.

CAROL. And I give you that, you'll let me live?

DEATH. Decide.

CAROL. ...So muscle tone; breasts west, southwest. Girlish laughter. Okay. *(DEATH points his staff at her and beckons with his free hand. DEATH begins to laugh, pealing off a laugh of healthy, young laughter.)* What is so funny?

DEATH. You, Carol. I would have settled for your muscle tone.

CAROL. You mean—

DEATH. Yes!

CAROL. I could have kept my girlish laughter? *(DEATH laughs more in response.)* So what? I can still laugh. So what if it's not girlish laughter? What's the advantage of shrieking like a nitwit?— Stop it. Stop laughing.

DEATH. You don't get it. Carol, you gave away the *store.* What do you think keeps me young?

CAROL. I'll have the last laugh. Laughter's not like muscle tone.

DEATH. I think you'll find it is.

CAROL. Everybody loses muscle tone. I can laugh *anytime,* a young laugh, a *girlish* laugh.

DEATH. Try it.

CAROL. Say something funny.

DEATH. After a quarrel, a husband says to his wife, "You know, I was a fool when I married you." "Yes, dear, but I was in love and didn't notice." …See?

CAROL. Not funny.

DEATH. A boy says to his father, "Is it true, Dad, that in some parts of Africa a man doesn't know his wife 'til he marries her?" "That's true in every country, son."
(CAROL realizes she needs to laugh and tries but can't.)

CAROL. I can't laugh at something that's not funny. Anytime *anybody* says or does something funny, I laugh first and I laugh *loudest.* Say something funny and you'll hear me howling.

DEATH. Husband and wife argue over finances. Husband says, "Well, if you'd learn to cook and clean this place, we could fire the maid." "Oh yeah? Well, if you'd learn how to make love, we could fire the gardener."
(CAROL tries to laugh, but it is a sad, tired middle-aged laugh. DEATH laughs anew, with a fresh sparkling laugh full of life.)

CAROL. Bad jokes.

DEATH. To you *now.*

CAROL. It's called growing up.

DEATH. Whatever you say.

CAROL. And this is supposed to be the big loss? Not laughing at bad jokes?

DEATH. And life's absurdities. And life's little ironies. And life's little sudden, unexpected pleasures. Never again will you laugh the way you did the first time you got your first kite to rise into the sky. Never again will you laugh during sex. What do you think keeps me young? But for you, all gone.

CAROL. I don't have to laugh! I'll find joy in work! *(DEATH laughs anew.)* And art!

DEATH. You people kill me. *(DEATH exits laughing.)*

CAROL. Herb...Herb! Wake up!

HERB. Hmm?

CAROL. Herb, talk to me.

HERB. Whaaat?

CAROL. Say something funny.

HERB. My butt hurts.

CAROL. Tell me a joke, anything. Talk to me and be *funny!*

HERB. Did you eat beans again?

CAROL. I mean it! I need you to be funny! Right now!

HERB. What's the matter with you? Are you going through the change?

CAROL. Help me laugh!

HERB. I need every hour of sleep I can get. I'm trying to compete with those young bucks at the office and you want to *talk?! (He turns over.)* Go to sleep.

CAROL. I'm serious! Help me laugh! I'm serious! I'm serious!

END OF PLAY

I'LL FLY AWAY

By
David Rush

CHARACTERS

RACHEL: About 30.
POPPY: Her father, old and frail.

SETTING: A clearing in a forest preserve.

TIME: October. Six a.m.

I'LL FLY AWAY

AT THE CURTAIN: *RACHEL leads her father, POPPY, on. She has a large bag filled with items as needed, and carries a folding canvas chair.*

POPPY. Come on, we can't be late.

RACHEL. All right, all right.

POPPY. Did you bring the harmonica?

RACHEL. Yes, I brought the harmonica.

POPPY. And the tambourine?

RACHEL. Yes, I have it all. How's this, this good enough?

POPPY. ...We're too close to the water, the water'll scare them away.

RACHEL. Where would you like to be?

POPPY. By the trees. Those tall trees. Those tall oak trees.

RACHEL. But then they won't see us. I think we should stay by the water.

POPPY. The water'll scare them away. They won't be able to land.

RACHEL. Poppy, please. Now come on, here, sit down. *(She unfolds a portable canvas picnic chair.)*

POPPY. The water'll scare them away. They won't stop. They'll go right on without me.

RACHEL. It's a little stream, Poppy; nobody's going to be afraid of a little stream.

POPPY. They won't know what it is.

RACHEL. Poppy, their civilization is a million years older than ours; they've figured out how to sail through black holes, and they talk to you through your electric razor. I think they should know what water is.

POPPY. Maybe they don't.

RACHEL. Think about it, Poppy; how do they take baths, how do they keep themselves clean, how do they replenish their vital bodily fluids? They must have water. Now, here, sit down.

POPPY. They wash themselves with machines.

RACHEL. Sit down, Poppy. You'll wear yourself out.

POPPY. ...I'm afraid they'll miss me. I'm afraid they won't see me.

RACHEL. Then we'll go back home.

POPPY. They'll go right on, won't they? They won't stop and wait. They'll just go right on ahead without me and I'll be stuck here.

RACHEL. We'll go back home and I'll make you French toast.

POPPY. I'll be stuck here for another two thousand years. We should move away from the water.

RACHEL. How about a Pop-Tart; you want a Pop-Tart? I got strawberry and apple cinnamon. Take your pick.

POPPY. I'm not hungry.

RACHEL. You sure? You might be later.

POPPY. Later I'll be asleep.

RACHEL. Asleep...?

POPPY. Of course; how else do you travel a thousand light years away? They put you in frozen sleep, I told you.

RACHEL. No, you didn't. You never told me that part.

POPPY. Well, stop and think, it's the only way it has to be. They'll land. They'll make sure it's me, they don't want to make mistakes, but then, when they're sure, they'll take me up into the ship. They'll be glad to see me. They'll all come to shake my hand and slap me on the shoulders, so glad to see me; and then they'll ask me if I'm tired, and I'll tell them, yes, I am very tired. They'll understand. They won't ask me any questions but they'll understand. So they'll take me down the hall and give me my cabin and wish me pleasant dreams, and then I'll go to sleep and when I wake up...I'll be back home.

RACHEL. ...You've thought it all out.

POPPY. I've had years.

RACHEL. But what if they don't come, Poppy. Have you thought about that too?

POPPY. They'll come.

RACHEL. But just suppose they don't? I mean—

POPPY. Why wouldn't they come?

RACHEL. I don't know, I'm just saying. Maybe you heard them wrong.

POPPY. Don't talk about it; you're trying to scare me.

RACHEL. I want you to be prepared, that's all I'm saying. If they don't show up, you'll come back home with me, I'll make you some French toast and you can take a long nap. Doesn't that sound good?

POPPY. I'm not listening. Did you bring the harmonica?

RACHEL. Poppy, don't change the subject; now come on. We'll wait half an hour and if they don't come I'm taking you back home.

POPPY. You know something, don't you?

RACHEL. Poppy...

POPPY. What, they talked to you? They said something.

RACHEL. No, of course not.

POPPY. You're lying. I heard last night, you were talking to them in the bathroom. I heard the noise.

RACHEL. That was my hair dryer.

POPPY. Tell me what they said.

RACHEL. They didn't say anything, Poppy. How could they; they don't exist!

POPPY. Stop it.

RACHEL. It's all in your head, when are you going to understand? There are no outer-space people coming for you. The noise you hear in the razor is the razor.

POPPY. Then why are we sitting out here? Why are we waiting for them?

RACHEL. Because you kept insisting and Dr. Martin said I should prove it to you once and for all.

POPPY. Dr. Martin doesn't know anything. They told me to watch out for him.

RACHEL. ...All right. But when they don't come, when you see for yourself, we're going home and it'll be over.

POPPY. I'm cold.

RACHEL *(taking out a blanket, wrapping him)*. Of course you are. It's the crack of dawn in the middle of October; polar bears would freeze out here. I told you to put on your long underwear, but no; you insisted you wouldn't need it.

POPPY. I didn't say I wouldn't need it *here*. I said I wouldn't need it *there*. They have two suns; it's always seventy degrees. You don't listen.

RACHEL. Yes, of course. Here. Are you hungry? You want a Pop-Tart or not?

POPPY. What kind did you bring?

RACHEL. Strawberry and apple cinnamon.

POPPY. I'll have strawberry.

RACHEL. Fine. And your pills; you have to take your pills.

POPPY. I don't need them.

RACHEL *(dishes out small pills from a pill box; maybe three)*. Yes you do, Poppy. Dr. Martin said you'll need them for the rest of your life.

POPPY. Not anymore. The people will cure me.

RACHEL. Poppy...

POPPY. That's why they're coming. They know exactly what to do; they have machines. They put you in this machine, it's like a bathtub, and they fill it with some kind of warm stuff and it cures you.

RACHEL. ...You never said that, Poppy.

POPPY. I don't have to tell you everything.

RACHEL. Then tell me now; what did they say?

POPPY. Why should I? What do you care; you don't believe me anyway.

RACHEL. We're talking about your pills, Poppy; this is very serious.

POPPY. I asked them, I said, "What if I'm too weak or something?" and they said, "Don't worry, Mr. Liebowitz, we have machines. We know exactly what to do. You don't need those silly pills anymore." And they were right.

RACHEL. Christ, Poppy.

POPPY. So you can flush those down the toilet for all I care.

RACHEL. When did they tell you this?

POPPY *(struggling with Pop-Tart wrapper)*. I can't open this. Open this for me.

RACHEL. Poppy, please; when did they talk to you about the pills?

POPPY. A couple weeks ago. Wait, wait, I got it.

RACHEL. Look at me. How long has it been that you haven't taken your pills? This is very serious.

POPPY. A week, maybe two. So you can put them away.

RACHEL. Oh, Poppy, for the love of God. I thought you were just sleepy because you were sleepy. Don't you know what you did? Don't you know what you're doing to yourself?

POPPY. I'm getting ready to leave. What do you have to drink with this? You brought tea or something?

RACHEL. That does it. Come on, we're going home right now.

POPPY. No.

RACHEL. I have to call Dr. Martin, come on. *(She starts to pack up whatever she's unpacked.)*

POPPY. No, I told you.

RACHEL. Maybe it's not too late, maybe there's something he can do.

POPPY. It doesn't matter, I won't do it.

RACHEL. Poppy…!

POPPY. I'm not going back, why don't you believe me.

RACHEL. You have to.

POPPY. They'll be here in fifteen minutes. You said you'd wait.

RACHEL. Poppy, there's *(no time to fool around)*—

POPPY. Have a little pity, for the love of God. Maybe you're wrong. Maybe once in your life you could be wrong. You don't have to be Hitler all the time, do you?!

RACHEL *(stunned by this)*. All right. Fifteen minutes. It is now twenty-seven minutes after six. At precisely quarter to seven, we are getting in the car and I'm taking you home and then, then we'll see who's wrong. And there won't be any more of this, this crap. No more...voices and...spaceships and... *(She stops, fighting tears.)* Jesus fucking Christ, Poppy, that was a shitty thing to say.

POPPY. Let me have the harmonica.

RACHEL. I'm the one who stayed, you know. I'm the one who took you in.

POPPY. Nobody asked you. We should practice.

RACHEL. What do you mean, nobody asked me? Where else were you gonna go?

POPPY. I don't want to talk; it's too late for talk. Where are the instruments?

RACHEL. Come on, where else were you gonna go? Answer me that; come on, before you start resenting me.

POPPY. With them! That's where; with them. I should've been there years ago. I missed them the last time they came, I'm not going to let that happen again. Sally, give me the goddamn harmonica.

RACHEL *(a moment)*. I'm not Sally, Poppy. Sally died when she was ten. She was killed by a car. I'm Rachel.

POPPY. No. Rachel's the one who was killed. You got that wrong too. You get everything wrong. That's why we should practice. If I miss them, if they don't hear the signal, I'll never never forgive you.

RACHEL *(takes out the harmonica)*. All right. Then here. Play it loud, Poppy. I hope they hear you.

POPPY. You take the tambourine.

RACHEL. Yes, Poppy. *(He blows on the harmonica, as:)* Would you have been happier, Poppy, if it was like that? If I was the one who was killed and Sally was still around?

POPPY. Why talk about it now? Why dwell on the past? In ten minutes, I'll be gone and you can do whatever you want. We'll both be happier. Now, remember, it has to be loud.

RACHEL. I know all this, Poppy. I think I know everything now.

POPPY. They particularly said it has to be loud so they hear it. Otherwise they won't know for sure it's me. They'll think it's somebody else trying to get in my place.

RACHEL. Yes, Poppy. I'll play it as loud as I can. And I hope you're right about them. I hope to God you're right about them.

POPPY. One...two...three...

(He blows on the harmonica, making what he thinks is music. RACHEL beats a rhythm on the tambourine. The noise is horrific, but loud. They continue as LIGHTS fade.)

END OF PLAY

PHONING IT IN

By
Michele Markarian

Phoning It In premiered in 2003 at the Piano Factory in Boston, Mass., as part of Devanaughn Theatre's "1st Annual Dragonfly Festival." The play was directed by Andrew Sarno, and featured Carl Schwaber and Molly Kimmerling.

CHARACTERS

BRIAN
STEPHANIE

SETTING: A city park.

TIME: The present.

PHONING IT IN

AT THE CURTAIN: *BRIAN and STEPHANIE are seated on a bench. They are holding hands.*

BRIAN. You know, I really love you.

STEPHANIE. Oh, that's nice. I really love you, too.

BRIAN. Really?

STEPHANIE. Yeah. Really. *(BRIAN tries to speak. Cell phone rings.)* Excuse me. *(Answers cell phone.)* Hello? Oh, hi! Hi! How are you? I'm—oh. Oh. Really? Really? You like him that much? Of course it's a lot! Carrie! Come on! You're telling me you want to marry the guy, well, that's liking someone an awful lot. Wouldn't you say? Oh. Yeah. *(Nods head.)* Okay. Carrie, I'm kind of—oh, is that your buzzer? It could be him? All right, I'll let you go. Bye. *(She hangs up.)* Sorry.

BRIAN. What was that about?

STEPHANIE. Oh, Carrie's just— *(Cell phone rings.)* Excuse me. *(She picks up phone.)* Hello? *(She hangs up.)* Wrong number.

BRIAN. So anyway, I really—

STEPHANIE. I was telling you about Carrie. She wants to marry this guy.

BRIAN. What guy?

STEPHANIE. The guy she's been seeing!

BRIAN. What's wrong with that?

STEPHANIE. Brian, come on! I mean really!

BRIAN. What, really?

STEPHANIE. I mean, she's only been seeing him two months!

BRIAN. So?

STEPHANIE. You can't just marry someone you've been seeing for two months! It's not right!

BRIAN. Why not?

STEPHANIE. Well, jeez, we've been seeing each other for eight months.

BRIAN. Yeah? *(He leans closer.)*

STEPHANIE. Exactly!

BRIAN. What do you mean, exactly?

STEPHANIE. Exactly!

BRIAN. Are you saying that—you think we shouldn't— *(A cell phone rings.)* Excuse me. *(He answers phone.)* Hello? Scott. Yeah. Yeah, well, I'm kind of—no. No, not yet— *(He looks at STEPHANIE.)* What? What do you mean, don't do it? You said last week that—what? She *what?* Scott, are you sure? Uh-huh. Yeah. Yeah. Yeah, that's pretty serious. That's really serious. Just be sure you got your information right, buddy. You wouldn't want to—oh. That's your call-waiting. Okay. Good luck. *(He hangs up.)*

STEPHANIE. Who was that?

BRIAN. Scott. *(He looks glum.)*

STEPHANIE. Oh. *(BRIAN starts to speak, then stops.)* Why the face?

BRIAN. What face?

STEPHANIE. You know. *(She exaggerates glum face.)*

BRIAN. I don't wanna talk about it.

STEPHANIE. Is it about Scott? *(BRIAN nods.)* What about Scott?

BRIAN. I don't wanna talk about it.

STEPHANIE. Brian!

BRIAN. What?

STEPHANIE. I thought we agreed to tell each other everything!

BRIAN. This is—so wrong.

STEPHANIE. Maybe it's not so bad. Tell me.

BRIAN. Oh God. Where do I start? *(A cell phone rings.)*

STEPHANIE. Oh, Brian, I'm sorry. This could be Carrie. I'll just be a minute. *(She answers phone.)* Hello? Carrie? Hi! What? He *what*? Oh my God! *(She screams.)* That's incredible! Oh, Carrie! *(She jumps up.)* When? July? Oh, perfect! Seriously? Seriously? Oh, I'd be honored. Oh my God, yes! Oh, can I tell Brian? I love you too, sweetie. Tell Conrad congratulations! *(She hangs up. BRIAN sighs.)* Well?

BRIAN. Well what?

STEPHANIE. Aren't you going to ask what that was about?

BRIAN. Why?

STEPHANIE. Why? What is wrong with you? *(BRIAN sighs.)* Carrie is getting married.

BRIAN. That's nice.

STEPHANIE. To Conrad.

BRIAN. Conrad. Conrad. Wait a minute. Is that the guy she's been seeing for two months?

STEPHANIE. Yeah.

BRIAN. This is good news?

STEPHANIE. Yeah. She's my best friend.

BRIAN. But I thought you said it wasn't right.

STEPHANIE. What?

BRIAN. You said it wasn't right for a couple who's only been dating for two months to get married?

STEPHANIE. That was before.

BRIAN. Before what?

STEPHANIE. Before—I just had to get used to it, that's all.

BRIAN. You're unbelievable. How can you change your mind, just like that?

STEPHANIE. Brian, I didn't change my mind. I just— adjusted it, that's all.

BRIAN. Are all women this fickle?

STEPHANIE. What kind of stupid remark is that?

BRIAN. It's not stupid. It's—uh, I'm sorry. I think I'm still upset about Scott. He just told me—

STEPHANIE. And I can't believe that Conrad proposed to Carrie after only two months! *(She glares at BRIAN.)*

BRIAN. Yeah. *(Pause.)* Are you—not happy about this anymore?

STEPHANIE. We've been going out for eight months!

BRIAN. Yeah.

STEPHANIE. And—

BRIAN. What?

STEPHANIE. I'd just like to know where this relationship is going, that's all. *(BRIAN shrugs.)* Maybe it's time to just end things.

BRIAN. I don't know. *(Cell phone rings.)* I'm sorry. *(He answers phone.)* Hello? Oh, hey, Scott. How's it going? Really? Greg made it up? Why? You gotta be kidding me. I told you not to sleep with her. Yeah. Yeah, I know. No kidding. No kidding. Wow. That's great, Scottie. No, I mean it. That's really cool. Yeah, I'll be seeing you, man. What? Who, me? No, I haven't. Yeah, yeah, she is. *(He smiles at STEPHANIE.)* Yeah, yeah, I will, though. See ya. *(He hangs up.)*

STEPHANIE. I don't know what I was thinking.

BRIAN. About what?

STEPHANIE. Nothing. Never mind.

BRIAN. Stephanie, there's something I want to ask you.

STEPHANIE. Go ahead. *(Cell phone rings. She answers it.)* Hello? Carrie?

BRIAN. It's pretty important.

STEPHANIE. Wait a minute, Carrie, I can't hear you. *(She motions for BRIAN to stop talking. He sits back and sighs.)* What? I still can't hear you. Okay. *(She hangs up.)*

BRIAN. I think you know how I feel about you.

STEPHANIE. Oh?

BRIAN. You're a special girl—uh, I mean, woman. I feel like the luckiest—

(Cell phone rings. STEPHANIE answers it.)

STEPHANIE. Hello? Yeah, that's much better. Yeah. What? He *what*? No! No way! Stop it! *No!* Carrie, that's not even funny, that's just plain sick. No way. You tell him that there's no way in hell you're going to marry him. Seriously. Lose him. You hear me? No, I won't tell Brian. No, don't worry. I promise. I won't say a word. I'm sorry, sweetie. I'll call you later. Bye. *(She hangs up.)*

BRIAN. As I was saying—

STEPHANIE. I can't believe it.

BRIAN. Don't tell me—I don't want to know.

STEPHANIE. I can't tell you. I promised Carrie I wouldn't.

BRIAN. Oh.

STEPHANIE. So what were you saying?

BRIAN. Stephanie, I— *(Cell phone rings.)* Wait a minute. Hello? Scott. No, no I haven't. No! Just—leave it to me, will you? Yeah, yeah. Later. *(He hangs up.)*

STEPHANIE. You didn't tell me what happened with Scott.

BRIAN. I don't want to talk about Scott.

STEPHANIE. What do you want to talk about?

BRIAN. Stephanie, I love you more than any woman I've ever been with. I can't imagine living withou—

(Cell phone rings. STEPHANIE answers it.)

STEPHANIE. Hello? Who? Oh. Oh, you're very smooth. Very smooth. I can't believe you told my oldest friend that I had a great ass. What do you mean, it's true? You ask a girl to marry you and then you tell her that her best friend has a great ass? What kind of sick pervert are you? Oh. That kind. I'm not interested. And if you ever bother Carrie or me ever again, I swear to God I'll have you arrested, you hear me? Same to you! *(She hangs up.)*

BRIAN. What the hell was that about?

STEPHANIE. Don't even ask.

BRIAN. Yeah, I'm gonna ask! Some guy tells my girlfriend she has a great ass, I wanna know about it!

STEPHANIE. It's no big deal. He's just a jerk.

BRIAN. How can you say that?

STEPHANIE. What?

BRIAN. It *is* a big deal! It—wait a minute. This isn't what I want to talk to you about. Stephanie, I love—

(Cell phone rings. STEPHANIE answers it.)

STEPHANIE. Hello? Carrie? Carrie, I can't understand you. Stop crying, sweetie. You what? You miss him? You think you overreacted? You want to take him back? Uh-uh, huh. Yeah. I just don't think it's a good idea, that's all. I—if you really want me to be your maid-of-honor I will, but don't you think—no. No. Yeah. Call him. *(She hangs up phone and stares straight ahead, dejected.)*

BRIAN. Stephanie? *(No answer.)* Stephanie? Stephanie, I— *(He realizes she's not listening, picks up his cell phone and dials a number. Cell phone rings.)*

STEPHANIE. Hello?

BRIAN. Stephanie, I love you. Will you marry me?

STEPHANIE. Who is this?

(She turns and looks at BRIAN, sees him on phone, and is surprised.)

END OF PLAY

4-1-1

By
David Fleisher

4-1-1 was first produced in New York City in 1996 by Expanded Arts as part of its "Bread and Circuses Festival of New Plays."

CHARACTERS

OPERATOR
CALLER

SETTING: A telephone company, and a private residence.

TIME: The present.

4-1-1

AT THE CURTAIN: *LIGHTS up on OPERATOR.*

OPERATOR. Information.

(LIGHTS up on CALLER.)

CALLER. Yes, Operator, I'd like the number for a Dr. Phillip Carey on Ridgemont Avenue.
OPERATOR. Carey?
CALLER. Yes, that's right.
OPERATOR. Is that spelled C-A-R-E-Y?
CALLER. I believe so.
OPERATOR. Checking.
CALLER. Thank you, Operator.
OPERATOR. With a C?
CALLER. Yes, with a C.
OPERATOR. I don't see a Dr. Phillip Carey with a C on Ridgemont Avenue.
CALLER. I wonder if he spells his name with a K.
OPERATOR. I don't know, sir.
CALLER. Would you see if there's a Dr. Phillip Carey with a K on Ridgemont?
OPERATOR. K-A-R-E-Y?
CALLER. Yes.
OPERATOR. Checking.
CALLER. Thank you.
OPERATOR. There's a Phillip Carey with a K on Columbo Circle.

CALLER. Columbo Circle?

OPERATOR. Yes, sir.

CALLER. But I was told his office is on Ridgemont Avenue.

OPERATOR. The one I've got listed here is on Columbo Circle.

CALLER. Columbo Circle?

OPERATOR. Yes, sir.

CALLER. Wonder if that's the same Phillip Carey.

OPERATOR. I wouldn't know, sir.

CALLER. I don't even know where Columbo Circle is.

OPERATOR. Question.

CALLER. Yes, Operator?

OPERATOR. Could he have moved?

CALLER. I don't know.

OPERATOR. Is there a way for you to find out?

CALLER. Not until I get the phone number and ask him.

OPERATOR. Would you like me to give you the number?

CALLER. I just don't think that's the correct Phillip Carey. I never heard of Columbo Circle, plus I honestly believe he spells his name with a C.

OPERATOR. Did you say you would like the number?

CALLER. Yes, give me the damn number.

OPERATOR. Beg your pardon, sir?

CALLER. Please give me the number.

OPERATOR. The number is…are you writing this down?

CALLER. Yes, Operator, as we speak.

OPERATOR. As what?

CALLER. Nothing. Just give me the number, thank you.

OPERATOR. The number is 689-3417.

CALLER. Operator?

OPERATOR. Yes?

CALLER. I don't mean to be a pest, but I changed my mind. I want you to check again for a Phillip Carey on Ridgemont Avenue. I'm sure he spells his name with a C, and I know he hasn't moved.

OPERATOR. You want what?

CALLER. Check again for a Dr. Phillip Carey with a C on Ridgemont Avenue.

OPERATOR. Again?

CALLER. Yes.

OPERATOR. But there was no one by that name with that spelling at that address.

CALLER. Operator, this is very important. He's a psychiatrist.

OPERATOR. A psychiatrist?

CALLER. Yes.

OPERATOR. I'll check under "Psychiatrists."

CALLER. It's for my wife.

OPERATOR. Beg your pardon?

CALLER. My wife.

OPERATOR. Life?

CALLER. Wife! It's for my wife!

OPERATOR. No reason to raise your voice, sir.

CALLER. Sorry, Operator, I'm just a little upset right now.

OPERATOR. Beg your pardon?

CALLER. Nothing, damn it! Just find the number! Can't you see I'm in a hurry, for God's sake!

OPERATOR. Question.

CALLER. What, Operator?

OPERATOR. Why is it necessary to be rude?

CALLER. I shouldn't be taking out my frustration on you. It was wrong.

OPERATOR. I'm only trying to help you.

CALLER. You don't understand. See, my wife is a very sick woman, and I need to get a hold of Dr. Carey as soon as possible. He's a psychiatrist, and he was highly recommended for my wife.

OPERATOR. Your wife's a psychiatrist?

CALLER. Operator?

OPERATOR. Yes?

CALLER. Did I say my wife's a psychiatrist?

OPERATOR. I thought you did.

CALLER. I said my wife's a very sick woman and she *needs* a psychiatrist.

OPERATOR. I'm sorry.

CALLER. Operator, it's not your fault. You're only trying to help. It's me, I'm the one causing all the problems here because, see, I'm...my wife is...well, she has an unusually severe chemical imbalance in her brain, and she's been experiencing psychotic episodes.

OPERATOR. I see.

CALLER. She poisoned our cat last night because she thought it was from outer space. And now she's threatening to kill *me* because she's convinced I had sex with the cat, that I got pregnant, and I'm now going to give birth to alien creatures.

OPERATOR. I see.

CALLER. My wife sleeps with a knife under her pillow!

OPERATOR. Is your wife there with you now?

CALLER. She's lying down upstairs in the bedroom.

OPERATOR. Do you need a psychiatrist?

CALLER. Yes!

OPERATOR. Do you have the name of a psychiatrist? Because if you don't, sir, I can give you the number of social services, and I'm sure they would be more than happy to recommend one.

CALLER. Operator.

OPERATOR. Yes?

CALLER. I already have the name of a psychiatrist.

OPERATOR. And that is?

CALLER. Dr. Phillip Carey.

OPERATOR. Carey?

CALLER. Yes!

OPERATOR. Someone called just a moment ago and asked for a one Dr. Phillip Carey on Ridgemont Avenue.

CALLER. Operator?

OPERATOR. Yes, sir?

CALLER. That was me. *I* called for a one Dr. Phillip Carey on Ridgemont Avenue just a moment ago. You're still talking to the same person. We haven't hung up yet.

OPERATOR. Is this some kind of joke? Are you playing games with me? Because if you are, I can assure you the proper authorities will be notified.

CALLER. Let me see if I can make this as simple as possible for you.

OPERATOR. Please don't patronize me, sir.

CALLER. You have no idea what I'm going through with my wife.

OPERATOR. I don't appreciate being talked *down* to. I'm doing the best job I can. I want very much to help you and, believe me, I understand this is an emergency. Your wife's pregnant, and she's feeling out of sorts.

CALLER. My wife is not pregnant and she's not feeling out of sorts. She's *sick. Very sick.*

OPERATOR. Has it ever occurred to you that maybe I have feelings too?

CALLER. I didn't mean to show any disrespect, Operator.

OPERATOR. Have you considered for one second that I might have a few problems myself? That maybe *I'm* experiencing difficulties in my own life? Oh, I know what you're thinking. She's only an operator.

CALLER. No, I don't think that.

OPERATOR. Well, let me tell you something, Mr. Carey, you are not the lone ranger. We all have problems. In fact, you know who could really use a little help right now?

CALLER. God knows, I'm sorry, Operator…

OPERATOR. Me! You know why?

CALLER. I'm afraid I don't.

OPERATOR. My husband told me last night, after we had sex mind you, that he was leaving me for another woman.

CALLER. Beg your pardon?

OPERATOR. Don't beg-your-pardon me! You heard what I said. *(Silence.)*

CALLER. Did you hear that?

OPERATOR. My own husband…cheating on me. Do you know how that makes me feel, Mr. Carey? Like I don't matter anymore. It makes me feel worthless.

CALLER. What is that?

OPERATOR. What is *what?*

CALLER. That clicking noise.

OPERATOR. I don't hear anything.

CALLER. Is someone else on the line?

OPERATOR. We were so happy in the beginning. Life was full of magic and infinite possibilities.

CALLER. Operator, I think my wife might be awake upstairs. Susan, is that you? Are you on the line?

OPERATOR. Then he started drinking. He would come home drunk every night. I think he started seeing that other woman then. Her name was Stella.

CALLER. You can talk to me, sweetheart. I'm here for you. I will always be here for you. Talk to me, Susan.

OPERATOR. Mr. Carey, you're such a sweet and patient man, but my name's not Susan.

CALLER. Operator! I think my wife's listening in on our conversation from the extension upstairs. Susan?

OPERATOR. Okay, first of all, let's get something straight. My name's not Susan, it's Gloria. And I apologize for getting so emotional, but I put my pants on one leg at a time just like everybody else. I...have... feelings.

CALLER. I can hear you breathing, sweetheart.

OPERATOR. Stop that!

CALLER. I'll be upstairs right away to tuck you in. *(Silence.)* Operator, I think my wife just hung up. I need to go upstairs to check on her. *(Pause.)* Susan?

OPERATOR. Susan...Myra...Gertrude...whatever. What difference does it make? I'm just the operator. You know what, Mr. Carey? You're starting to remind me of my husband. Know what he did one night? He yelled that bitch's name out while we were making love... *(Yelling.)* Steh-lah!!

(CALLER cups the receiver in his hand, looks up, then offstage.)

CALLER. Susan, is that you? *(Into phone.)* Operator, I've got a situation here. My wife's coming downstairs.

OPERATOR. Question.

CALLER. Make it quick!

OPERATOR. What did I do to deserve being treated like this?

(LIGHTS fade slowly on CALLER.)

CALLER. Listen, I don't have time for this. I need the number of that psychiatrist now! Dr. Phillip Carey on Ridgemont Avenue. Operator! Operator!

OPERATOR. Checking...nothing yet. Let's see, Carey... Carey...here it is. Dr. Phillip Carey, 1213 Ridgemont Avenue. That's interesting. Sir, he spells his name with two r's, not one. It's *C-a-r-r-i-e.*

(LIGHTS up, slowly revealing CALLER slumped over in his chair, with a knife in his back)

OPERATOR *(cont'd).* That number is 632-1445. Are you writing this down? Hello? *(Silence. OPERATOR dials.)* Is this Dr. Phillip Carrie's office on Ridgemont Avenue? Good. I need to make an appointment to see Dr. Carrie as soon as possible. *(Breaking into tears.)* It's about my husband.

END OF PLAY

LET ME COUNT THE WAYS

By
Jay D. Hanagan

Let Me Count the Ways was originally produced in 2002 by Gatesinger Company, Ltd. in Pultneyville, N.Y. It was directed by Jay D. Hanagan, and featured Sara Blankenberg, Andrew Meyer and Mike Mulberry.

CHARACTERS

SHE: A woman.
HE: A man.
FATHER: A father.

SETTING: A living room/bare stage.

TIME: The present. Evening.

LET ME COUNT THE WAYS

AT THE CURTAIN : *SHE and HE about to embrace and kiss…if they're lucky.*

SHE. I love you.

HE. I love you.

SHE. Kiss me. *(HE immediately leans in and SHE just as immediately—)* Wait!

HE. What?!

SHE. My father. He will hear.

HE. I'll be quiet.

SHE. I love you.

HE. And I love you.

SHE. Kiss me. *(HE leans in.)* Wait!

HE. I'll be *very* quiet. *(Leans in.)*

SHE. Do you say you love me because you love me, or do you say you love me so that you may kiss me.

HE. Yes.

SHE. "Yes" to what?

HE. "Yes" to whatever it is that will allow me to kiss you.

SHE *(turns)*. So you admit you do not love me.

HE. I admit nothing of the sort!

SHE *(turns back)*. But you do not deny it!

HE. I deny nothing of the sort!

SHE. You don't.

HE. And I shan't!

SHE. So you love me?!

HE. I suppose I do.

SHE. And I suppose—

HE. —I love you! Kiss me! *(Leans in.)*

SHE. Wait!

HE. Should I have said it the other way around?

SHE. *Why* do you love me?

HE. I don't know.

SHE. You don't *know?!*

HE. I mean, I know, but…but my love is far too great for mere words.

SHE. It is?

HE. I just said so, didn't I?

SHE. Kiss me! *(HE leans in.)* Wait!

HE. You will not be-*lieve* how quiet I can be!

SHE. Are you saying you are not attracted to me?

HE. Of course I'm attract—…is this a trick question?

SHE. Would you still want to kiss me were you not in love with me?

HE. Of course!

SHE. So love has nothing to do with it.

HE. Of course not.

SHE. So you would nigh be happy going about kissing whomsoever you fancied with nary a thought of love.

HE *(beat)*. No.

SHE. No!?

HE *(confused)*. I don't *think* so.

SHE. Well I wouldn't think so either.

HE. Love truly hurts.

SHE. Aye, it does. But wait! You hurt?

HE. Sorely.

SHE. So you love me!

HE. If this is heading where I hope it is, then "yes."

SHE. Kiss me, my love!

HE. Then yes! *(Leans in.)* Wait.

SHE. What?

HE. Would you be so shallow as to not allow me the pleasure of your lips were *you* to not find me to *your* liking?

SHE *(beat)*. Huh?

HE. Do you want to kiss me of love, or rather of taking pity on one who otherwise you may find repulsive?

SHE. I don't find you repulsive.

HE. You don't.

SHE. I never have.

HE. Would you find me fair of face?

SHE. Probably. Kiss me.

HE. And the rest?

SHE. The rest of what?

HE *(indicating himself)*. Rest! Rest!

SHE. I am not yet tired. Kiss me.

HE. The rest of *me*. Do you find all of me to be fair?

SHE. Fair would do it.

HE. But no better than fair.

SHE. But no worse.

HE. How can you say you love one whom you yourself can only describe as being, at best, average?

SHE. You have a good heart. You have a good soul. Above average.

HE. A good heart and soul does not reflect well in a mirror. *(Reflective.)* In song perhaps—

SHE. —But it dost reflect well in mine eyes.

HE *(impressed)*. Good line. I love you.

SHE. I thought you might. Kiss me. *(Leans in.)* Wait!

HE. If your father hasn't heard us by now he's as deaf as a post!

SHE. What of *my* heart and soul.

HE. What of them?

SHE. How do things reflect in *thine* eyes?

HE. They reflect as they might looking down at a pond in the coolness of a bright, still summer morn. When all of nature is in tune with its harmonic tendencies which inevitably leads us back to the heart and soul song alluded to briefly prior.

SHE *(unimpressed)*. So you see me reflected in a murky, scummy, biologically suspect colloidal suspension.

HE. Home schooling has done you well in the sciences.

SHE. Is it *me* that you see reflected in your experiment in soil and water conservation—-

HE. My analogy seems to have eroded into something heretofore unthought of.

SHE. —or are the eyes you gaze into belonging to some aquatic menagerie of frog, perch and bullhead.

HE *(aside)*. My thoughts tend to lean towards the latter.

SHE. *Why* do you toy with me thusly?

HE. If I were toying with you, then most assuredly I would be having fun right about now.

SHE. You would?

HE. *Most* assuredly.

SHE. Then you *do* love me!

HE. Do you come with CliffsNotes?

SHE. We both see beyond the physical. Don't we. We see not with our eyes, for they are blind. We instead see with our hearts. Our hands. Our fingertips.

HE. Our lips?

SHE *(lovingly)*. Aye. Our lips.

HE. I was hoping you'd say that. *(Leans in.)*

SHE. Wait!

HE *(rubbing his neck)*. I'll have to check to see if chiropractic treatment is covered by my health insurance.

SHE. Let us not waste this moment.

HE. As we have so many others.

SHE. Let us make a pledge.

HE. As we wax poetic and polish our verse.

SHE. Never to quarrel again.

HE. We were quarreling?

SHE. Aye.

HE. Where was *I?*

SHE. Do you so promise?

HE. If that's what it'll take to get your tongue in my mouth.

SHE. Shh! My father! He will hear!

FATHER *(off)*. Your father doesn't care!

SHE *(calling off)*. Good night Pa-pa! *(To HE.)* I love you.

HE. And I you.

SHE. You me what.

HE. I blew it again, didn't I.

SHE. You cannot say the word?

HE. I have said the word. Anon and often.

SHE. But you say it not now.

HE. It sounded romantic the way I said it. *(Poetically.)* "And I…you."

SHE. I don't know. It sounds as though you lack conviction. That you are not committed.

HE. Let us both be committed in the profound, undying and unwavering love that courses through our very veins with every beating of our hearts.

SHE. My darling!

HE. My beloved!

SHE. Kiss me!

HE. Here goes! *(They kiss, long and passionate. Then stare into each other's eyes.)* Anything?

SHE. Not a thing.

HE. Me neither.

SHE. Shit.

HE. You'd have thought with that kind of buildup—

SHE. —anticipation—

HE. —that we would have felt something.

SHE. Timing.

HE. We missed our moment.

SHE. That we did.

HE. Now what?

SHE. "Law and Order" is on the television.

HE. New or a rerun?

SHE. Who can tell?

(As they exit off.)

HE. Do you have anything to eat?

SHE. Do you like cold pizza?

HE. Love it.

END OF PLAY

ABOUT THE PLAYWRIGHTS

CASS BRAYTON spent several years performing in all kinds of offbeat venues, and is an original member of the Sisters of Perpetual Indulgence, San Francisco's radical drag street theater/political/spiritual/charitable troupe. He was known as Sister Mary Media and frequently performed on stage with his back-up singers, the Cass-ettes. In 2003, PlayGround produced his play, **I'd Like to Buy a Vowel**, as part of the Best of PlayGround Emerging Playwrights Festival. He is presently a member of Rumpus, a group of Bay Area playwrights.

KENT R. BROWN See inside front cover.

DOMENICK VINCENT DANZA is a network playwright at Chicago Dramatists whose works have been featured in Chicago Dramatists Ten-Minute Workshops and Circle Theater's New Plays Festivals. From 1993-2003 he served as founder and artistic director of Chicago's Green Light Performing Co., which created and toured educational performances to schools, museums and libraries throughout Illinois. During that period, Danza wrote, directed and choreographed 15 musical performances including **The Time Keepers**, **The Underground Café** and **What's Up With Albert?** He has taught jazz and musical theater dance at Lou Conte Dance Studio in Chicago, Indiana University Northwest, Northwestern University and Loyola University in Chicago.

LISA DILLMAN is a Chicago-based playwright whose plays have been produced, most recently, at Berkeley's

Transparent Theatre, New York City's Hypothetical Theatre and in Chicago at American Theatre Company and Steppenwolf. In 1991, **Terre Haute** received the Julie Harris Playwright Award and in 2003, **Separate Rooms** won the Sarett National Playwriting Contest. She has received two commissions from Steppenwolf Theatre and fellowships from the Illinois Arts Council, the Tremaine Foundation and the Millay Colony for the Arts. In 2003, her play, **Rock Shore**, was workshopped at the O'Neill Playwrights Conference.

BATHSHEBA DORAN began her career as a writer and performer at Cambridge University, where she studied English Literature. Her plays include, among others, **Fifteen Minutes, Odes and Gameshows, The Parents' Evening, The War Play** and **Feminine Wash**. She has been produced at the Edinburgh Festival, The Atlantic Theatre in New York City and The Old Vic Theate and the Drury Lane in London. In 2002, her adaptation of Henrik Ibsen's **Peer Gynt** was directed by Andrei Serban at the Theatre of the Riverside Church in New York City. Her newest work, **Living Room in Africa**, was workshopped in 2004 at the O'Neill Playwrights Conference. She is the recipient of a Liberace Playwriting Fellowship, a Howard Stein Scholarship and the Lecomte de Nouy playwriting award.

JEANETTE D. FARR has written and developed several plays including **The Burning of White Trash, Accidentally on Purpose, Human Wonders, IceSPEAK, Blue Roses** and **Pitchin' Pennies at the Stars**. Her works have been produced off-off-Broadway, as well as in Washington, D.C., Texas, California, Nevada and Virginia. In

1999 and 2000, her plays, **For Kicks** and **But Seriously Folks**, were presented as a part of the Edinburgh Fringe Festival. She has been commissioned by Sierra Repertory Theatre to adapt Yoshiko Uchida's children's story, **Journey to Topaz**, for their 2004/2005 outreach tour. She is presently the literary associate at the Pacific Conservatory of the Performing Arts.

CATHERINE FILLOUX is an award-winning playwright and librettist whose work has been produced internationally and throughout the United States. Her plays include **The Beauty Inside, Eyes of the Heart, Silence of God, Arthur's War, Escuela del Mundo** and **Photographs from S-21**. Her opera, **The Floating Box: A Story in Chinatown**, with composer Jason Kao Hwang, premiered in 2001 in New York City. She is the recipient of the Eric Kocher Playwrights Award, an Asian Cultural Council Artist's Residency grant and is a four-time Heideman Award finalist. Filloux has also been a James Thurber Playwright-in-Residence and a Fulbright Senior Specialist. She is a member of New Dramatists.

DAVID FLEISHER teaches in the English department at Lynn University in Boca Raton, Fla. His collection of short, dark comedies, **Grave Concerns**, has been produced at theatres around the county. He co-authored, with David Freedman, the nonfiction book, *Death of an American: The Killing of John Singer* (Continuum Publishing). With author/songwriter Shel Silverstein and Nashville songwriters Mickey James and Sharon Spivey, he wrote a fact-based musical set in Utah entitled **Last Call at the Cozy**. A member of the Authors Guild and The Dramatists

Guild, his work is included in *The Best Men's Stage Monologues of 1999* and *The Best Women's Stage Monologues of 2000* (Smith and Kraus).

GREGORY FLETCHER earned a BA in Theater from California State University at Northridge, an MA in playwriting from Boston University and an MFA in directing from Columbia University. His plays have appeared off-off-Broadway at Intar 53, Manhattan Theatre Source and Greenwich Street Theatre. Regionally, his work has been featured at the Kennedy Center Theatre Lab, Boston Theatre Marathon, *Slam*Boston, Provincetown Fringe Festival, Provincetown Theatre Company and the Edward Albee Last Frontier Theater Conference in Alaska. Fletcher also works as a freelance director and stage manager.

NANCY GALL-CLAYTON has written several award-winning plays including **General Orders No. 11**, which won the Streisand Festival of New Jewish Plays award in 2002, and **The Colored Door at the Train Depot**, which was a finalist of the 2003 Southeastern Theatre Conference New Play Project. **Felicity's Family Tree** won the 2003 Eileen Heckart Drama for Seniors Competition, 10-Minute division. She has been a three-time finalist of the Actors Theatre of Louisville National Ten-Minute Play Contest and is the recipient of grants from the Kentucky Foundation for Women and the Kentucky Arts Council. She is a member of The Dramatists Guild.

MEGAN GOGERTY is a playwright, musician and performer based in Los Angeles. A Playwrights' Center

Jerome Fellow, she recently completed her MFA in Playwriting at the University of Texas at Austin, where she received a James A. Michener Playwriting Scholarship and the Ellsworth P. and Virginia Conkle Endowed Scholarship for Drama. Her music-play, **Love Jerry**, toured southern England in 2004 in association with Dartington College of the Arts in Devon. Other titles include **Hobo Season**, **Fireproof Baby** and **Ragnarok: A Glamtastic Opera** for teenage audiences Her solo performances, including **Phrenology Explained** and **Passing Out**, have been presented throughout the Midwest.

MARK GUARINO has had numerous plays produced at Chicago theatres including Zebra Crossing, the Curious Theatre Branch and Chicago Dramatists where he has been a resident playwright since 1995. He is the recipient of the national 2003 New Play Prize by Chicago's Prop Theatre for his play **All Dogs Must Heel**, the 2001 Tennessee Williams Scholarship by the University of the South for his play **From Hutchinson Street**, and the John Gerrietts Award for Creative Writing from Loyola University Chicago. He is also a four-time finalist of the Chesterfield Film Project Fellowship.

JAY D. HANAGAN is an internationally produced playwright whose works have appeared at Devanaughn Theatre in Boston, Source Theatre in Washington, D.C., Playwrights Circle in Palm Springs and Chicago's Artistic Home, as well as numerous festivals including the Riant Strawberry Festival in New York City. His play, **Along For The Ride**, was a Samuel French 28th Annual Off-Off-Broadway Original Short Play Festival winner in

2003; and in 2004, **First Kisses** won first prize in the Backdoor Theatre's 20th Annual New Play Project. **Softly Sara Falls**, a play dealing with domestic violence, was produced in 2004 by Marist College of Poughkeepsie, N.Y.

FRANK HIGGINS is the author of **The Sweet By 'n' By** which was staged at the 1992 Williamstown Theatre Festival with Blythe Danner and Gwyneth Paltrow. His works, including **Miracles**, **Lovers Leap** and the musical play, **WMKS: Where Music Kills Sorrow**, have been presented at the Fulton Opera House, the Old Globe Theater and other regional theaters. **Gunplay** has been produced widely across the country, with scenes read on Capitol Hill prior to the passage of the Brady Bill. His play for young audiences, **The Slave Dancer's Choice**, is published by Dramatic Publishing.

CALEEN SINNETTE JENNINGS is the author of over 70 plays. She is the recipient of Washington's Theater Lobby Award and the Source Theatre's H.D. Lewis Award. In 1997, she was a finalist for the Jane Chambers Playwriting Award, and in 1999 she received a grant from The Kennedy Center Fund for New American Plays. In 2000, she received a Heideman Award from Actors' Theatre of Louisville for **Classyass**. Her children's plays, **A Lunch Line** and **Same But Different** are published by New Plays, Inc.; **Inns and Outs**, **Playing Juliet/Casting Othello**, **Sunday Dinner** and **Free Like Br'er Rabbit** are published by Dramatic Publishing. She is Professor of Theatre and Director of Theatre/Music Theatre in the Department of Performing Arts at American University.

JULIE JENSEN is a playwright whose works have been produced in London and at the Edinburgh Fringe Festival as well as in New York City and theatres nationwide. Her titles include, among others, **White Money, The Lost Vegas Series, Two-Headed, Wait!** and **The Dust Eaters**. A three-time winner of the Mill Mountain Theatre Playwriting, for **Tender Hooks, Last Lists of My Mad Mother** and **Two-Headed**, she has also won a Joseph Jefferson Award for Best New Work and an *LA Weekly* Award for Best New Play. She has received grants and fellowships from The Kennedy Center Fund for New American Plays, the Pew Charitable Trusts and The Playwrights' Center. She is currently the resident playwright at Salt Lake Acting Company. She is published by Dramatic Publishing, Dramatists Play Service, Playscripts, Inc. and Smith and Kraus.

JANET KENNEY is an award-winning playwright who is the recipient of a Tanne Foundation Residency and an Edward Albee Theatre Conference Panelist's award, as well as awards from Perishable Theatre, the Provincetown Theatre Company and the O'Neill Playwrights Conference. She recently completed **Globus Hystericus**, a commission from Theatre Emory in Atlanta, Ga., and is preparing **My Heart & My Flesh** for production by Boston's Coyote Theatre. Several of her short plays have been performed nationwide and published in various anthologies. She holds a BA in theatre arts from the University of Massachusetts at Boston and an MA in playwriting from Boston University.

BARBARA LINDSAY is a fifth-generation Californian, who presently lives in Seattle, Wash. In 1989, her first full-length play, **Free**, won the New York Drama League's Playwrighting Competition and premiered at the London New Play Festival in 1991. Since then, there have been numerous productions of her work internationally and throughout the United States. In 2001, ten of her short pieces were produced under the collective title **Snapshots** by El Portal Center for the Arts in Van Nuys, Calif. A long-time member of Golden West Playwrights in Los Angeles, she has taught writing classes throughout Washington, California and West Virginia.

DAVID MACGREGOR is a playwright, screenwriter and critic. His plays include, among others, **The Waiting Room**, **Paternity Ward**, **Revelation**, **The Hero's Journey** and **Towards the Perpetuation of the Human Species**. In 2002, his play, **The Late Great Henry Boyle**, premiered at the B Street Theatre in Sacramento. His screenplays, **Phobos** and **Double Bind**, have won awards from the American Cinema Foundation and *Fade In* magazine. He has contributed critical articles to *Cashiers du Cinemart*, including "The Lost Art of the Made-For-TV Movie: Evil Roy Slade" and "The 5,000 Finders of Dr. T."

MICHELE MARKARIAN is a Massachusetts writer whose works include fiction, sketch comedy and plays. Her short works, including **Old Friends** and **Eight-Minute Dating Man**, have appeared in several New England Festivals, among them The Firedog Theatre Inc.'s Staged Readings Series and the Devanaughn Theater's Annual Dragonfly Festival. She has collaborated on other stage works with The Common/wealth Theater Collaborative, The Newbury Street Theater and Ace Theatricals. Her full-length play, **I Enjoy Being a Girl** (co-written with Anne Pluto), was commissioned in 2002 by Lesley University for their Women's History Month. It was also performed in 2003 at The Firehouse Centre's New Works Festival in Newburyport, Mass. She is a member of The Dramatists Guild.

CHERISSE MONTGOMERY is a playwright and poet whose plays have been performed at Venus Theatre, Southern Writers Theatre and at Seattle's Mae West Fest. Several of her poems and short stories, including "Beware of Dogs," "Fortune Cookie Explains U.S. Foreign Affairs Policy," "Riding in the Carpool Lane to Mt. Rushmore" and "Micronesia 1954-72," have been published in the *Washington Square* literary magazine, *The Residential College Review*, *Voices Magazine* and *Xylem* magazine.

BRETT NEVEU is a Chicago-based playwright whose works include, among others, **Eric LaRue**; **Empty**; **Drawing War**; **the go**; **The Last Barbecue**; **twentyone** and **Eagle Hills, Eagle Ridge, Eagle Landing**. He has been produced by the Terrapin Theatre, A Red Orchid Theatre, Stage Left Theatre, The Factory Theatre and the American Theatre Company. Other venues include Spring Theatreworks in New York City and Asylum Theatre in Las Vegas. He has been commissioned twice by Steppenwolf for their New Play Initiative, and in 2003 was the winner of the Goodman Theatres Ofner Prize for New Work. Neveu is currently a resident playwright at Chicago Dramatists.

EDWARD POMERANTZ is a playwright, novelist and screenwriter who is a member of the writing faculty of Columbia University and SUNY-Purchase. His plays and screenplays have been read and performed in New York City at the New Federal Theatre, the Actors Studio, The Kitchen and the Westside Theatre. In 1996, *Caught*, for which he wrote the screenplay based on his original novel, *Into It*, was released by Sony Pictures Classics. His stage titles include **Man Running, A Long Story, Brisburial, Shenanigans, Nothing Personal** and **I Hate When It Gets Dark So Early**. His numerous awards include two Writers Guild awards, a CAPS grant, a Ford Foundation grant and three John Golden Awards. He is the creator of the Writers Guild of America East Foundation Screenwriting Workshop dedicated to seeking and nurturing writing talent in the Harlem community. He also serves as creative advisor at the Toscano Foundation Screenwriters Lab in Oaxaca, Mexico.

BRUCE POST is the executive director of the Maxwell Anderson Playwrights Series, where he produces the annual Young Connecticut Playwrights Festival each spring. His plays have been produced in New York City, Los Angeles, Kansas City, Washington, D.C., and on Martha's Vineyard. His plays include **The Whipping Boys**, winner of the UMKC Award for Playwriting; **Band**; **The Master Race** and **Size Matters**, which received the John Gassner annual playwriting award in 2003. He teaches high school drama at the world famous Waterbury Arts Magnet School. His work is published by Broadway Play Publishers and Dramatic Publishing.

388

MONICA RAYMOND is an award-winning playwright and poet based in Cambridge, Mass. Her plays have been produced frequently throughout Massachusetts, as well as by Stage Left in Chicago and at the Vital Theater, Circle East and Looking Glass Theater in New York City. In 2001, **Safe House** won a Panelist's Choice Award at the Last Frontier Theater Conference. In 2004, **Hijab** was featured in "Occupied Territories: Palestinian- and Jewish-American Playwrights on the Middle East" at Boston Playwrights Theater, and included in New York City's Samuel French Festival. Her poems have been published in *Heresies*, *Sinister Wisdom*, the *Iowa Review*, the *Village Voice* and others; and, most recently, in *Poems from Sojourner: A Feminist Anthology* (University of Illinois Press, 2003). She has been a resident at The MacDowell Colony and the Atlantic Center for the Arts and is the 2005 Nadya Aisenberg Fellow at the Boston Writers Room. Raymond has taught writing at Harvard University, Lehman College and the School of the Museum of Fine Arts, Boston.

REBECCA RITCHIE is a health lawyer and playwright who writes frequently about the breast cancer experience. Her plays include **Rachel Calof**, **The Shiva Queen**, **The Gratz Delusion** and **Box Lunch**, among others. In 1996, **An Unorthodox Arrangement** won *ArtVoice Magazine*'s "Artie" award for outstanding new play, and the Dorothy Silver Play Writing Competition. In 1998, **The Crustacean Waltz** was co-winner of the Helen Mintz Award and winner of the "Artie" award for outstanding new play. She is a graduate of Goucher College and the Law School of the University of Pennsylvania and has served on the New

York Foundation for the Arts playwriting/screenwriting grant award panel. She trained in the Western New York Playwrights workshop under the direction of Emanuel Fried. Her works are published by Smith and Kraus and Broadway Play Publishing. Ritchie is a member of The Dramatists Guild and the International Centre for Women Playwrights.

DAVID RUSH has had productions of his work at Manhattan Theatre Club, Playwrights' Horizons, Chicago Dramatists, the Mark Taper Forum and Chicago's Stage Left, as well as other regional theatres across the United States. Recent plays include **Germinous Seeds**, **Feathers in the Wind**, **Police Deaf Near Far**, **Cuttings**, **The Prophet of Bishop Hill** and the musical **Prairie Lights**. He is the recipient of several Jefferson awards and citations, and three After Dark awards for best new work, including **Dapples and Grays**. In 1997, his Civil War drama, **Leander Stillwell**, won a *Drama-Logue* award for Excellence in Writing and was voted one of the *Los Angeles Times*' 10 Best of the Year. He is also the recipient of two Midwest Emmy awards, for **Dona Gracia's Candles** and **The Two-Hundred-Dollar Willie Mays**. Rush is a member of Stage Left Theater Ensemble and a resident writer emeritus at Chicago Dramatists. He currently heads the Playwriting Program at Southern Illinois University, Carbondale.

MARK SMITH-SOTO is a Costa Rican American poet/playwright and professor of romance languages at the University of N.C. at Greensboro. The author of three books of poetry, his poems have appeared in *Nimrod*, *Carolina*

Quarterly, *Literary Review*, *Americas Review* and the *Kenyon Review*, among other journals. He is the recipient of the North Carolina Writers' Network Year 2000 Persephone Competition award and the 2002 Randall Jarrell/Harperprints prize. His first full-length collection, **Our Lives Are Rivers**, was published in 2003 by Florida University Press. Several of his short plays, including **A Night at the Bistro, A Private Hell** and **The First Day of the Rest of Our Lives,** have been produced by the Greensboro Playwrights' Forum.

LISA SOLAND graduated from Florida State University with a BFA in acting and received her Equity card working as an apprentice at the Burt Reynolds' Jupiter Theatre. Her romantic comedy, **The Name Game,** was published by Samuel French in 1995. Other titles include **An Afternoon With Shirley, Cabo San Lucas, The Lord's Last Supper, Matt and His Crazy Writing Machine** and **The ReBirth**. Her play, **Waiting,** is featured in *Women Playwrights: The Best Plays of 2003* (Smith and Kraus). Soland leads "The All Original Playwright Workshop," a group of actors, writers and directors whose purpose is to develop new and original material for television, film and theatre.

DONNA SPECTOR is a member of The Dramatists Guild, Poets & Writers and The International Centre for Women Playwrights. In 1986, **Another Paradise**, her first play, was produced off-Broadway at the Players Theatre. Other titles include **Hanging Women, These Are My Adults, Manhattan Transits, Strip Talk on the Boulevard, Dancing With Strangers** and **A Sense of Move-**

ment. She has received two N.E.H. grants to study in Greece, and grants from the Geraldine R. Dodge Foundation and the New York Council for the Arts. Her poems, scenes and monologues have appeared in many anthologies and literary magazines. **Golden Ladder,** is published in *Women Playwrights: The Best Plays of 2002* (Smith and Kraus).

WANDA STRUKUS is a Rhode Island-based playwright whose works include **Blink and She's Gone, Wingwalkers, Salt, D'Arc Comedy** and **Robbie 2 is Drowning**. Her plays have been produced by the Contemporary Theater Series in Tucson, Wild Frontier Theater in Chicago and the Boston Women on Top Festival. She has received play-development support from the Chicago Women's Theater Alliance, and has had her work published in *Grain Magazine* and *Writer's Digest*. She attended the Sewanee Writer's Conference as a Tennessee Williams Scholar in playwriting and presently writes, directs and teaches in the New England area.

JULES TASCA is a playwright, librettist and performer whose works have been produced in numerous national theaters including the Mark Taper Forum, and internationally throughout Austria, South Africa, Germany and England. Titles include **Theater Trip, Old Goat Song, The Spelling of Coynes** and **Deus-X**. His libretto for C.S. Lewis' **The Lion, the Witch and the Wardrobe** played in New York and London. His works have won the Thespie Award for Best New Play, the Barrymore Award for Best Play, a grant from the Pennsylvania Council of the Arts, the Dorothy Silver International Playwrighting

Award and the Bucks County Writers Club Screenwriting award. His radio writing, including **The Grand Christmas History of the Andy Landy Clan**, has been produced frequently on National Public Radio.

JERRY THOMPSON has had readings and/or performances of his plays, including **Hello, I'm Will Shakespeare** and **Eddy and Benny**, in Massachusetts at the Provincetown Theatre Company, The Firehouse Center for the Arts in Newbury Port, The Eventide Arts Festival in Dennis Port, The Barnstable Comedy Club in Barnstable, The Academy of Performing Arts in Orleans and at Another Country Productions in Boston. Other works, including **Small Town Girls**, **The Elevator** and **Back Yard Apartment**, have been performed in Valdez, Alaska, at The New England Academy of Theatre in New Haven and at The Research Institute at Ohio University. Thompson is a member of the Provincetown Theatre Company's Playwrights Lab.

CHRISTOPHER WALL has written numerous plays including **Couldn't Say**, **Some Other Place**, **No One Talks to the Mailman**, **Elmo on the Half Shell**, **Forks and Knives** and **Head Games**. His awards include a 1999 Washington Theatre Festival H.D. Lewis Award for playwriting, and a 2001 Washington Theatre Festival Literary Prize. His work is featured in *The Best Men's Stage Monologues of 1999* and *The Best Stage Scenes of 1999* (Smith and Kraus). Plays and essays have also been published in *The Pacific Review*, *The Saint Ann's Review* and *Dartmouth Alumni Magazine*, among others. Wall currently teaches expository writing at New York University, where he is earning his MFA in dramatic writing.

KATHLEEN WARNOCK has had her work performed in a variety of venues throughout the country, including the Carrollwood Players in Tampa, Fla., and the Turnip Theatre and Homogenius festivals in New York City. Her plays include **I'm Gonna Run Away**, **A Bushel of Crabs**, **Grieving for Genevieve**, **The Audience** and **To the Top**, which was a winner of the South Carolina Playwrights Festival in 1990. **The Space Between Heartbeats** was produced in 2004 by London's Short & Girlie Company at the Blue Elephant Theatre.